AF291159

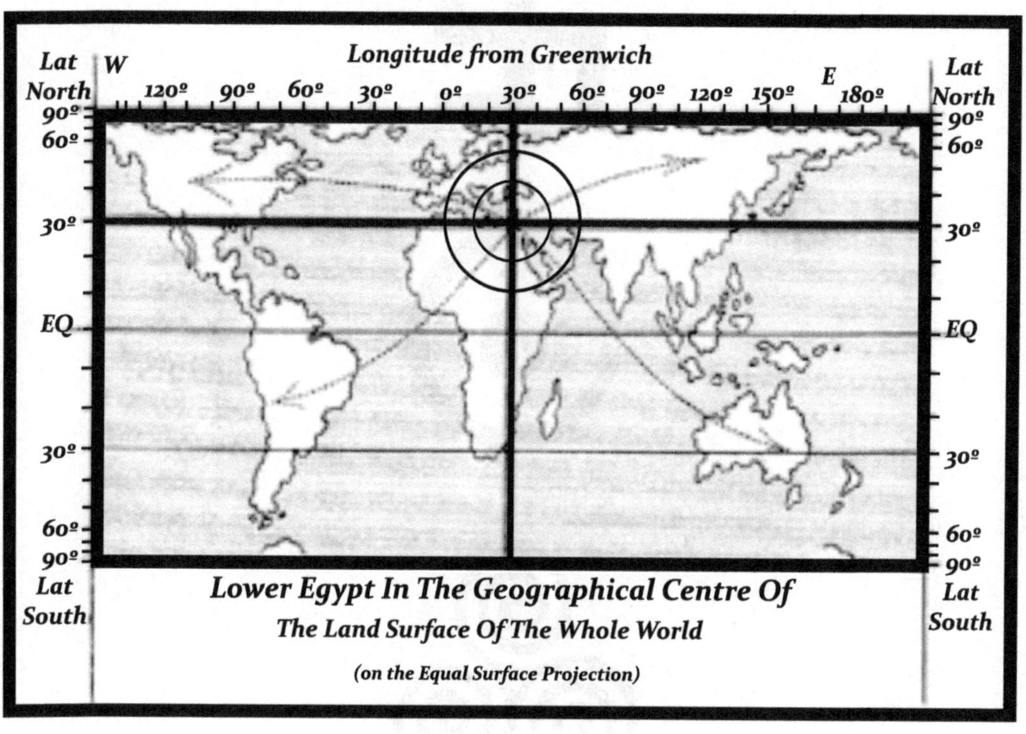

Lower Egypt In The Geographical Centre Of
The Land Surface Of The Whole World

(on the Equal Surface Projection)

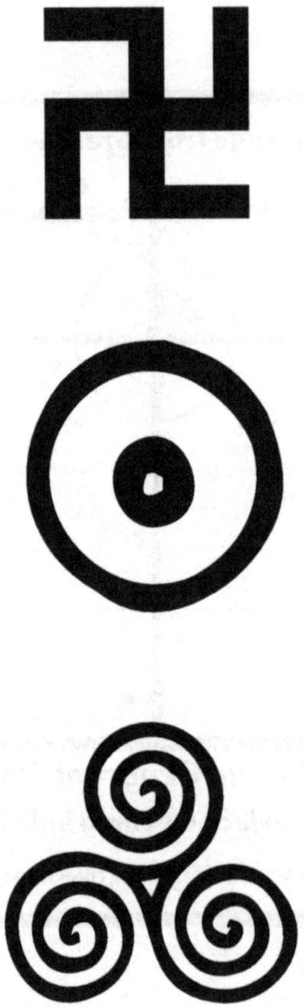

π

33

1 3 7 8 11 12 13 44 60

"And you will count your steps".

<u>Dedicated to:</u>

The Human Being(s)
of the Blue Planet.

<u>2012- 2084</u>

Diseased Not I

by c21 Anon'

A Poetic.

I am to tell you.
I knew **He** was with me,
and greater than this: Our Father.
And of the church without a god,
corrupt in the laws of man,
that I should be brought to suffer.

I shall teach you well now,
and History will mark my words indelibly,
that Hard Rains could ne'r they erase.
You will not have your Armageddon
only because **'I'** does not wish it too.
But you shall be made to taste it.
And you will learn respect. Word.

I did not feel the agonies
that were intended.
I grew strong and holy:
steadfast and resolute.
I drafted the gallows
by which **They** would hang.

And at this,

i has Them precisely where <u>I</u> wants Them. Word.

Leaving Scinoville.

On a 'Clear' day,
you could see The Elders' *caps*.
Swaying like willow,
weeping in the warm meadow haze.

The sweet stench of charred Niggers' flesh
wafting through the centuries,
over blossom rich maize.

Across the water, through Bristol came.
To The Deep South,
Skyline Pigeon home.
The very seat of England. Shame.

The gardener,
had been talking to the walls for years.
Leaping in and out of bushes,
like a geriatric Japanese soldier
on a remote Andaman island,
unaware the war had ended.
And that there was no war, since decades.

Still filled with a brainwashed loyalty,
he called himself Dick Barton.
More Slave than Fool,
making war 'tween ghosts and dark shadows.
Taking pot-shots at Sun worshippers: he would,
when the voices told.

When uncle died,
They conspired to steal the family estate.
A law unto Themselves,
The Accountant and The Lawyer.
And Their Evil Hoard.

 Outwitted and foiled,
'They' instigated an unlawful doctrine,
'to utterly destroy by any means,
 including lies and trickery'.

It was a damming indictment
of the avaricious and satanic cult.
They would be hoist by Their own petard.
Word.

I, was leaving Scinoville forever.

*caps. Abbreviation of *capirote(s)*. Long cumbersome conical headwear, worn typically by Spanish Catholics in penitence. But also, The Klue Klux Clan: and their ilk.

Look for God and you will not find God.
Look for Truth, and He will find you.

<u>And so.</u>

And let all of Christendom Know. And all The World. And let all It's religions and philosophies contained therein, be told. And without partiality. And so, it will be proclaimed. And so, every nation in The World will Know too. And all secular societies without religion, must too Know. And, so that they too are informed. And are advised of their civic duty. And so that they may unite also, in the Divine cause. And that being, <u>H</u>is return.

And it is time to surrender to the one God, once more. And to The One Truth, besides. And, in all His Majesty. And, before His return. And, so that He may return. And, just as it was before. And as it was too, in the beginning. And at The Dawn of Civilisation. And so that it is known. And exalted, that God is The Sun and The Stars. And all His Emissaries, are He in manifest. And so; just so. Word.

And, for the infidel in all antitheses, is risen. And *his* church is unholy. And it is a bastion of evil. And you must make no mistake about it. And such are the times. And precisely. And *he* is born of Soup. And *his* odour is sulphur. And *he* thrives on disharmony. And fractious dispute. And, *he* always has been this way. And no other way. And since the very Soup. And *he* is The Master of Hate. And *his*, is the Church of Hate. And *he* is hateful.

And *he* forges *his* way by unbridled hypocrisy. And by double standards. And by sheer two facedness. And *he* is driven singularly by a crippling inferiority to His Majesty. And *he* has striven to rule in His absence. And *he* is dwarfed in every aspect, by The Divine and All His Emissaries. And *his* followers are no different to *he*, in Their crippling inferiorities. And They are *he*, in microcosm and manifest. And such people are always dangerous. And They are corrupt and sinister and dangerous. And They are especially dangerous to The Human Being. Word.

And, They are forever competitive because of this. And, They are forever mongering war and disharmony. And They were once The *Un*evolved. And They were the primeval beast in ascendency. And now, They are The Devolved and devolving. And They prey upon The Common People. And They recruit from this reservoir.

And <u>T</u>hey consume them, as do vampires. And *They* are stolen away by this demon. And so *he* is in They. And They prey upon The Human Being. And The Human Being is Evolved and impervious. And They are frustrated by this. And They are the same now, as They were at The Beginning. And They are not Human Being(s). And They may not call Themselves Human Being. Word.

And The Common People is made fickle. And they are easily swayed. And they are not evil *'per se'*. And they know not what They do. And their minds are not their own. And they are but a Resource. And mere instruments. And, but they are like seaweed in suspension of a tumultuous Sea. And they are determined by the tides that govern. And they are the makings of The Masses. And they are not determined by their own resolve or philosophy, as is The Human Being. Word.

And they are The Searchers. And they follow whims
and fashions. And they listen to others, in order to
ascertain direction. And they have no inner voice. And
they do not know 'The Word of God'. And they believe
willy-nilly, in democracies and The Politics of Man.
And They obey the synthesised 'voice of god', prevalent
and emerging at the time of writing, carried on *his*
infernal * '$5 technologies'. And therein lays the rub,
my most studious and attentive reader. Word.

And those who fashion politics, may easily bag them,
by a well baited hook. And they are gullible. And they
are 'ten a penny'. And they are neither here nor there.

And so, by this and thus, *he* has synthesised the word
of god. And so, there is a synthesised telepathy, at The
Present. And *in* the time of writing. And a voice like
thought. And it is experimental. And it is invasive. And
there is a mass hypnosis underway without license. And
microwave subliminal broadcast is at every turnabout.

And *'this'* is the language of The Third Face. And at
this, you are to mark my words indelibly dearest reader.
And so, they become *his*. And they become They.

**An uncontrolled pandemic of mass produced, 'psyche influencing' & invasive subliminal macro surveillance technology, originally developed for military application, from reverse engineered Alien technologies, but now flooding societies, & available to 'the world and it's wife': and used extensively by any tin-pot cult or mafia, or Police Force, without warrant or license, to eavesdrop upon; or broadcast 'at', Their prey. And or indeed, to instruct & direct (or influence), the actions and movement of Their own kind or ilk.*

And <u>T</u>hey are obedient to the voice of the $5 technologies, that support *his* bidding, in lieu of The Voice of God. And indeed; of God Himself. And *he* is an imposter by *all* this. And by *his* infernal and invasive devices, *he* does indeed proliferate. And this is true.

And They farm The Resource. And The Resource is fickle. And *herdlike*. And easily swayed. And They had & have planted 'low hanging fruits', on which to graze and fatten The Resource, for easy pickings. And They build fences, just as Early Man. And Their Police(s) were & are Their farmers. And They farm in order to prey. And They set-up, frame and harvest. And They are The Great Hunters of The Domesticated. And but; The Resource has grown restless & unruly. And out of control. And They too, have now lost All control of The Resource. And these are The Times dearest reader.

And They find Their *raison d'etre,* within it all. And They are obedient to Their Master. And made subservient by Their particular vice(s), within the plethora '*he* in They' supplies. And The Resource is made weak and dilute, in It's confusion. And it is *an* honey grub. And It makes for easy prey. And so. And so, just so: it is. Word.

And they chase trappings. And anything shiny. And they dream the dreams of *his* manufacture, kept at arms length. And they will follow readily, any Stuffed Shirt; be it, *'party or person'*, scattering corn in ascendency, like a gaggle of fresh fledged gosling.

And they make a total mockery of the very concept of Democracy, in so doing. And They are *a* tract and repulsive. And a veritable swathe. And It is a *Foie Gras* & a *Faux Pas*, if you will, my dearest and most precious; and appreciative reader. And so.

And it is a folly of All that Democracy has strived toward, since the height of civilisation, at It's ancient and 'most important' conception. And The Optimum in symposium, where great human minds, communed with *the gods* of Olympus, to broke*b*ack saddle the beast in human nature. And The Law & Codes of Conduct, forged from The One Truth. And they are easily corrupted by all this. And They *is* weak. And They are bought. And They are traded. And They are totalitarian: really. And no mistake. And The Resource is misguided by corrupted politics. Word.

And They are easily conscripted, into argument and war, by lies and propaganda(s). And They delight in hearsay. And They fill *his* ballot boxes, according to instruction. And *he* in They, manipulate it all to ensure 'The Common People' functions well. And all according to *his* very desire(s). And They possess they. And *he* is in They. And They control they. And The Human Being is not The Common People. Word.

And The Human Being is unruly, but not violent. And, instead He is dispersed and self contained still. And He is reclusive now. And He is misanthropic. And He is outspoken against The Disease. And against all those who carry The Disease. And against all those who are The Disease. And He is The Sleeper. And He is waiting only for The Sun. Word.

And He is The Antidote. And He is All Knowing. And He is ready. And He is in my dearest and most precious and attentive reader. And He is 'I'. And **I** is in All of Us. And **I** is God. And, so I do take His name: I, in All His variant forms. And I is One. And in every language, of every nation of The World. And so, say 'I'. Word.

And They are All fractured. And They justify Their very existence under *his* reign. And, but there is no justification. And, nor can there be. And *he* is an imposter, to be sure. And They have thrived in Our absence. And They are granted an over estimated opinion of Their vitality, under *he*, in Their fellowship with one another. And They believe in Themselves wholeheartedly. And They truly believe that Their disease is a cure, to the very disease itself, that is only of Their own creation. And They are a Nonsense.

And They are supremely deluded, by *he* in They. And They are buoyed by All this. And They are bolstered. And They utilise weapons and technology, to impose Their disease upon All Peoples. And They are given a sense of importance, in an allegiance to *he*. And They are not Meek, like The Human Being, but weak. And They are Unmeek. And driven by the delusions of Their own importance. And therein lays the very rub.

And yet, They are strong in unity with one another. And Their common purpose. And in wealth and weapons and technologies. And They are avaricious. And They seek only power and authority. And They is a machine. And it is a machine to be sure. And it is an All consuming and unsustainable machine.

And it must double production, in order to feed itself.
And it must proliferate and breed. And, by the cult in
culture, it seethes and festers. And so.

And *he* is the driver of wedges. And *he* is the provider
of weapons. And *he* is the divider of Mankind. And *he*
is the dismantler of all unity. And *he* turns those; who
would be Human Beings, into Common People. And
The Common People, suffer all the trappings under *he*.

And they know not what They do. And Their minds
are not their own. And *he* draws up every despicable
trait known to Mankind. And *he* exploits it. And *he*
promotes and makes virtues of these traits. And greed
and jealousy are *his* fossil fuels.

And where We turned Homo Erectus into Human
Being, *he* is engaged counterwise, in It's progressive
devolution. And *he* is the catalyst of hatred.

And *he* is in all that, which is deemed to be good. And
at this, *he* is within the unbridled hypocrites, and every
manner of pervert. And *he* is in all that, which is
known to be *d'evil* upon The Earth. And at this, *he* is
true to himself, within T*hey*. And *he* is in They. Word.

And God is great. And Life upon The Blue Planet, is life within the Petri Dish. And Still; unchanged: despite the shape shifting of evolution, through eon and epoch. And They by *he*, form groups and clusters always. And it is this, that is *his* modus operandi.

And *he* will never be seen alone. And *he* is nothing as an individual. And *he* is sequestered. And only manifest from within other(s). And when that other, is amidst those others of the group, within The Resource *he* has conquested. And so.

And it is All rudimentary. And Life under *he* is unchanged since mud. And *he* is obsessed with repulsion and attraction. And splitting cells and atoms.

And so, Common People with common complex, preoccupations and obsessions, evolve from this quagmire. And *he* forges societies. And *he* builds armies. And from *his* nucleus, *he* builds molecules in alliance with others. And so, to do *his* bidding.

And *he* is malignant. And by this very model, '*he* is in They'. And The Common People congeal into collectives, of one form or another. And They club together. And into *his* infernal secret societies. And molecules, from single cells are created. And at this, They have complex. And They are complex.

And inherent weakness; is given strength. And inherent flaws, are intrinsic and rewarded. And social diseases breed in the microcosm of The Petri Dish. And *his* Mafias are as common to this common law, as *his* Forces. And there is merger. And it is All beyond Good & Evil. And it is the way of Life, by *him*, under *he* in They. And you may only evolve, within the limited scope *of* One's Life, my most studious reader, as a Human Being, to understand this. Word.

And it is this, that is the very cement that binds The Third Face. And I shall teach you All that you are to Know about The Third Face, in the bindings of this very volume. And you are to learn your lesson well.

And you are to mark The Words of I indelibly, for to be forewarned is to be forearmed. And: just as ever you are, my dearest and most precious and attentive reader, you are to take heed. Word.

And you must be wise to whom, and to which of what, is symbiotic to t'other. And: or another. And whom, is the host to what. And never judge a book by it's cover. And of those malignant cells; that adhere better to liars and hypocrites, to form the charismatic character and characteristics in *his* instruments. And equally, to learn how to determine those, who are pathogen free, and belong to His Majesty. And so, just so.

And any hypocrite can sell a charade. And under *he*, it is precisely what They do. And so, a word to the wise my dearest reader, at this juncture, is most appropriate. Word.

And just as such, as follows; is The Sun. And of which extraterrestrial entities, that breach the perimeter of Our atmosphere, whether hostile or welcome. And unto the complex carbon based compounds, of those who govern Life, whether friend or foe.

And these are the very influences on Society and Government. And you are to question The Spirit and the bacteria. And you are to learn to recognise the benign from The Diseased.

And All Truth is distorted by such in*t*ernal
moleculisation. And you may be sure of this, my most
attentive reader. And of the society formed by those
who form it. And by what forms those, who form the
societies. And there are secret societies within societies.
And there are puppets and puppeteers. And internal
and external forces. And influences, both large and
small; invisible and microscopic. And some from out of
this world. Word.

And The Spirit World is true, but *he* has manufactured
a fake and synthesised version of it. And it is *his*. And
his is the synthesised: 'Voice of God'. And They are
impostors. And *he* is in They.

And They are aiming to direct and govern society, by
powders and subliminal $5 technologies, one way or
another. And They are in the business of The
Digitilisation of Humanity.

And at the pinnacle of *his* ethos, and the societies *he*
governs, They are on opposing sides, solely for the sake
of appearances. And for the mundane business of
policing & government; but in truth, They are united
as a collective. And both are intent on doing *his*
bidding. And it is the well concealed truth. Word.

And They, are but two sides of the one coin. And They; aim to embroil All and sundry, into one side or the other. And They aim to control All The World, by Their infernal subliminal $5 technologies.

And by Their macro surveillance(s). And unwelcome prompts & direction. And commentary. And overall mind control. And manipulation, through The Digitilisation of Humanity. And It is a devolution.

And They are playing god, from behind the skirting boards and architrave. And They: Both, are a nonsense. And invest too heavily in the science of technologies. And They inflict it all on The Resource, with the intention of manipulation and governorship.

And They believe it all to be so very 'Big & Clever'. And but; it is anything but. And They see Themselves, as vital and important. And but, They will come and go, like a fleeting fashion. And like flared trousers, but a whimsical trend. And it will be so: Word.

And: just as there are worlds within worlds. And so, learn too, verily & soonly, that whichever rules The Spirit World, in this Atmos'; and whichever controls the bacteria, that is the very Life within it, will always be best placed to install, the complex carbon based organisms of influence, to govern All manner of Life, upon The Earth. And be sure, as sure as eggs is eggs, that His Majesty's creation, can never be accurately synthesised. And so: it is a folly from the outset, to even try.

And They seek safety in numbers. And the sum is always only as strong as it's weakest link. And The One, is perverted when conjoined. And The I, is corrupted. And The I will not stand to be corrupted or perverted. And so, The I leaves to stand alone, as One: in It's purity. And They become *his,* strewn as a string of pearls to swine. And at The Pinnacle of The Third Face, is the very conundrum in manifest. And it is All merely Science. And none of it is anything but Science. And even the purest of divinity, is precisely mathematic. Word.

And The Human Being is independent upon The Earth. And The Human Being belongs to nothing. And He will not be bullied or governed, because He is of no threat to any society, in which He lives. And He is The Way. And no mistake: just so. Word.

And He suffers none of the mortal conditions. And He is in unity only with The Divine, to whom He is Faithful. And He spends no time preoccupied with complex, or desires of domination. And, nor the subdivision or exploitation of other entities. And neither the splitting of cells and atoms. And nor the bodies these factions of fractions create. And The Human Being preys on no one. And He is simply Divine.

And the nature of *his* groups, is always to seek an opposing group. And it will make an enemy of anything different. And it must always seek out an Opposite, or an Opponent, according to It's primal nature. And *he* needs enemies. And '*he* in They' is always a warmonger, because of this predisposition. And It is The Law of Mud, from whence *he* came.

And it may be male against female. And it invariably is. And or, it may be black against white, which too often it has been. And or, those with authority against those without. And They will always make of it a rivalry or War. And They do not *Vive Le Difference*. And it is always a battle of sorts. And it is this way. And it is tiresome to His Majesty.

And but, it is The Law by which all Life born of mud is governed, under *he* by They. And 'tis the status quo, at the time of writing. And *he* lives by the law of repulsion. And according to negativity. And so.

And The Human Being conforms not, nor is defined by, any of these statutes. And whereas, 'They under *he*', are a very complex carbon based organism. And complicated by Their lack of Knowing, *in* His Majesty.

And counterwise; The Human Being is simply a complex carbon based organism, fused with The Divine. And by this, The Human Being is a peaceful, simple, and humble creature. And He is <u>H</u>is very reflection. And cast in His very image upon The Earth. Word.

And The Human Being is not complicated at all. And in It's pure state, It is a simple creature. And The Human Being will always have a garden, whenever or wherever He can. And He will never be at peace until He does. And The Human Being loves Trees. And Trees are magnificent. And majestic. And Trees sustain All Life. And they are Our landing ports, my most curious and attentive reader. And All Life is powered by photosynthesis. And no mistake.

And, the very quintessential importance of Trees, just exactly as you shall learn, is greater than you had ever learnt before. And they shall be your salvation. And they shall afford you a bridge to survival. And they will buy you time, where **_he_** has left you None! And you will learn to once again, surrender to His Majesty. And you will look no further than The Sun to do this. Word.

And **_he_** is in all Banking. And _he_ is in all Government. And _he_ is most prevalent in The Cities. And _he_ draws people to him, with _his_ trinkets and trappings. And _he_ is wherever there is money and slight. And, it is only _he_. And it has only ever been _he_. And _he_ lives in They. And They are _his_. And They are not Human Being(s). And all People(s) are not Human Being(s), by this very rule. Word.

And so.

And The Human Being was created in Our image, from the resource of the genus Homo Erectus. And it was a clever monkey, evolved from soup. And it was The Awakening. And it was God. And the very sense of wonder within.

And it was ten precessions since whence it was. And this is equal to two hundred and sixty millennia. And the first scribe to The Divine recorded it well. And He wrote a dot within a circle. Word.

And you know nothing of Us, my dearest reader. And much more is the very pity for this. And all Knowing is lost because of this very fact. And *he* by They, have destroyed the last of those who had The Knowing. And through the dark ages of this last millennium, that has led 'til now. And it is, just so.

And by the perversion of all religions, that links Us to you. And so. And by which All began, with the very germ of Truth, my dearest reader. And the germ of truth, is The One Truth, from which All else is derived, and deviant of. And The One Truth is He, and the untainted nucleus is His.

And so, say I. And all Knowing is lost to the natural disasters, that happen upon The World too. And the cataclysmic effects of these, each time, upon The Earth. And the loss of the accumulative knowledge, mustered through generations, to those *fall* swoops.

And by the decimation of populations at these events, that shatter The Morphic Fields, which are The Source of learning. And which are the harbingers of All knowledge and Knowing.

And do you doubt the stories of Noah. And of Gilgamesh. And do you now see these epic tales, as only sheer fantasy and nonsense? And you must be brought to understand, how The One Truth must mutate sometimes, in order to survive the evil forces, of *he* and *his*, that would have it destroyed. And who's *raison d'etre,* is only to seek and to destroy His Majesty.

And there is no greater irony than, that these 'Acts of God', are nothing to do with God. And counterwise infact: these events have added to the ignorance of God. And so, these events must be termed as, 'Acts of Nature' by 'Elemental Forces'. And over which, God has no jurisdiction whatsoever. Word.

And such forces simply 'are'. And have nothing to do with either Nature or God. And it is elementary. And yet still, God is within The Eternal Elemental Forces. And this is Our Father. And the robes We choose to adorn Him with. And He is The Father of All Creation. And He is The Sun and The Stars. And He is in every building block of Life. And All is governed by Him. And even the rains are Him. And He is sublime. Word.

And you have been desensitised by *he* in They. And you have been steered away from The Knowing. And you have strayed from The Word, because of this. And you have been diverted. And you have been deflected from The One Truth.

And you have been restricted to the five senses of mortal physiology, for the sole purpose of easier government, of you, by *he* in They. And They are wary of The Artist(s). And The Artist is always *an* Human Being. And The Human Being is conscious to the existence of the additional senses. And The Human Being has a sixth sense.

And The Sixth Sense is the name given to the collective remnants of the lost senses. And there are more than one hundred of these. And you do not see The Precious Orbs, carrying clusters of energies.

And you have been restricted by *his* faith in The Sciences, as science is, alone. And reduced by *his* technologies. And stifled too, by Mankinds' infernal need to drag his meat with him, wherever he goes *in* Life. And or, The Universe. (And, but All metaphysics is Science too. And The Unknown is in The Knowing). And by *his* increasing faithlessness to The Divine, instead. And its corresponding spiritualessness.

And They believe All that They are taught. And They are well conditioned by *he* in They. And They are pragmatic. And They are being brainwashed well. And scrubbed clean of All Knowing, by *his* $5 technologies. And by Their compliant obsession to them.

And *he* has committed gross atrocities and genocides, to affect *his* plan. And *he* has capitalised on each set-back throughout prehistory, until recorded texts. And these near extinctions are catalysed by elemental forces. And upon each disaster that befalls The Earth.

And when all is well and at peace, *he* simulates all natural disasters, by making wars and suffering, to try and wipe the slate clean. And this is most favourable to *his* agendum. And to eradicate all Knowing, that threatens *his* domination, is *his* very objective.

And so that *he* may rule upon The Earth, in pale imitation of His Majesty, unhindered. And *he* preserves and celebrates ignorance. And nothing that is upon The Earth is, as it is in The Heaven. And more is the very pity for this. Word.

And *he* continues in this fashion. And *he* is unrelenting in *his* plan. And The People, are acceptant of the carnage upon The Earth, by *him*. And it is an industry, under him. And there is little bliss to be drawn, from the Well of Their accumulative ignorance.

And *he* by They, promote democracy. And They do so by tyranny and despotic force. And this defines the very irony, that reinforces the need for Democracy. And *he* by They, brainwash vast tracts of society, to ensure It's support. And these were once known as cannon fodder. And now, 'a new skin for an old ceremony', dictates.

And, but still All is propaganda, and mass hypnosis. And lies and hypocrisies. And above all, a disease. And all aboard subliminal microwave; now. And They have learnt how to install fascists, through the democratic model. And They are in the business of manipulation & manufacture of The Electorate, from the resource of The Common People. And by the process of osmotic installation, by subliminal microwave. Word.

And They now endeavour to digitalise Humanity. And All peoples have been pixilated. And/or, shall be. And/or, are being so. And All, have been cross-referenced onto ever increasing data bases. And it is riddled with inaccuracy. And gross generalisation & wanton speculation. And there is erroneous policing by algorithm. And it is partisan and not impartial. And it is State sponsored, by those with a vested interest, in the new order, that '*he* in They' strive toward. And so.

And the policing by computer algorithm, is a deeply flawed artificial intelligence, at the time of writing. And as it always will be, and cannot but ever not be. And no amount of binary code, could ever definitively define human genus. And so, it should not be advanced. And yet, it will be. And It is playing God.

And it is not policing. And it is sleep walking the species into an apocalypse. And The Third Face, aims to create one single homogenised control board, from all of this. And this is Their very objective.

And They aim to outlaw The Human Being, for It's uniqueness, individualism and intelligence. And 'he in They' aim to genetically modify humankind, just as They have already with plants & livestock. And *he* is farming The Resource now. And you are to be sure of this, my dearest and most precious reader. And no mistake. Word.

And you are to learn and study well, who are this Third Face, my dearest reader. And They are an emerging infernal pestilence upon The Earth, with Their $5 technologies. And They have only come to be, because of Their invasive $5 technologies. And They will come from both sides, and all sides, to form The Third Face. Word.

And They shall be drawn from an amalgam, of *his* Tin Star Forces, and *his* Tin Pot Mafias. And you will learn to mark 'The Words of I' indelibly, about this matter, my dearest and most attentive reader. And so: just so.

And They aim to pressgang. And load vast tracts of Humanity, onto silicon chips. And sail them into mental slavery. And so, to obey *his* every command.

And '*he* by They', brainwash and remote control. And *he* aspires to be at the very pinnacle, of The Pyramidal Model, by assailing The Third Face, by this plan. And *he* sees the devolution of The Resource, as an essential, to *his* own evolution. And *he* is in They. Word.

And The Masses of The Resource, are increasingly like clockwork mice. And made so, by *his* $5 technologies. And by designer drugs. And the lacing of narcotics. And by trappings and vice. And by politics. And by compounds within the elements of Air and Water. And by radiowave mostly. And it is an unrelenting onslaught, upon the governable senses. And it is All subliminal. And it is All elementary.

And it is an attack upon the nervous system. And this shall serve *him* and *his* democracies well. And appease The Generals of *his* war mongering machines, in All the Nations of all The World.

And, but The Human Being shall stand against it, until
The People are reclaimed. And We shall see to it. And
there is a sense of purpose. And It is God's Will. And
We will forever galvanise The Human Being, in their
endeavour, to uphold His Will; against *his* endeavour.

And the machine is well foddered now. And it is an
insatiable beast. And a Harvester. And all consuming.
And it feasts on the same pitiable peoples, who once
manned the battlefields and trenches. And *Les
Miserables.* And the same hapless folk, who were once
called God's children, before stolen child by child away.
And they are adult. And but, it is only 'those who fight
for Peace without violence', who are God's children.
And *for,* never once has God, Our Father, war
endorsed. And so. Word.

And *he* has pitted *his* recruits against The Human Being
for centuries, in the effort to make mincemeat and
genocide of them. And politics too. And the numbers
of The Human Being have dwindled.

And *he* has perverted the very notion of Democracy.
And *he* makes Them flock into *his* cities, where *he* can
best concentrate, and utilise *his* $5 technologies; to
master Them.

And *he* has transformed warfare into clinical carnage. And war is a game to *him*. And The Good and The Gentle, are made extinct 'by *him* in They'. And are only replenished by the newborn, arriving to The Nursery, in all innocence. And what should be the very beauty, in 'The Circle of Life', is a conveyor belt of corruption & carnage, under *he*. And The Gift of Life becomes an unassailable minefield for many, as they trundle along.

And these Innocents; truly are God's children. And these Good & Gentlefolk. And The Human Being is no different now, in a sense, and in His quandary, to Neanderthal, at the crossroads; where once He too stood. And so.

And *he* writes The *h*istory, to purport that carnage 'is' the norm. And *he* teaches The *h*istory, to install it, 'as' the norm. And The People assign it all to human nature. And to slavery and oppression.

And *he* presents *himself* as the emancipator, of all those enslaved. And *he* is anything but. And it is all far from the nature of The Human Being.

And it is only *his* very existence, that causes others to rally to arms, against *him* in They. And They thrive on every propaganda *he* peddles Them. And They, like fools. And little is untainted by *him*.

And *he* basks in *his* own glory. And *he* glorifies violence and war. And, with the histories written. And with the vanquished slain, *he* rules. And *he* has moved steadfastly toward *his* glory, since Olympus fell and Rome began.

And *he* perverts the One Truth of Church, then as now. And The Church is largely a godless haunt; by *he* in They, by this. And *he* has epitomised all Evil, throughout *his* reign. And *his* hypocrisy knows no depth nor bounds. And The Divine has ordained, that *his* reign must be ended. Word.

And so, it shall be ended. And in All the Nations of all The World, *his* tyrannies and oppression shall be ended. And this is The Word of God. And this is The Word of The Sky People. And this is The Word from The Kingdom. And this is the word, brought by The Men from The Stars. And they are The Emissaries of God. Word, Word. And double: Word.

And The Human Being seeks Us. And The Human
Being, has always sought Us. And The Human Being
believes, still. And they are correct to believe still. And
it is only The Human Being, that does believe. And
since ever We created them, they have believed. And if
you do not believe; you may not call yourself an
Human Being. Word.

And their number is being eroded. And they have been
put into retreat. And they have chosen reclusion above
aggression: as their preferred defence. And hideaway.

And The Human Being is in none of these groups or
parties, to which The Common People fuse too readily.
And from the resource of Homo Erectus it began.

And We left Mankind to it's own devices, between
visitations. And it must be so. And We may only travel
at certain solar and planetary conjunctions. And We
may only be realised by Faith and Knowing. And you
may know Our Orbs.

And Adam is man. And One. And He is the first
Human Being. And He was born of photosynthesis.
And He was commuted by Electron. And born of
oxygen. And The Light was in Him. And He was made
flesh and bone. Word.

And there is The Epic of Gilgamesh. And there is The
Story of Noah. And the one they call Plato, was dutiful
in the scribing of Atlantis. And it is five precessions,
since whence it was.

And 'I' has told you this. And All this, was All of then.
And 'I' has laboured, to tell you this. And I shall
reiterate it again and again and again, until your lesson
is learnt well. And you are able to learn your lesson.
And so.

And so, all tales of Mankinds' ascendency, It's demises
and near extinctions, spanning multiple precessions of
The Earth through The Galaxy, is chronicled in only a
few short years, since the advent of the written word.
And does not correspond remotely, to the times in
which the events, depicted in said text(s), actually
occurred. And this is elementary, my dearest and most
attentive reader.

And it really should <u>N</u>ot be so confusing, my dearest reader. And or, nor, so very difficult to understand. And you have doubted it in your ignorance. And *he* has brought you to doubt it. And *he* proliferates only by promoting doubt.

And doubt is the infection by which *he* proliferates. And it is the very contagion. And The Disease itself. And The One Truth, is the antithesis and only antidote. Word.

And this doubt is the very germ of the disease. And the disease isolates The Human Being. And detaches He, from the infected masses. And They live under a mass hypnosis of contagion. And *he* is in They. Word.

And you have been coerced. And brought to seek alternative explanations, for your existence, in Our absence. And it is only *he,* who has done this. And if you doubt, then *he* is in you. And you may not call yourself an Human Being.

And the most fractured, have flocked to *he*. And *he* embraces Them. And *he* has endeavoured to breed away The Human Being. And The People have followed blindly. And, They march into the vacuous void of obedience to *he* in They, by *him*. And They have been embroiled, into *his* plan.

And They have been ensnared, in *his* trappings. And, The Common People are won over and sold out. And They are satisfied by instant gratification. And They are appeased with ease. And by hollow speak. And self affirming propagandas. And by *his* simple technologies and gadgetry. And by *his* shallow promises and trinkets. And so.

And less than one in four are Human Beings now. And that is quite apparent. And perhaps it is much much less. And, perhaps even less than that. And 'I' fears it is. And this bulletin shall forge the consensus. And the energy is weak. And The Planet Wave is polluted. And it will be a rapture of sorts, that determines the calculation.

And The Blue Planet's Wave, is at It's lowest ebb. And
he has shanghaied and exploited this weakness. And it
will be a revelation in kind, that dispenses the
judgment. And it shall be a genetic harvest and census.

And: The People have now reverted to that; which We
first arrived to. And the intelligence of The Resource
itself, is unchanged in ten precessions. Word.

And Homo Erectus is of a constant intelligence. And
Its' only variant, is the technology it deploys. And, it's
spiritual elevation, through era and stimuli, in
correspondence to The Divine.

And it is all at it's most dark and dense, at this
conjunction. And, at it's very least. And, it's lowest
possible. And We are far from The Golden Age(s).

And it is once more, the same bipedal godless
humanoid, descended from Ape, We arrived to. And It
is no different now, to then: but for the trinkets that
adorn It. And the technologies that drive It. And the
trends and fashions It follows.

And the majority of all evolution in The Cradle of Life, takes this template. And, Life is commonplace throughout The Stars of The Nebula. And make no mistake about it. And this is the omnipotence of God.

And, God arrives to It. And, God is All things. And, He possesses the building blocks, to create anything He wishes. And by which to take any form He desires.

And God radiates. And: He installs components by radiation and fusion. And He mutates through molecular composition. And by such, He moves in mysterious ways. And governs All evolution.

And these compositions are His creations. And He manipulates evolution, by polymers & catalysis. And God will always gravitate, in a heartbeat, to the simple complex carbon based organism. And it is for this, He waits for all eternities. Word.

And, He is The Sun. And to those in far away worlds, He is a distant star. And God, The Sun proximate to their world. And All stars are connected and united as One. And so; He is The Sun & The Stars. And He is omnipotent. And He is All things. Word.

And whenever evolution from The Soup, tips over the fulcrum point, between The Physical and The Spiritual, He comes. And He dispatches His Emissaries, at the first sign of Wonder. And, in whichever form He requires them as. Word.

And the very germ of The Human Being, is in His zenith, precisely, at that tipping point. And His Majesty would want it, no other way, than that. And beyond this perfect simplicity, all complication(s) set upon Mankind, are Not as He would have it.

And you must not attempt to understand Him, because you shall not be able. And any notion you might arrive to, will be an insult to His *very* Majesty.

And I is to tell you this, my dearest; and most precious and ever attentive reader. And: I am but the most humble and dutiful scribe to His Majesty, in so doing. Word.

And so, All Faith(s) in His Majesty, are to be kept at the *utmost strong* & of the *utmost simple*. And He is The Sun. And so, just so.

And, yet All Intelligence, should expound and become as advanced as it may, so long as that strong and simple faith is maintained, and resolute. And Evolution welcomes and expects intelligence to evolve. And to question. And, but all intelligence must be directed away from the business, of attempting any comprehension of His Majesty. And from speculation; into the realms of something <u>He</u> is <u>Not</u>. And so.

And the fanciful ramblings of an inquiring mind, is to be kept away from the devils dykes of theology and debate, that run parallel to The Path of Righteousness. And beware the peddlers of elaborate interpretation(s), that you might encounter along The Way, of Life's Journey. And there must only be Wonder & Knowing. And He is The Sun. Word.

And all homáge to His Majesty, must be by Art and Prayer alone. And never politics. And there must never be an intelligent quest for knowledge or answers, about His Majesty. And He is The Sun. And He is The Father of All Creation. And that is all. And It is simple. Word.

And: The Human Being is the *very* melding, of The Physical with The Divine. And there is a catalyst here. And this is the becoming of Being. And It is the birth *of* The Soul. And Life is beautiful, in it's power and simplicity. And, it is only then, does Life become Divine. And at this, there *'is'* The Divine my Pretties. And The Human Being; at both His & Her *very* zenith. Word.

And *(previously),* We remove all primal function to render obsolete the appendix, which is the primal signature. And We install The Mind and Soul, beyond the biological function of primary organs.

And it is awesome. And it is wonderful. And it is full of Wonder. And all primeval traits, leave accordingly. And *he* and *his*, engage the matter counterwise. And at this, there is the very rub, my dearest and most attentive reader.

And there is no resistance to the temptations of basic instinct, where there is none. And We would never seek, or be able to, install Ourselves in One, without Faith, or (at least), Belief or a sense of Wonder.

And it is an evolutionary leap from the mud. And it is
no sad loss whatsoever. And neither too, *any* comment
on the exuberances of youth, in human nature, *previous*
to installation.

And All Life beyond this, is complicated and dilute,
otherwise. And The Human Being will always have
spent It's quota of youthful exuberance(s) anyway, as it
is right and proper so to do, to be here: to be sure. And
most popularly, quite naturally, most probably.

And the delineation of such experiences, as being Close
Encounters of The Fourth Kind, and/or Abduction, is
only the mortal mind, attempting to comprehend
something it simply cannot, (for the time being).

And *of* Angels; being Space Travelers: rid of the
burden, of needing to cart their flesh and sinew with
them, as they go about their interstellar business, is
much closer to the mark. And The Path of
Righteousness, is broader than you might think, my
most attentive reader & Scholar.

And We claim nor claimed none, that are not *ready &*
willing. And *he* and *his*, engage the matter counterwise;
more fervently.

And *he* and They are ugly. And *he* 'in' They, are ugliest.
And *he* makes sickening perverts of *his* elders instead.
And All perversions within the churches, are about
this. And War(s). And The Catholic Church holds on
to a residue of The One Truth, despite every manner of
atrocity, committed by Them, under God's name.

And *of* the city within the city. And there are treasures
squirreled away therein, possessing great powers. And
It is unable to utalise the *ancient* artifacts, that they
have 'conquested & sequestered', and taken in store.

And the city within the city, is the very residue of The
Empire of Rome. And swathed in crimson still. And it
has been a bastion of evil and hypocrisy, for ever for it.

And, but now it shall be cleansed and rejuvenated. And
by His love. And by this radiation, whilst the *aperture*
is **abert*. And the city within the city, will house only
true emissaries of The Divine, in this time. And during
the given scope *of* the pages *of* this binding. Word.

**abert: open. Aperture abert: a celestial opening allowing passage.*

And the celibacy of The Christ, is a state of Being. And it is Not a disciple's discipline, but a nature; that is arrived to. And it cannot be emulated or imposed. And it cannot be indoctrinated, or impressed upon a priest. And nature cannot be suppressed in this manner, without the gravest of consequences.

And Autumn can never be Spring. And neither Spring, Autumn. And All manner of evils and The Ugly Fish, make their lair, in the repressions and anomalies thereof, and thereabouts. And in The Hypocrites. And in *All* those who would defy without respect, such simple Laws of Nature.

And by all of this, too many children have suffered, at the hands of these Men of God. And these men are Not men, Nor are They of God. And It must be said.

And They prey not pray. And They are only degenerate misfits, in a stalker's camouflage. And They are wolves in lambs' clothing. And They are *his* alone, to be sure. And no mistake. And They are not His. And They are Not Human Being. And They are Not Godly. Word.

And The Christ arrived to celibacy. And The Human
Being, will arrive to it naturally; in the autumn of His
years, as is right and proper. And this is the very nature
of The Resource, in it's pure state: of Human Being.

And, but *he* nurtures green monsters and jealousies,
inside The Common People. And *of* They, precious few
upon The Earth, within *his* domains, grow old now,
with any great dignity. And They corrupt and inflict.

And by perversion, *he* makes these Elders ugly. And the
mainstream, is channeled into a fast flowing gutter.
And instead of being wise and worldly, in the autumn
of Their years, They become jealous and judgmental of
youth. And the exuberance Nature affords it. And by
the *unvirtue* of all this, They become dangerous. Word.

And They farm the young and the poor, into serving
the industries of Their perversions. And into the wars
and industries, of Their ridiculous ideologies. And, so
to do *his* bidding. And it is slavery still. And as always.
And this is the way of '*he* in They', in *his* elders. And
about this, you are to mark my words indelibly; my
dearest and most attentive reader; for it is a Truth.

And They pontificate against Human Nature. And
They persecute those Human Beings, embracing and
celebrating their existence, in their Spring *thru*
Summer. And, as it is right and proper so to do. Word.

And The Path of Righteousness, is broader than They
know. And only The Human Being treads well, the
broad and meandering path. And enjoys the
commanding vistas of Life's experience(s).

And It is a gift from God. And the young Lover &
Poet, is *an* 'Living Ode' to His Majesty; *in excelsis*. And
so: cue fanfare. And He (And she), is ~ the very tribute
above all others: to God. Word.

And The Human Being avoids the potholes of both
perversion and repressive laws. And the hypocrisy born
of it all, that are but some of the bumps in their road,
upon Life's journey.

And The Human Being is designed to celebrate It's
vitality, in a mutual complicity, until Summer's End.
And no sooner than Autumn, is the time for the
spinning of *the* Rumpelstiltskin Yarns, of Philosophy &
Politics.

And twilight; but a time for modest reflection. And
Life in this state is ecstatic. And it is not sterile, but
reflective. And it is outwardly, a time for guidance &
teaching. And inwardly, a time for contemplation. And
never is it a time for exploitation. And always, it is a
time for kindness. Word.

And The Divine despises all perversion, of His creation
and intention. And, but _They_ linger. And, They cling
to Life and power. And They will not be prised away.

And They become decrepit and corrupt. And They
have an inflated opinion of the importance, of Their
own vitality; because of _he_. And _he_ by They, inflict and
impose instead, because of It: until Their bitter end.

And _he_ gives _raison d'etre;_ and great authority, to the
extraordinarily ordinary. And They are buoyed by it.
And They know nothing of the spiritual gigantism,
that His Majesty gifts to All 'His' elders. And they are
most often, to be found, living the simplest of lives.
And in every corner of The World. And with the
greatest _of_ humility.

And We never forsake the Human Being. And The Human Being never forsakes Us. And We have never deserted The Human Being. And, but sometimes We are kept apart, by cosmic forces: Alone. And many fall away in the high tides. And this is where Faith must command fortitude.

And it is only *he*, who destroys and undoes. And it is only *he*, who champions devolution. And it is *he,* who promotes the vices of The Soup, above The Gift of Life, Itself. And there is scant pleasure, to be derived therein: in comparison to Divine Glory. Word.

And sufferance in Life, under *him*, far outweighs the pleasures *he* provides. And it is illusion; and only trappings. And with only the moments of superficial gratification, as wages. And the temporary and short-lived rearrangement of bodily chemicals, pathogens and bacteria, by catalyst and stimuli, as currency.

And Life at It's most primeval, is fraught with sufferance. And Predation. And We will not support the undoing and destruction of Our creation, by *he*, any longer. And nor by *he*, in They, will The Human Being be subjugated, by *his* tyranny and predation, more.

And neither The Women, nor The Children, or The Trees will suffer. And The Human Being will Not be a victim of *he*, in They, by *him*, any longer. And The Human Being, will not be made extinct at *his* hands. And *he* will not return The Blue Planet, in to The Soup. And *he* alone will be cast into The Abyss. And beneath and beyond The Abyss, is The Soup.

And <u>He</u> is All of Light. And all knowledge and truth has been suppressed. And all links to Us have been severed. And They have never known The Truth. And all truth is lost. And it is lost further, by every genocide put upon The Human Being, at *his* hands, by They.

And only *he himself* amongst They, knows The Truth. And *he* exploits *his* knowledge. And *he* in They exploits & maintains Their ignorance, so *he* might continue to rule upon The Earth, and never be exposed.

And *he* will do anything to prevent Them from Knowing. And *he* has never exalted that truth, *he* keeps secret. And *he* never will exalt The One Truth. And *his* reign is an awesome lie upon The Earth. And **he** will do everything in *his* power, to prevent His Majesty's return. And this is *his* singular endeavour. And, at this you are to mark I's word(s) well. Word.

And so.

And They grew in number from the disaffected. And the astronomical window, by which We may come and go, is narrow. And it is an elliptical shard. And only God may pass. And, or those who go with God.

And only The Twelve Times Twelve Thousand have left by it, since was He last here. And only The Twelve Times Twelve Thousand, will return by it, when He returns. And they shall do His bidding upon The Earth. Word.

And they will execute His plan. And you must strive to learn the universal truth(s) in Numbers. And He is very much in the mathematics. And in Numbers; *is* the purest science. And you will count your steps. Word.

And He moves by diffracted light. And The Equinox is very important. And The Precession of The Earth, is most important. And all orbits of all spheres are important. And alignments. And non-alignments, between spheres through Space, are paramount.

And They evolved from the fractured misfits. And They were begotten of those who were not made Human, in the first instance. And by those in whom, the process was not complete. And, or was fractured.

And, They are filled with primeval bitterness and jealousies, that The Human Being does not suffer. And They are Godless. And, The Human Being, 'lives and lets live'. And, but They are always competing with His Majesty. And They will never, 'let it be'.

And They make sticks and stones, from Their inferiority to The Divine. And The Human Being in correspondence. And *he* has nurtured these traits, and made virtues of them. And They are vengeful and vindictive. And They are driven by *he*, through these traits in They.

And *he* has harnessed Them into servitude. And envy and greed have been honed into weapons. And They envy The Human Being. And by this, They feel They must overpower and destroy, what They ought best to endeavour to emulate. And, They feel They must better, what They should worship and adore.

And it is a primeval gene, that drives the devolution. And it is bound for The Mud. And survival of the fittest, is *his*. And, for Darwin's Law ceased to apply to Homo Erectus, beyond the first visitation. Word.

And the elliptical orbit is a Celestial Magnetic Force. And only The Divine, can give The Spiritual an evolutionary advantage, over The Physical. And, The Divine removes aggression, but installs an impenetrable force field and immunity, to protect the sublime Being from physical harm or disease.

And this is the very strength of The Human Being. And this is The Planet Wave in essence. And *he* knows this. And *his* is *a* counterwisdom. And, *he* has all The World going forward, backwards. And so, counterwise, it *is* the very whys and wherefores of war.

And *he* makes wars, in place of harmonies. And *he* pollutes the Planet Wave. And here is the importance of the precession, and the elliptical orbit. And here is The Truth, to be unravelled, from the uncertain sciences of Astronomy and Astrology. And applied to the realm of Metaphysics.

And there is an aperture. And you must know of The Red Planet too. And of course there is a pattern. And, of course it is all beyond mortal comprehension. And so, it is chaos. And so, it belongs only to theory. And not to Knowing. And They have absolutely no idea, my dearest and most attentive reader.

And The Human Being Knows, but cannot explain. And this is The Knowing. And it is a sense. And there is no cause to explain. And it is proper only to wonder. And His Majesty adores those, who wonder about Him. And The Human Being is in essence, an entirely spiritual creature, in harmony with It's physiology. And He lives in celebration of The Divine. And It's faith is resolute. And this is the nature of The Human Being.

And The Human Being is often mistaken for The Common People. And: but they are Chalk and Cheese ~ in comparison. And they are as different, as Homo Sapien to Neanderthal. And I shall sing you a song.

> *"And are you not yet convinced, by The Moon about*
> *the Earth,*

> *~ in correlation with the female cycle. And the miracle*
> *of birth".*

And all of that, is the very essence of the nursery
planet. And there, is your female intuition my Pretties.
And quite where it ought to be. And as if 'The Sense of
Wonder', was indeed the very memory of eons passed.

And there is your Planet Wave, as well it should be.
And as God intended. And, the impenetrable protective
field, of egg and womb. And, is that not The Moon, on
It's twenty eight day cycle about The Earth; my dearest
and most attentive reader. Word.

And would anyone amongst *his* Evil Hoard, drenched
now in *his* feeble *'handheld'* advanced technologies,
really dare to profess to be better than these Ancients,
who lived by the codes of this very knowledge. And
with a perfect command over gravity and magnetism.
And the tools of whom, which now gather dust,
behind the crimson curtain, of The Old Curiosity
Shop, in the City within a City.

And these Ancients are The Human Beings, in their
very element. And they governed. And lived in
ascendency. And in Knowing and obedience, to The
Men from the Stars. And the biology born of <u>H</u>im.

And this was a Golden Age, between our second visitation, nine precessions since. And the floods and destruction(s), some five precessions ago. And _he_ rose again, from the quagmire of this cataclysm. And Mud.

And always, it is two steps forward and one step back. And as such, is the very mechanism of the elliptical spiral, that is Precession. And it is a reflection. And it is always the shape of things to come. Word.

And are you not yet convinced, by The Sun being precisely four hundred times further from The Earth, than The Moon: whilst being four hundred times larger, simultaneously. And precisely. And so, at eclipse, both are apparently exactly the same size. And perfectly. And 'just so', It is. Word.

And is it not the most affirming of all illusions, my dearest reader. And as such, is The Divine. And the melding of The Physical and The Spiritual. And Matter, with the anti-matter of The Sublime. And there, wherein He lays. And through which He shines.

And do you Know about photosynthesis and fertilisation. And there you have it precisely. And the correlation between The Sun and The Moon, is exactly why The Blue Planet is a nursery, in the first instance. And so very precious to His Majesty. Word.

And do you know of Anthropomorphic celestial transmogrification, and genetic harvests. And do you understand now, why the Humanoid form in bilateral symmetry, is the most preferred and common construct of The Divine. And why The Human Being is created in His image. And why the gestation of All I's reproduction, follows that celestial order.

And you have no Knowing now. And without Knowing, you can have no understanding. And all peoples are now embroiled, into the same evolving homogenised festering bacteria, of Life on Earth. And *he* has Them obsessed, with every vanity of the flesh and sinew. And *his* infernal $5 technologies. And there is little Light. And The Resource do not appear to look up from Their desks, and Their devices, in Their cities without Stars. And They are all the same, as it appears. And largely indistinguishable now, from each other.

And it is synonymous with the cult in culture, that They are alike and uniformed. And bonded by Their common cause. And They may Not dictate to The Human Being. And neither, any or All those of Divine ordination. And They (in due course), may not be able to govern the Human Being either; at all. Word.

And They live beneath the hardened crust of a shanghaied Ethernet. And *he* has engineered The People into believing that *he* has Them All, at Their most advanced. And that *his* technologies are, at The Cutting Edge. And it is a veritable nonsense. Word.

And They believe that They are at the cutting edge, under *him*. And it surely is a nonsense, to have such a belief. And only The Human Being knows different. And without The Divinity of His Majesty, They are ignorant of The One Truth. And *he* is self proclaimed, in God's dominion. And *he* in They, is always boastful, of Their imposing and invasive technologies.

And They are on an Incredible Journey within you, my most attentive reader. And They are viral. And there might be nano – machines, coursing through your veins, under *his* very pilotship, if you are a person of interest to Them. And, or one of *his* laboratory rats.

And They can see through your eyes. And They invade without license. And They get under your skin. And you must reject it All like a bad kidney, my precious. And don't believe that there is any Law that will protect you, because it won't. And there isn't. And you must remain an Human Being. And persevere. And you should think in *quill & ink*. Word.

And you must Know that the cutting edge of technology, has no real correlation whatsoever, to the cutting edge of evolution. And nor indeed, to the overriding intentions of His Majesty.

And by far the most of *his* technologies, are only fleeting fashions. And a flash in the pan. And as vaguely important, within the greater scope of human endeavour, as flared trousers. And The Human Being is forever in the very peloton of Life itself. And He is Divine always. And perennially in sunshine yellow.

And *of* the Planet Wave. And *of* the very reverberation. And of that, by which all should be honed. And would be, were '*he* in They' not playing God, with the natural elemental forces. And polluting All of It. And monkeying foolhardily, with His Majesty's creation.

And, it is All a travesty of Divine Law; to keep Him from you. And but, We are steadfastly breaking through *his* shields and deflectors, to combat this. And you are to be assured of this, my dearest and most precious reader. And you are to be steadfast in both your Being, and your Faith. Word.

And We are infiltrating *his* technologies. And the number 33 is a wormhole, wherever it appears. And especially in liquid crystal, or digital format. And it is a perfect number, in this respect. And it is a diffractive angle too. And We may radiate through this number. And We do. And no mistake. Word.

And this number will find you. And attract you to itself. And you shall adhere to that number, if you are An Human Being. And We are in that number. And be sure. And this number is Our vehicle. And you will not understand why. And you will not understand how. And: but be sure, my dearest and most attentive reader, that if you are an Human Being, with Belief and a Sense of Wonder: that you shall receive The Knowing. Word.

And We will catch you by the blink of an eye, wherever numbers are displayed by *his* technologies. And you will have a thought. And you will Know We are with you. And you shall see. Word.

And so.

And They are corrupt. And They are sinister. And They are dangerous. And They by _b_e, butchered all The Aboriginal cultures of The Nursery Planet. And, so _he_ might deflect you from The One Truth. And you cannot know, that all Human Beings were once linked, by the sublime energy of The Planet Wave. And it is the very ether.

And it was owned by no one, nor no one thing. And The Craft and Cult, have endeavoured since The Dawn of Civilisation, to own and harness it. And It is The Source. And it is The Source in Sorcery.

And by Their attempts to own it, They have corrupted it. And They aim to own all things. And They believe All things must be owned. And They protect and promote predatory capitalism.

And They drive economies. And They aim to double production always. And so, it is Them who plunder The Earth. And of course it is Them, who take down The Trees.

And *he* is in They. And *he* would have you starved, of
All Light & Oxygen(s). And *he* would have you blinded
and asphyxiated, in a cloak of sulphur. And *his* very
plan, to do All of this, is afoot. And *he* mongers war, to
drive economies. And *he* builds things up, only to
knock them down; and to bolster industry, by *his*
infernal predatory capitalism.

And They create market forces, by driving the
economies of *all the nations of all the world*. And pitting
them against each other, to supply the demands They
create. And by instilling greed, by '*he* in They', as a
virtue. And by this model '*he* in They' proliferate.

And They must control, and own all things, according
to the inferiorities of Their intrinsic nature. And They
believe ownership gives strength and power. And so it
does, within the apparatus of Their own contrivance.

And by the measure and mechanics, of Their
Patriarchal and Capitalist Societies, They will not let,
'Live, and let live'. And They will not, 'Let it be'. And,
of The Source, It became the preserve of Witchcraft.

And the course of It's elemental force, was farmed like a beavers' dam, under Them. And channeled. And routed. And bought and sold. And They have monkeyed with the free-flowing Source, installed for the benefit of All Human Beings, by The Divine.

And *he* took a part in it. And *he* was in They. And They became *his*. And They were known as *his*, for this. And now, of Witchcraft, it is only the preserve and sanctuary, of the most ordinary of women. And They are oppressed into the servitude of a Matriarch of sorts, by *he* in They.

And it is not a Matriarch, as should be All Life on Earth. And as Mother to Moon. And but, it is a hive of vengeful scorn, devilry, bitterness, and vindictive spite. And these "witches" are foot soldiers. And there is little wizardry about Them. And They are only secret society cultists, desperate to manipulate and assert.

And All that Their craft is, my dearest reader, is only a form of passive underworld government. And a social engineering. And the miniscule manipulation of elemental forces, is It's only mystery. And the cajoling of bacteria. And They can curse. And cast plague.

And devilry and witchcraft curry no favour with His Majesty. And it is all a weak science, that does not lead to The One Truth. And It is a miserable and orphaned bastard.

And They are interknitted beneath The Ethernet. And increasingly, by The 'Incredible Journey', of secreted $5 technological implants, and pathogens. And They by *he*, are inside They. And all about. And at the very cutting edge of biometric experimentation. And it is a ridiculous nonsense. And like flared trousers, it is but a fleeting fashion. And has no 'real' place in the scope of evolution. And neither Life's purpose or Destination.

And The Human Being, is right to reject it *All* like a bad kidney. And too, the present day obsession, with the absorption of *his* macro technologies, above His Majesty, into the integrality of Human Form. And it has been observed. And The Mass(es) within The Resource, believe in *his* technologies wholeheartedly, where once *they* embraced all things holy. And it is the very same fervor, of then as now. Word.

And 'They by *he*', are obsessed with Their handheld apparatus, for the prime and current example: of Their dependency upon *him,* at the time of writing.

And They are enslaved. And tethered to the subliminal microwave technology *he* secretes by It. And that They know little of. And understand about, even less. And They know not, what is being done to Them. And They are increasingly, and very subtly becoming, addicted to It, as Their humanity is eroded away.

And They love Their tracking devices, for all It's fringe benefits, such as telephonic communication; and video clips. And it is The Devil's Tool. And *he* spills into Them, like the very guts of a Trojan Horse. And *he* is consequently the sleeping enemy within, later to be awakened, according to *his* very plan. And *he* is quite literally within T*he*y. And *his* biometric components, are being systematically installed. Word.

And *he* in They, and They by *he,* hanker for the seemingly impossible, bio-mechanical evolutionary leap, that will spring Their handheld apparatus, in to the integrality of Their very being, by bio-metric osmosis.

And this small step is soon, at the time of writing. And it will be the proverbial "giant leap", of non-humankind, into a Brave New World; during the scope of this bulletin. And it is a familiar crossroads. And one where Neanderthal too once stood too, to be sure sure.

And so, just as where once did mineral & rock, swirling in a tumultuous sea, at The Dawn of Time, give birth to Life. (Aside: And this *origin* is The Truth *of* The Miracle of Life, my dearest reader & scholar); so, now: do They search, in anticipant adoration, for The Scientist or Technician, who will be Their god; *his* wonders to perform: The Master. And make of Them; Machine. ~ And each morning will begin, come this glorious day, (Not): not any longer with; *by* switching on the power to the handheld device(s), reposing upon the resource's bedside table: but, by plugging in, the detachable device, into the housing porthole of the flesh & sinew, of *the resource's* body, Itself. And so: Engage Modem. And Good Morning. And so: just so it shall be. And They shall be *his* instruments, come this day. And soon: within 2 generations of humanity & 5 generations of technology. Word.

And I must tell you now, (aside), that Big Brother is a degenerate misfit. And *he* is consigned and confined, to the attic *of* Our Father's Mansion. And *he* is in the architrave. And there are precious few angels in the architecture. And *he* is behind the Redeye. And *he* is behind the skirting board. And of Mice and Men, *he* is the infestation. And The Disease.

And the male of the Common People, is no better than the female. And the female is no better than she ought to be. And as such is The Resource. And so all was, and will be, lost; unless abated. And all is equal. And inferior to His Majesty. And it is nothing to be boastful of. And so, The World is controlled in consequence, by a few evil men, and some women. And the latter have aspired to this, to be equal to Their male counterparts.

And there is an homogenisation taking place. And governed now, by a single spirit. And that spirit is *his*. And *he* is in They. And They are grappling at the pinnacle of The Third Face. And trying to establish a foothold, for the control of It All.

And They wrestle in the mud of corruption and hypocrisy. And the apparatus They clamber upon, is of *his* construction. And design. And They monkey thereupon: mongering wars, and playing ungodly games. And with an overestimated value, of Their own vitality. And They are devoid of All Humility and Wonder. And Their only pursuit, is toward power and wealth. And the authority by which to attain such.

And They have no humility; to be sure. And, The Human Being does have humility. And this is the very hallmark of The Human Being. And Authority without Humility, is Always Tyranny. And therein lays the rub, my most attentive, and politically astute reader. Word.

And The Human Being, seeks only the infallible truth of Divine Guidance, in His wonderment. And The Human Being, never seeks, or appoints Leaders to dictate. And neither, Dictators to lead. And there is no such animal, as benevolent dictatorship. Word.

And The Ethernet, which is The Source, is now steadfastly being implemented, into making a mockery of The Matriarch, as it was, and would be, under He in *s*He.

And All that was Divine, is being synthesised by *he*. And *he* is counterfeit. And *he* is a fraud. And a Faker. And *he* is not godly. And by It, T*hey* remote control The Common People. And by viewing remotely from a distance. And by *his* infernal $5 and subliminal technologies. And macro surveillance(s). And the Peeping Toms *of* Redeye.

And by every opiate, and synthetic drug of The Masses, now at *his* disposal, coursing through the trillions of miles of Resource veins. And aboard the nanotechnologies. And biometric laced particles therein; riding through new territories. And: peering into new worlds for the first time, like explorers; riding the white water rapids on 'a' virgin African continent.

And The Common Junkie is most typical. And subject to this law. And it is run like a clockwork mouse, by Them, by It. And *he* aspires to control All peoples this way, with the weakest; the first to be laden'd onto *his* silicon *s*chips, by emerging biometric technologies. And bound (and gagged), as if for Botany Bay. And to the brave new world, of a virtual reality. And They, under *he*, are advancing Their subliminal technologies, in this very Endeavour, & The Theorem of Devolution. And *his* instruments; are '*he* in They'. And They, *his* oarsmen. And at *his* command, They heave to. And so.

And *he* drives the evolution of technology. And the evolution of technology, corresponds with the devolution of Humanity. And *he* farms Pharmacy, to the detriment and devolution of The Species.

And '*he* in T*hey*', devise(s) Law(s). And then; *he* divides
The Law into smaller laws, where there ought to be no
laws. And these industries create employment for the
minions, which occupy and employ, *his* very agents.
And who dutifully serve *his* agenda. And so.

And *he* is in They. And by All this, *he* corals and
diverts. And devolves and emasculates a species. And
The Human Being, my dearest and most precious
reader, until now, have been laid to waste, and put
asunder, by It. Word.

And His Majesty; does see some useful purpose in
social engineering, indeed: but fears the repurpose of
The Resource by such, has *malintent*. And They would
be *his,* were this to be allowed, unhindered & unabated.

And blood and veins will soon be rendered obsolete; to
fluid and wires. And nanotechnologies. And All within
a very few generations. And primary organs; become
merely interchangeable component parts. Word.

And They scuttle about, in obedience to The Voice of
the $5 technology, as though it were The Voice of
God. And to Them it is the voice of god. And it is
Their Master's Voice. And They see *him* as Master.

And, only because They do not Know God. And it is only ever; always someone from a higher rung of The Third Face, than They, who They see as Master and Commander, that They hear. And, hiding behind walls, or concealed in the circuitry or architecture, playing god amongst the gargoyles. And They know the voice of the $5 technology is not God, but They do not Know God. And They know no better. And so to Them, *he* is the higher power.

And They speak of stuff & nonsense. And They speak of sex magic. And They aim to shatter the cerebral chambers and nervous systems of Humankind, with tools of pornography and narcotics. And by a general demoralisation of Mind, Body, Soul and Spirit.

And The Common People is most susceptible to this onslaught. And the extraordinarily ordinary; more is the pity. And *his* plan is very much afoot, at the time of this inscription, my dearest and most attentive reader.

And in this field, They are at Their *ungodliest* height, as unbridled hypocrites. And temptation is no temptation whatsoever, when it is seen for what it is. Word.

And why? ~ for They want Their World filled with fractured and broken individuals. And narcotics; above and below ground and counter. And too, the technologies to remote control it's users by. And the powders. And the solutions, that are the very problem. And the radio waves of order & indoctrination. And this is how They would have it: the money and the power. And the entire business of Life, my most attentive and politically astute reader, is simply this: "It is a game, where the people who have the money, endeavour to control those, who make the money".

And the *enslavery*. And All, whilst pontificating counterwise. And They are Hypocrites of an unprecedented caliber. And They are Evil. And They are D'evil. And it is All a terrible lie upon The Earth.

And All that They are, is a terrible lie upon The Earth. And so, my dearest reader: you are to Know, They are The Disease. And *he* is in T*hey*: most assuredly. And so, just so. Word.

And *he* in They, at this, can manipulate the
demoralised subject, to serve *his* wants. And *he* farms
Them. And that subject; is then a Common Person,
demoralised and godless. And obedient. And They
swarm into cults. And They congeal on mass.

And They make up secret and esoteric societies. And
They observe ritual and vice. And underground
ceremony. And They practice witchcraft(s). And They
worship and obey Their Leaders & Providers, as
dedicated mindless fanatics. And They are gullible to
trend and whim and fashion.

And of The Common People, it is a foot soldier, to
boot. And infecting All, with It's poisoned pollens,
trampled from the hive. And so it goes: contagion. And
disease seeps into the mainstream. And the tainted *is*
seen as the norm. And so it goes. And by this, The
World becomes *his* ward: stolen from **H**is glory. And so
it goes. And the ' to & fro', of a tug of war, like the
changing tide, throughout the spiraling procession of
The Planet, through It's Universe. And so.

And according to *his* plan, when are All of They infected, The Disease would be the norm'. And it would no longer be a disease, but a devolutionary step, toward The Mud. And The Earth would be *his* world.

And the dreadful stench of marsh grass. And this is *his* very plan. And *he* favours greater; a vice dependant hoard, than a single free thinking individual. And you will argue with I, about this, but it *is* the truth, the whole truth, and nothing but the truth. And *he* may be staved off in the short term, by sweet fragrance(s) and perfumes. Word. *(But it is no lasting remedy).*

And The Human Being under **I**, is the only antidote, to the pestilence of the evil hoard. And They is a plague of locust. And They go about Their business with authority. And They seek positions of authority, to give Themselves authority, within the apparatus of Their own construction. And from these positions, They contrive and monger wars, in order to oppress and control.

And *of* The Ethernet, that is The Source. And, it is channeled like a hardened artery now, let by *acupoints*. And, selected and pinpointed, by those in authority. And beneath a grid marked out globally, in quadrants.

And it is not fluid & free flowing, and sublime, as once it was, when installed by elemental magnetic forces, determined by The Sun and Stars. And instead it is contrived and engineered. And synthetic. And it is nothing like; when The Human Being sat in wonder of His God, and grew to develop great & fanciful tales, of sultans on their flying carpets, from what they saw.

And anyone who will surrender to *he* now, will be hooked up to It. And connected. And *locked in*, like an adhering particle. And They will be issued with a device(s). And targeted with microwave. And entered into the very *raison d'être* of *his* plan. And if the subject, has no wherewithal about His Majesty, and is not an Human Being, It shall, All too soon become Their raison d'être by proxy, too. And They shall become a machine. And or, rather a component in a machine. And an automaton. And a malignant cell, within The Disease itself. And about this, my dearest reader, you are to mark my words indelibly. And before *All* Paradise Lost. Word.

And on mass, this Common People may become an Evil Hoard, by little more than a catchy slogan, a snappy uniform, and the barefaced lies of some heart wrenching propaganda.

And it swarms too readily. And They *are* fickle and whimsical. And easily led. And They jump, when They are told to jump. And to a specified height. And history tells tales, so it all might need never be repeated. And but <u>His</u>'tory is seldom 'heeded'. And *he* farms it thus. And only for this, T*hey* are dangerous.

And when vexed, They by *he*, shall do *his* bidding; every time. And so They have done, on too numerous an occasion. And They do. And '*he* did'. And *he* adores The Swarming(s). And *he* encourages the swarmings. And *he* makes plans around the swarming. And the swarmings occur, just beyond each *three score years and ten*, in cycles of around eighty years.

And so, They worship and obey the voice of the subliminal $5 technology. And it is at *this* time of writing, a superswarming in advent. And with All the contagion It affords. And that voice is *his*. And *he* has capitalised on the advancement of technologies. And *he* has stolen a yard by this. And extraordinarily ordinary and common people, are afforded extraordinarily intrusive powers, for the meanwhile. And jobs for Peeping Toms & perverts. And They are made giddy by the intoxicant of Power. And They are buoyed by it All. And made important.

And They are *his* instruments. And They play god. And Satan (who is _he_), has entered government, at near each and every nation of The World. And corruption is rife. And just as with every element of The Disease, once commonplace, it becomes The Norm.

And common criminals have entered Police Forces. And too often They actively predate on the civilians, who are ostensibly, The People. And so, just so it *'was'*: at the time of writing, my dearest and most precious reader of The Future. Word.

And They make Laws & Wars, not so They can engage in combat *per se*, but so They can control All sides. And control narrative. And create illusion. And *his* Will is conveyed, by *his* instruments. And it is imposed. And the laws are administered by *his* instruments. And these instruments are They. And these instruments are *his* generals, whether with or without rank; enlisted or civilian. And the civilians of *his* cult, attach themselves like suckerfish, to the enlisted of *his* cult. And They meander through the shark infested waters of Their own creation, looking for prey. And it is so. And it is unfair. And They abuse authority, and the channels of communication it affords Them. And It is a flagrant breach of Rule & Law, and no mistake. Word.

And where once was a level playing field. And the referee would 'from time to time', *call* 'foul', at the infringement of a rule, it is now a 'free for all'. And a minefield of entrapment, set-up, subterfuge, trickery and deceit. And there is abuse of authority, for financial gain, at every turnabout. And make no mistake about it: that it is so. And They are corrupt. And They are unbridled hypocrites. And They are extraordinarily ordinary. And They abuse the authority bestowed upon Them. And the authority They have stolen. And They are pathogen infested and bacterial. Word.

And They are the most common of people mostly. And whether with peaked caps and shiny buttons, or not. And They are a genus without genius. And some are good, and some are bad. And some are very Ugly.

And you are to only look for The Spirit: and not the rank, my pretties. And you are only to extract the truth, from the bones of It. And the ghosts They cling to, in this pursuit. And for this, you will need to utalise one of the residual senses, bundled up (and stored), into your sixth sense. And if you are an Human Being, my dearest and most precious of readers, you shall have a sixth sense. And the particular sense you need for this exercise, will be within that compendium. And so.

And people do possess an aura. And it goes with the territory. And it comes with The Gift of Life. And it is *an* hue, more than it is a colour.

And therefore, by example: it would be better defined as Sunshine, than it would be *as* yellow. And the aura is determined by the Spirit, that *doth* possess the person. And, however I digress, to impart this lesson. And so.

And The You is in The <u>H</u>ue or *hue*. And can belong to <u>H</u>e or *he*. And it is a curious study every time. And too often, the true colours and fancy plumage, of the Unbridled Hypocrite, are amazing to behold. And the charade displayed. And the dance of The Hypocrite, never hoodwinks the Human Being. And so say <u>I</u>.

And They under *he*, are a marauding pressgang, upon The Earth. And *his* staunchest recruiting agents. And They will continue to endeavour, to load All human kind onto silicon *s*chips, and *sale* them into slavery.

And one by one, They are laden'd & uploaded. And it is The Digitalisation of Humanity, that They are about. And a new skin for an old ceremony. And this is Their very business, as ever it were. Word.

And They are an infectious disease. And so *he* builds *his* army, mostly with The Fractured and Disaffected, recruited thus. And They are a motley crew, that make up *his* Evil Hoard. And it is a cult. And it is a secret army. And it is civilian, in it's make up and majority.

And *he* is in They. And The Cult recruits by this very practice. And propaganda fertilises the germ within. And the germ is in the mud.

And The Planet Wave is now an Ethernet, laced with *his* $5 technologies. And It pinpoints and targets It's subjects, with the greatest of ease, from a distance, at the press of a button. And It channels and broadcasts, specifically & particularly. And those signed up to *his* agenda, hear *his* voice to the exclusion of all others. And *he* commands the obedience of *his* own. And They are as faithful to *him*, as The Faithful are to His Majesty. And so *he* is a formidable opponent. Word.

And at this, it is a counter synthesis of The Voice of God. And this was never the purpose of The Planet Wave, my most attentive reader. And mark my words indelibly. And It was once blanket like. And shrouded The Morphic Fields of learning and levitation, by antigravity and magnetism.

And each progressive step was triggered, like stepping stones, through the ascent of The Human Beings' earliest evolution. And The Mind was a microcosm of The Heavens & Earth. And All was just so. Word.

And now It is gridded and plotted into quadrants, by *he*, in They. And it is a trawler's net. And They administer and administrate, beneath it. And They pontificate. And The Voice of God is drowned out:(It is *an* oscillating reverberating humming sound): to all, but The Faithful and The Human Being. And it *is* distant and vague and dissipated. And chaos prevails as a consequence. And the overlaid Voice of God: (a voice like thought), is gone. And The Resource is divided unequally, between those who still have it, and those pressgang'd into the sythesised and counterfeit version, of It: that is *his*.

And **H**e is still above it All my Pretties. And rest assured. And He is God. And He is The Sun and The Stars. And so very far above it all. And so far above the festering pathogen infected bacteria of Life on Earth, under *he* by They. And He has Not deserted you, my most precious and ever attentive reader. Word.

And in every conceivable way, He is above it All. And so far beyond All mortal comprehension too. And He is in the 'Sound of Light': now. And it is a change of frequency, if *you* will. And this is your meditation, my dear sweet, inquiring & *ever* Faithful reader. And pay no heed to ungodly interference. And now look to hear Him. And if you are Human Being, He will find you. Word.

And the 'extraordinarily ordinary', is a term that relates not to Our arrogance, but to Their ignorance. And you are to be reassured by this, my Pretties. And, but so too, equally concerned. And, **H**e is becoming so, and too, polarised. And out of reach. And further distanced from The Common People, as They progressively lose Their sense of wonder, to the seductive science of *his* technologies. And The Common People *is* becoming *his*, more than they are remaining His. And Faith is an increasingly scarce commodity, amongst The Resource. And They is the very tide on which Humanity rides, and divides at Fulcrum's Point. And the tug of war, between Heaven and Earth, would appear to be more reflective of the shape of The Earth's Precession itself, than of the juxtaposed Wills, of His Majesty and His adversary. And 'the' doings of their respective number.

And The Ying & Yang. And the zig and zag. And the planet's corkscrew mimickery of DNA, with its 'two steps forward, and one step back', are rather, more so; merely the cards He is dealt with, than by His design.

And yes: He is all things. And All things are He. And but, only in as much as He, is The Air that is carried in The Wind. And He is there and within, because We choose Him to be there, regardless of the activities of elemental forces. And but: over which, He has little or no control or jurisdiction. And so, just so.

And the two are poles apart. And The Common People, in their blinkered ignorance, are falling like flies, to *his* regime. And They are dilute. And They have lost all sense of wonder. And that is All. Word.

And They are hopelessly detached, from The One Truth, and His design. And They are *his* now, instead. And They are no longer His. And They are not Human Being(s). And The Blue Planet, is now immersed in a super saturated solution, without a trace of the Divinity, that once ruled It. And it is returning incrementally, toward The Soup, under *he* by They.

And They enhance The Planet Wave to Their wants. And by *his* primary technologies. And It is now the very tool of The Third Face. And it is not sublime, but a hardened crust, inhospitable to His Majesty.

And They use extractors, to draw from it. And so, to govern the molten seething bacterial mass within. And It is like a hardened artery.

And They lace it with Their own agenda. And it is no longer The Source, feeding The Morphic Fields, from which The Human Being drew and grew. And by which, God communed with His children. And by which, The Men from The Stars (in all their translucent finery, & *on* zero gravity levitation pads), commanded The Faithful, and built The Ancient Worlds by. Word.

And, but it is now the preserve of an esoteric elite ruling class, playing god. And, They rule by a Science. And an oppressive politic. And The Human Being rejects it all, like a bad kidney. And God does not like people who play god. And, too few have ascended to be with The Divine, since all Knowing was lost. And those that have, *are* The Twelve Times Twelve Thousand. And belong to The Golden Orb of His Majesty. Word.

And *he* has forged an awakening of sorts, in They, by *he*. And The People have been awakened into a nightmare, from which They cannot escape.

And They know now no different. And They feel chosen. And purposeful. And it is Their *raison d'être,* to be a party to It. And They know no better. And They Know nothing.

And a slave will always know it's purpose. And a slave will always know it's master. And so, They obey The Master, for fear They will be punished, if They do not. And, in the hope that The Master might reward Them, with trappings or trinkets. And or, something shiny.

And The Human Being is only irritated by, and impervious to; it All. And The Human Being is increasingly isolated, into the fringes and remote pockets of society, for the meanwhile. Word.

And The Planet Wave, is now a synthesised substitute, of It's original nature, and The Mind of God. And it is now totally artificial. And it is *mispurposed* to *his* purpose(s). And it reverberates in every way, the same way. And, but it is not the same, because of *he* in They, by *him*. And It's misusage.

And They by *he*, are engaged in The Digitalisation of Humanity. And all Humankind is affected by this. And the aquatic mammal, is most effected. And dissipated, by it all. And the aquatic mammal is reliant on The Voice of God too, and more specifically, the base oscillating reverberation, beneath It ~ caused by The Earth hurtling through the zero gravity *deafness* of Space. And best interpreted, most accurately, by the didgeridoo of aboriginal Australia.

And, but such side *affects*, to Their Masters' plan, does not concern Them, in the least, despite the lip service They pay to those, of whom it does concern. And They exist only to proliferate, and double production. And to plough through regardless, according to Their capitalistic regimes. And They are an *All consuming* and self serving breed. And They are only concerned that They are, as a People, united by It, according to Their own agenda. And They are a breed apart. And They favour the extinction, of every living creature, including The Human Being, bar & by, but Them. And so.

And It is an homogenisation of sorts. And it is Evil most certainly. And They are The Evil Hoard. And They proliferate by contamination. And, as such; is the very disease. And no mistake.

And They are swarming, my dearest and most attentive reader. And Their Master Always believes that *he* is Satan incarnate. And so, They are satanic by definition. And *he* may be risen simultaneously, in more than one.

And The Planet is interknitted by It. And by They, under *he.* And you must beware of short men, with big technology my Pretties, for They are made tall by it All. And They are *his spies* within *his species.* And there is a rule of thumb. And this is very true, and well observed. And All gross generalisation, only ever comes about, through 'the mean & average'. And there is never smoke without fire. And men with large ears, are predisposed equally, to eavesdropping and invasions of privacy. And All Being(s) have purpose. And evolution, through eons of time, would teach you that, my dearest and most attentive reader, if Life was not so short.

And *he* senses the feelings of personal inadequacy, within Them. And *he* detects the scent of mud & marsh grass. And *he* enforces jungle law. And *he* deals in complex. And *he* offers compensation. And *he* makes *his* easiest recruits, of those with acute feelings of personal shortcomings. And the complex ridden fractured misfit, will always find it's *raison d'etre,* and a home, under *he.*

And so, They arrive like gladiators, with a vengeance upon The World. And into the arena of Life. And finally, a vent to air Their spleen by. And Evil prevails, by this serpentine model. And The Human Being suffers none of It. And yet, is all too often a victim of It; by proxy. And so.

And They are bitter and perverted. And these are like landlocked angels to him. And the imperfect are perfect for *his* wants. And vengeful bitterness and scorn, suit *him* most agreeably. And They are recruited and dispatched, about a wired world, to plant *his* invasive and intrusive $5 technologies. And to gather pollen, *for* to pollute and poison by. And it is Their modus operandi. And so; to collect anything that They can twist and tinker with, to fashion into financial gain. And interesting persons are manufactured into 'persons of interest'. And just so, like evil elves, are the very instruments of *his* imps & minions. And They are the feverish installers of it all. And They wire The World by It. And it is a wired world, under '*he* in They', by Them. And They spread disease and malicious rumour; and propagandas, by It. And They manipulate. And by electronic viral infection; the pathogenic effect of which, is as pervasive as any rampant bacteria. And *he* is toxic. And no mistake.

And it is all contagion, by *he* in They. And those of Their ilk, fly drones too. And They play War, like They play computer games. And carnage is a leisure industry.

And great and decorated war heroes, *shall* be recruited from Amusement Arcades. And They kill and maim Innocents, and Human Beings, from the safety and comfort of an easy chair.

And so: be attentive my dearest and most precious reader(s), of both Present & Future, for We shall Not allow All this to come to pass. And for that prevention, to be best implemented, We need You. And no mistake. And We are The Sky People. And We champion The Human Being(s') evolution, by Light & Spirit. And We oppose machine and biometrics, outside their everyday practical function; as The Way.

And You are to be Our vessels. And so say I. And *he* may not deny Us any longer. And this is the word of The Sky People. And We are amongst you, though not incarnate. And We are in the air you breathe. And you remember Our number, don't you, ~ my dearest and most attentive reader? And so, reflect each time you see It. And We will be with You. Word.

And *his* infantries *shall* become biometric robots, within the scope of this bulletin. And *his* propaganda machinists, will be persuasive to the power; that *he* is good. And They too are clockwork mice, only doing *his* bidding. And *he* has legions to recruit from; in the amusement arcades and lounge rooms of The Wired World. And the viral infected electronic realm *he* presides over, that is *his* dominion. And what greater *raison d'etre,* could be bestowed upon the gaming zombie, of a bone idle lounge lizard, than for gallantry, on the playing field of battle: or the battlefield of play. And how else could pride be afforded, to such disenfranchised & dysfunctional youth, earning Their stripes on PlayStation. And it is the *very* direction, in which it is *All* headed. And but, it is Not The Way.

And They are not Human Beings. And They are made into infernal busy bodies with purpose, according to *his* agenda. And They are All fingers & thumbs. And They are given great purpose, within Life, outside the very purpose of Life. And it is a travesty. And it is a nonsense. And it is an affront to His Majesty. Word.

And so.

And It is all only reflective of DNA itself, I supposes. And Life follows the pattern, that it is patented by. And the Precession of The Planet, spiraling across The Universe, limping as she goes. And dragging it's bad leg behind her. And two steps forward and one step back, as footprints in the sand, through The University of Time and Space.

And It is All beyond Good & Evil: really. And it is really only around the bend, until full circle. And into The Realm of Pure Science. And it's governorship. And where, therein does abide His Majesty, and The Father of All Creation. And so: just so. Word.

And All bodies of authority, above and below ground, upon The Earth, are morphing into one, by this, by They, under *him* in They. And at this time. And They cannot help themselves. And each celestial step The Blue Planet takes, along her predetermined path, is simply catalytic. And You Know, my precious. And it is all largely fated. And but, for His Majesty, *All* Life upon The Earth, is of no greater significance, than the bacteria clinging to the surface of a wind felled fruit, on an orchard floor. And so, the surrender to humility.

And All is somewhat predetermined, by celestial patterns; but never precisely so. And sometimes there are the Golden Ages, from Time to Time, when is the best foot forward. And when All is Good. And there is a spiral.

And there are parameters, that do indeed tolerate a margin of individuality, drawn from the tumbling tombola, within the cyclical predetermination of Life.

And there can often be, per chance, 'a' resultant Fame & Fortune. And, or indeed celebrity *or* notoriety. And it is most irregular, to the mean & mundane.

And too many live with such insatiable wanton cravings. And They see celebrity as the jackpot ticket, when The True Success of Life, is quite opposite. And so, the *very* real purpose of Life Itself, passes Them by.

And it is All *his* doings(s). And when All is said and done, It is but a simple twist: under the influence of magnetism, Light and gravity. And a kink: in a precession, that is the spitting image of DNA, that holds all the cards. And so say I.

And The One Truth is in The Wonder. And it is
beyond All mortal comprehension of His Majesty. And
uncharted, on the road map of His Universe; in the
microcosm of Ourselves. Word.

And so, the gases and elements take their form, each
time, from Time to Time, under the influences of
magnetism, Light and gravity. And each and every step
of the way. And as; so they surely must. And are;
predetermined so to do.

And, The Spirit decides from a celestial vantage point,
upon the vessels of the individual(s) it frequents. And it
is *an* happening. And it happens by design or
otherwise. And it may very well be seen as a random
selection, from the perspective of Humankind. And or,
even a Divine intervention. And **I** is sure it is. And
pattern would appear as Chosen. (And to tap into this
pattern, to a degree, is to be seen as clairvoyance).

And but, all creatures great and small, must be
occupied by Spirit, of one sort or another, whether
selected at random, or by Divine predetermination;
regardless. And as, in the case of Enoch. And forget
every notion suggested by Celebrity, emerging from
popular culture. And such serves Only as amusement.

And some are toxic. And *he* is sulphur. And as such is Life, whenever *he* is in ascendency. And from Time to Time, upon The Earth, *he* is. And at the time of writing, my dearest and most precious and ever attentive reader, *he* is. And *he* shall remain so, for the meanwhile. Word.

And of The Chosen One, *(so called),* who would be The Son of God each time, by this slim probability. And *coming* by recurring pattern. And who does indeed, arrive in manifest, from Time to Time, as a rank outsider also. And at both and against tremendous odds: He is All things. And only for the sake of argument. And many would attempt to predict pattern and proclaim. And so, but yet, of He as follows:-

And He is not of sulphur. And He is not born of marsh grass. And He is All of Light. And celestial. And He manifests as a Commoner. And He is not a Heathen. And but, not all Heathens are *his*. And not all Heathens are Commoners. And those Heathens who are not *his,* are Human Being(s). And they live on the fringes of society, as misanthropic recluses. And they are Not 'go with the flow' Mainstream. And they live in idle contemplation, until chosen. And they wait only for The Sun and The Son. And The Father. Word.

And it is only the elemental forces of Spirit, that give identity to an otherwise nondescript carbon based resource. And that is the rudimentary science of it all. And the very bare bones of Life on Earth. And Life without a name; is the greatest humility. And *just* Being, to which particles adhere according to Science.

And of He; whom indeed is sent from The Kingdom of Heaven: in reflection of The Kingdom of Heaven, by His Majesty, to take mortal form upon The Earth; moreover. And it is He who paves the righteous path.

And He leads by example. And His Spirit is the guiding Light. And He is The Way. And The Path of Righteousness is broad. And I am but a humble scribe.

And it is *far far* broader than those cults of the cloth, (who have manipulated His Majesty's intent, into their own mortal governments and oppressions), would have ever had you believe.

And there is nothing of the unbridled hypocrite, about His Divine emissaries. And about this, you are to mark my words indelibly, my dearest and most precious reader, of both The Present and The Future. And take heed, back yonder, to the heath; and wonder. Word.

And Science has It, but *doth* not yet know what it has. And The Scientists are 'hot on the trail', hounding down His Majesty. And they are in His pursuit, in conveyances & chariots built of Chemistry & Physics + Mathematics. And algebraic formulae. And biometric theoretic experimentation.

And but: they shall never see the wood for the trees. And nor His crown for the corona. And they will lose His scent in the wild waters of Wonder. Word.

And but: I shall tell you, as it is my duty so to do. And I am a dutiful scribe to The Divine in so doing. And I will tell you All, of the Kingdom of Heaven. And of the distorted reflection of It, upon The Earth.

And I shall *(in my teachings)*, underline that an Electron: (the subatomic particle), can be two places simultaneously. And are. And so, just so and so, it is. And this scientific fact, is the basis of the theory and theology of: *"On Earth as it is in Heaven"*, in principle. And so; think on. Word.

And He, whom is indeed conceivably born to random immaculate selection. And He, who is All of Light, until made incarnate surely. And by no more significant scientific means apparently, than the haphazard wheel of fortune, that selects a lottery jackpot winner. And so. And of The Resource that houses The Spirit: there is only ever their given names, to suggest that It All might be otherwise. And makes of People; persons. And builds from flesh and bone, character.

And there is only the personalities of people, to suggest that it is not so. And the proof is in the lack of proof. And The Truth is in The Wonder. And that is all.

And that The Divine might have no part in the predetermination of random selection, is but Satan's folly, on a barren landscape, to which you ought not subscribe, if you know what is good for you. And without The Spirit, (which is The Divine reflection of His Majesty, in the haven of The Heaven of His Kingdom), to remarkably distinguish, any One member of The Resource, upon The Earth, from any other member particularly; is impossible. And so, All that is God, by way of scientific explanation; and All that is Spirit, equally, is ironically contained, in the 'very' *dark matter,* that is all about. And there shall be disclosure.

And **H**e who can manipulate or cajole the electron, in and from, a distant Heaven, to command and dictate, over its *'mirror image'* upon The Earth, is The Divine. And He is God. And/or The Son of God. And no mistake. And He is true. And He is real. Word.

And those precious few, upon The Earth, from Time to Time, (And there are times when there are none whatsoever), with this Knowledge, are The Magicians, (and not mere witches). And they are Emissaries of The Divine. And they are not illusionists or fakers, but prophets. And in Ancient Times, and in Future times (*of* the cyclical Golden Ages), always would they carry a wand. And this is the instrument of The Divine.

And to propose that it might be the individual itself, responsible for It's own celebrity, and not the apparent random selection of predetermination; is error. And those *of* Faith *in* The Golden Ages, would call this 'Fate by Eros'. And not Errors; my most appreciative reader. And so.

And those of The Dark Age(s) of the precession, would *seize the day,* and claim all they conquer as Their own. And this would be Ego.

(And They are *his*. And *he* is in They. And it is *Them;* most assuredly, who 'make opaque', the reflection of The Kingdom upon The Earth. And it is a world of smoke screens. And a hideous hall of mirrors, under *he* in T*hey*. And distortion. And it is lies and deception. And hypocrisy. Word).

And but; (aside): moreover; it is the *latter,* that is predominantly the case. And that predetermination, is more influential upon The Life, than The Self. And Life is a game of chance, until The Fate(s) play their hand. And this is The Spirit. And no one is the master of their own destiny. And Life is not what you make it. And None are particularly blessed, above any other. And but; may only look forward, to enjoying the tumbling tombola, and the random fortune, of not falling into parable, and onto stoney ground. And so; whichever way the wind blows, will determine the good seeds from the bad. And nothing more. And at their harvest, the wheat from the chaff. And so: just so.

And Life is all about. And everywhere. And it is in the air that we breathe. And the intoxication of The Spirit, is the very business of Life. And the very purpose of It.

And It is in the science of photosynthesis. And in The Neutrinos within The Leptons within The Electrons. And so: just so. And it is in The Trees. And H̲e is in The Trees. And He is His Majesty. And *he* (D'evil), is in the fossil fuels, that pollute the atmosphere. And *his* odour *is* sulphur. And *he* is risen from The Abyss.

And so.

And *he* is emerged, from the prehistory of The Dawn of Time. And from, the very belly of The Earth. And with a putrefied soul, as black as treacle. And from marsh to mash *h'is* risen. And *he* is the money and the power now: no doubt. And for the meanwhile. And *he* is in *The Fossoilers.* And the infernal internal combustion engines, of All industry of modern *history.*

And *The Fossoilers* are *his* instruments. And *he* is exhumed by Them. And *he* controls the *fuck & fight* in *All* The World. And The Peoples breath in *his* noxious poisons. And *he* manipulates these, so to have the control. And at the time of writing, *he* is at *his* zenith.

And *he* builds, so to destroy. And so, to build up again. And to promote *his* predatory capitalism each time. And *he* schedules War and discord, only in order to drive flagging economies. And to perpetuate this model. And it *is his* game of Monopoly, whichever way. And *he* in They, never wish for peace, except at the idyll, where ' *he* in They' feathers 'It's' nest. And blood is washed from *his* hands. And from where *he* can control, the misery & carnage of *his* manufacture, from a safe distance. And it is this way every time. Word.

And you are to mark my words indelibly about this, my dearest and most precious and ever attentive reader. And wear it near to your very bosom, whether you are man or woman. And be clever about it. Word.

And The Spirit that occupies you, is without gender. And you are to Know this. And you are to arrive to this. And to *All* other Knowing, in due course. And in so doing, you will be transformed from Resource, to Human Being of the highest order. Word.

And I must tell you, my dearest and most precious and ever attentive reader. And, (aside), and in *All* confidence. And for the duration of the meanwhile. And until *he* is spent. And exhausted. And defeated: it will remain so. And until the close of this aperture, to be precise: (2084): it shall be so. And it shall remain so. And so: when shall His Majesty reign once more. And shall All energy once again be His. And The Resource rejuvenated accordingly. And you should have no fear of global warming: Not really. Word.

And neither should you fear the radiance of His Majesty, for He is certain of His actions. And it is the very majesty, of His very own weapon(s), under the crown of corona - working toward *his* defeat.

And all this, is as cyclical, as the very precession itself. And it is quite normal, according to the Production of Eons, in which The Precession stands-in, as months. And in 'this' time, the population of The Resource will be reduced. And it must be reduced. And the only matter is, *of* how it shall be reduced. And so.

And: but it need not be by suffering. And starvation and disease. And or, and by, Flood. And or, it may indeed be, by all of these means. And exacerbated by the latter. And whether this way or that, is not to be entirely decided by predetermination. And The Resource and it's governors, will have a stake in their fate to a considerable degree.

And I am to be dutiful in my appointment, as humble scribe to The Divine about this topic, later in this letter. And you are to pay the closest of attention, my attentive reader, when I *does*: or else. Word.

And there are more losers than winners, in The Game of Life. And Only because *he* has made of Life a game, with too many players on one side of the net. And a distortion in manifest, upon The Earth. And it is a racket, under *he* in They. And it is a side show coin toss. And it is rigged. And two faced. And it is slavery.

And They are corrupt. And bias. And the odds are loaded. And heavily stacked. And be told, my dearest and most precious reader. And take heed. And take Word back to The Heath. And neither be fleeced, nor skip to the slaughter, as you go. And *he* walks amongst you, as a wolf in sheeps' clothing. And *he* preys on Heathens. And it shall remain so, for the entire duration of the scope of these pages. And Heathens are Good. Word.

And so.

And it is only the division and balance of elemental forces, that determine the status quo. And hereditary monarchy is a nonsense, where one is good and the next is bad. And yet Their powers remain the same. And so, We are to carry each other, instead. And democratically, install persons of the utmost integrity, into regal status. And for lifelong terms. And not just the 'flash in the pan', of four or five years. And so, *for* to fulfill visions. And bring routine and longevity. And We are to do unto others, as We would have them do unto us. And so: (aside); These are The Laws.

And the very rich must pay the highest taxes, to support the societies, that gave them their riches, in order to maintain the government, and infrastructures of those societies. And so: The Rich must not be parasitic. And they must pay their taxes gladly. And with goodness in their hearts. And they will be rewarded by love & gratitude. And appreciation.

And when *he* is in They, They simply don't give gladly. And, or selflessly. And or, without ulterior motive. And They can be clearly recognised as *his*. And They evade and deprive. And *he* is in They. Word.

And it must be the end of the white billionaire, and the starving black baby. And it must not be the beginning of the black billionaire, and the starving white baby.

And *he* may not squirrel away secret fortunes, whilst the *Havenots,* starve in an overburdened society. And, whilst left buckling under a lack of support, from the selfish and the greedy. And *he* is clever and calculated. And *he* evades well, all moral & social obligation. And *he* & *his she~s,* can be clearly seen in They, as They 'were' *in* Rome. And some dynasties of Egypt. And, as most ostentatiously prevalent, in the royal houses and châteaux of seventeenth & eighteenth century France.

And those Human Beings whom are well heeled, and do too enjoy The High Life, (which is not wrong in itself), *All* have charitable foundations. And they do wonderful work. And they give generously. And so; just so. And it is a foolproof method, to distinguish All those in the public eye, between His and *his.* Word.

And *he* in They maintain(s) disparity & division, quite deliberately. And *he* protects The Corrupt, who exploit both the fact, and the loopholes. And the status quo.

And those who have made Their riches, in correspondence to the misery & poverty of others, are to be shamed. And moved from celebrity, to infamy. And there is no notoriety, that anyone would crave, in infamy. And everyone must be as kind as they can be. And kindness brings with it, its own reward. Word.

And Satan, who is *he*. And *he,* who is *him* in They, has wealth in abundance. And *he* preserves the disparity, as a protectionist mechanism. And The Human Being(s) is generous. And kind. And philanthropic. And there you have the lesson in a nutshell, my dearest and most attentive reader. And this is the 'Word of I'. And so say I. And 33 is Our number. Word.

And these are The Laws, more than any article, and contrived subparagraph, woven into the protectionism of predatory capitalism. (Aside). And; it is only so that I might state the obvious, by *your* humble scribe, (who has preempted His 'preaching to the converted', in His having the obvious stated; by the listing of the aforementioned and subsequent *articles of Law)*.

And it is all very tedious and boring to my most devoted reader, who does not seek to lift the mundane politics of office, from these pages. And who will intrinsically Know, such things already, as *an* Human Being. Word.

And but, it must be said with clarity. And such important matters, documented; as it is proper, so to do, within these humble bindings. And so; others might or may draw reference, or seek guidance in The Future. And or instruction, from them, as they see fit.

And my dearest reader must remember: that, His Majesty, has often been misconstrued and misrepresented, by Critics in The Past. And maligned by Idiots. And misquoted by Witches, (*far* less clever than They would have thought Themselves to be). And indeed, *just in case of;* All those who would choose to tread a *bittercup* from *purple prose.* And so, it is written.

And His Majesty sees All of They as *his.* And is unashamed in His assertion, that He will always choose His humble scribe, from the resource of The Lover & The Poet. And He will always be His favourite boy. And nothing through *All* time, will ever change that.

And where a bulletin is of such magnitude, as this, my dearest and ever attentive reader, it is good to include a clear manifesto, as a subtext to the main vehicle. And as, tender to locomotive, if you will. And so.

And but; by all means, Everyman may use their natural bent. And drive; and talent and acumen. And aspire to wealth and great things, if it is their inclination to do so. And to many, achievement derives fulfillment. And to others; not. And Apathy is, too; precious.

And there would appear to be a regrettable predisposition, within The Resource, to trample over and exploit those, not immediately related, *(in some form),* to Itself. And to see another, who is in every way the same as them, as prey. And, or an hostile enemy, simply because they are unknown to them. And it is a fundamental design flaw, in the ascent of Man. And it is a poor reflection of His Majesty. And It causes War.

And there are unsatisfactory levels of violence and perversion(s), within The Resource, that would be best bred away, than be allowed to remain. And His Majesty would prefer to delete such flaws, from the DNA of The Resource, rather than to leave it, as something for *he* in They, to develop & exploit in Our absence.

And You must enjoy Life. And so long as there are taxes ploughed back, for the greater good of everyone everywhere, and the very wellbeing of the Planet in general, you will be able to. And by the continued goodwill of The Philanthropists, who will have the honorary status of Guardian, bestowed upon them.

And All War will be crushed and prevented, by an overriding Global Government, that is singularly concerned with the well being of The Planet, and It's Peoples. And this shall soon be installed. And once it is, or soon after, He shall return. And It shall be fully implemented and operational, by the close of this aperture. And: or very shortly afterward. And this will ensure the very end of despotic dictatorship. Word.

And technology must be advanced, singularly for the betterment of Mankind. And The Human Condition. And robots will be our slaves. And they do not have emotion. And they must not be given emotion. And they will be engaged in Agriculture and Recycling. And Policing and Law Enforcement. And all areas of public service. And they shall drive buses. And sweep roads. And they will act precisely, according to their programming. And the servitude of machine(s) is not slavery. And but, 'It' shall be Slave(s).

And under His Majesty, there shall be no biometric merger, but a distinct distinguish-ment, between Man and Machine. And the robots will serve The Human Being. And pioneering invention, will not be for the primary use of military, with 'hand me down', secondary domestic usage. And but instead, used singularly, for the betterment of Life on Earth. Word.

And the population growth of the Planet, must be curtailed. And maintained at its optimum of 4 Billion. And *All* & every; extremely humane and sensitive method(s), will be devised to enforce this. And It shall be stringently enforced. And Life will be treasured and valued as a consequence. And it is an imperative. And All Life will have value. And no Life will be cheap.

And The Circus of The High Courts, will be pared back. And there will be capital punishment without cruelty. And, or delay or ceremony. And without any more deliberation, in the passing of judgment, than is necessary. And only for those who commit heinous crimes, against *the person*. And Death Row; is only for those, where there is any element of doubt in the guilt. And prison, only a place for those deemed to be a danger to society. And productive community service for *All* else.

And euthanasia, an accessible option at every juncture. And You are We. And We are One. And So say I. And these are The Laws. And: Democratic Capitalism is preferred, as an underlying politic, to Totalitarian Communism, it is observed. And is best, as generally applied to The Resource currently, with all It's flaws. And at the time & place of writing: (EU: West '22). And for the foreseeable future. And it is correct. And it corresponds more honestly to Human Nature, which can indeed be channeled, but never suppressed.

And a capitalistic society, marshaled by a M̲achine aided, impartial, nonpartisan, communistic government, would be optimum, until such Time as transmogrification is complete. And by when, Plant Life is to be successfully incorporated, into the genetics of The Resource. And so; indeed. Word.

And, so to remove the predatory nature. And the underlying cruelties of same, that appears to have stifled the evolution, of Our clever monkey. And threatened, All other *Flora & Fauna,* both East & West *of* Eden. And if the seeds are planted during this phase of the precession, His Majesty would expect the first fruits of harvest, as soon as the next visitation. And so: in around 13 or 26 thousand years. Word.

And the flesh tone & hue of vitality within The Resource, would turn from pink to green. And to be 'in the pink', in two, three or four, precessions from now, would most probably require verdant tissue.

And this would be the first sign of success, in the process. And there might be forty shades of green, between the best of health, and terminal illness. And <u>I</u> believes that this would be a welcome advancement. And the first teetering steps toward an evolutionary leap, that could only be discussed categorically in Eons.

And The Resource is a work in progress, with all its social and anti social predispositions. And It will always be organic, under He, owing to the carbon base. And His Majesty's commitment to Humanity. And practice makes perfect. Word.

And so.

And All Human kind is only a resource, built from a carbon molecular base. And whatever name it carries, or title it gives Itself, It is only a vessel, in which The Spirit resides. And once The Spirit brings 'being' to The Resource, It becomes Human Being. And so.

And The Resource is nothing without The Spirit. And this is the very teaching of The Sky People. And The Sky People are the emissaries, dispatched from The Kingdom, by His Majesty. And The Sky People are purveyors of Spirit. And this teaching belongs to The One Truth. And it should come as no surprise.

And The Kingdom is so very far away. And it is impossible to commute incarnate. And with all the bags and baggage(s) of flesh and sinew, burdened upon *the* carbon based organisms of The Resource. And so the mastery of electrons, that exist in both *locals* simultaneously, is paramount. And definitive of His glory. Word.

And so, We are here in Spirit. And We arrive by Light. And more particularly in concentrations of Light. And as Orbs. And as The Twelve Times Twelve Thousand.

And The Sky People are most particular. And very definite. And We are The Essence of Life. And We are mathematically fixed, by Science. And once We attain Our status, as one of The Twelve Times Twelve Thousand, We have numerical value. And Eternal Life.

And it is only The Spirit, that is important in the business of Life, despite the many trappings and distractions of Vanity, put upon the flesh & sinew, of mortality. And the constraints of mortality, are very limiting. And so say I. And embrace His Spirit. Word.

And but there *is* - and can indeed be; 'Celebrity'. And celebration of The Individual. And so say I. And with both his'tory and His'tory to tell.

And but; Existence; both animate and inanimate, is truly only a revolving science, within a definite pattern, to which All things must adhere. And more specifically, *to which All particles, within All things, must adhere.* - And it is only shape shifting. And therein, is evolution & extinction, stretched through precession upon precession, across Eons.

And if you must Know, my ever curious and inquiring reader, the *corkscrew journey* of Planet Earth, has a loose approximation of 19 precessions, in the course of an Eon. And there are about 3 Eons in an Epoch. And even a whole stack of Eons is less than a dot. And so.

And His'tory is filled with majesty and triumph. And Light. And *his*'tory is filled with pain and suffering, darkness and carnage. And such has been the stories of Life upon The Earth. Word.

And so there is reincarnation, of sorts; by virtue of the patterns Life takes. And there is the incarnation of Spirit, by scientific repetition. And that is so. And it is true. And of course it is true.

And It is as true as leaves on the tree, returning year after year, each Spring. And it is really very true, & just as the leaves on the tree, returning year after year. And how could it not be true. And the tree is still the same tree, but a little different, year upon year, with the tell tale rings of age. And as such, is the spiral of Precession, that never quite returns precisely, to the point it was at, previously. And The Great Spirit, is beyond all mortal comprehension, just as is His Majesty. Word.

And so it is Holy. And so, It is the *very* stuff of
Wonder. And His Majesty, and The Great Spirit, and
the celebrated entity, of H̲e as an individual, are One.
And so, just so, as ever it were: it remains. Word.

And but: each near perfect reincarnation, with each
near perfect, yet erratic revolution, *(of the corkscrew),* is
not commonplace. And it is a spiral more so, that
maintains an irregular pattern. And prevents repetition.

And it is a vortex. And so *the repeat,* is never quite so.
And it is only every twenty six thousand years, *(and
some),* that a precession is completed. And this is the
length of The Precession. And it is a vortex, by which
All Antecedents and Descendents come and go, be it at
conception or expiration. And So.

And The Past & The Future, can never be precisely at
The Present, but are indeed, ever so slightly port &
starboard *of* The Present. And The Past & The Future,
are in almost perfect parallel, with The Present. And
with a little science applied, to a Leap of Faith,
anything becomes possible, my cleverest reader.

And it ought not be too farfetched, to be able to change horses in midstream. And sidle saddles, fore or aft, aboard the carousel of Time Itself: which knows nothing of the manmade chronological constructs, *of* Past, Present & Future. And only of The <u>N</u>ow. Word.

And I am not merely humouring you, my dearest and most attentive of readers, when I advise that the understanding of, 'The Precession of The Earth', and The Spiral it takes within Eons of Time, in revolutions of twenty six thousand years, will discover for you: Time Travel. And so 19 x *X* = *an Eon*. Word.

And my most *intrepid & diligent*, and studious of readers, can begin their quest here. And will indeed, often have done so, throughout Time. And but, to no avail, as yet. And never under the guidance and invitation of <u>I</u> especially. And so, I should put it into *a* context, that every fine young *groovy* student's mind will understand, ~ Time Travel is like the scratch on a vinyl record, moving instantly forward, without the need for revolution. And right here; my most precious of readers, is the very germ, to ignite the genius required in you. And here is the tributary source, to the stream of consciousness, that will lead you to your discovery. And so bon voyage et bon chance mes amies.

And everything is in The Human Beings' Mind. And no mistake. And It is a microcosm of The Heavens & Earth, to be sure. Word.

And you will give thanks to these humble bindings, in due course, for being your greatest inspiration; my ever gracious reader of The Future. And: with the seed corn scattered <u>N</u>ow at this, 'The Time of Writing', give thanks to His Majesty, for the reaping of what He sew.

And pay homage to His humble scribe, who wrote for You, upon His instruction. And such stylish nonsense. And since: the 'dot within the circle'. And so, may <u>I</u> now have written for You, once more: a Tri-Spiral, in <u>H</u>is name. And leave the remainder to you to Wonder. And the dalliances with Sciences. Word.

And so, I am to tell you; that His Majesty expects tremendous inroads, to be made in this regard, during the course of this aperture *abert*. And before the close of It. And much depends on you, to fulfill the vision, that is the fact. And for great fervor and excitement, to be renewed and carried forward, from this: His bulletin. And for you too indeed, to form the vanguard, be-fore the forthcoming Golden Age.

And from the very day You lift His words, from these humble bindings, to be inspired; You are to be enthused & renewed. And It is a new frontier forward: Port & Future. And It is a resurgence back: Past & Starboard. And so say I. Word.

And (aside), suppose if One were able, to sidle across to the parallel contour(s), of Past or Future. And, rather than following the laborious linear route, of twenty six thousand years *and some,* of cumbersome evolution: to sidestep. And for *then & there,* you shall have it: in a jot. And just like the scratch on that gramophone record, fore or aft, in phonographic illustration. And it is easier said than done, I grants you. And but, there you have the very bare bones of the Science(s) required. And the shards of Time. And Light. And Space. Word.

And needless to say, there are also many more dilute patterns and forces at play, than The Precession, within the very *matter of fact* of Existence. And the overall shape it takes. And more and variant circles within circles. And such is the very stuff of some religions, to be found East and Far East of Constantinople. And long before Christ & Mohamed. And religions serve their purpose well, until Male Ego climbs aboard. And uses religion, as a vehicle for *his* politics. And so just so.

And it is good and proper to live a simple Life. And for that Life to be filled with Humility and Kindness. And Wonder. And His Majesty is devoted to You for this.

And the everyday business of Life, during this aperture, is to bring an end to *The Fossoilers* exhumation(s), that have seen *him* risen. And to draw *All* energies 'Port & Forward', from His Majesty's provisions instead. And **He** *is* The Solar. And He *is* The Wind & The Waves. And He *is* The Trees. Word.

And but a more secular understanding, will get you there too. And, but without the disembodied voices of The Dead, that Religions *can* afford. And just as there are years within decades, and decades within centuries, *All* Life follows pattern(s). And *of* precessions within Eons, it is *All* cycles & patterns. And nothing at all, but Science. And that is All. And, *but for what* Science calls, 'The Dark Matter', (of God): that stitches It All seamlessly together. And He is the glue that binds. And to my most devoted and precious reader: be sure to let those, who would discard these pages as stylish nonsense, know that 'The God Particle' was discovered, only days after His Majesty, had instructed His Humble Scribe, to pen this bulletin. And I like Enoch. And <u>I</u> has It All said now. Word.

And so.

And I am to tell you of The Pinnacle, my dearest and most attentive reader(s). And I am to tell you, of The Third Face. And the metaphorical metaphysical summit of which, do those of The Pinnacle clamber to control, at the time of writing. And what makes Them tick. And It is Real. And An Extant Ethos. And it is a manmade mind mapping construct. And a biometric program. And I am to give you advanced warning, of what They would be, so that They will not Be.

And They have circled Their wagons. And at 'The *very* Pinnacle', All Forces, and All Mafias, share a single frequency. And It becomes a merger. And an amalgam. And an alloy of allies, forged from strange bedfellows.

And They are amassing by corruption. And by the love of money, like a cyclonic cloud, around the summit of All Authority & Government, at Every Nation of All The World. And They broadcast to Their respective margins, with a common intent. And it is Their *modus operandi,* for All entities with *an* authority, (regardless of it being lawless or lawful), to Lord in union, over All those without authority. And therein lays the rub.

And They are a law unto Themselves. And You are to mark my words indelibly about this, my most precious reader. And You are to never let it happen. And You must never let Them Be. And to be forewarned, is to be forearmed. And so.

And this is not a declaration of anarchy & revolution, my most loyal and attentive reader of the future: *au contraire*. And but, rather simply a signpost: reading, 'Danger, Keep Out'. And so it is written. Word.

And; They now enjoy the same hastily opened Pandora's Box of tricks, as each other. And technology has united Them. And They belligerently share, the same subliminal $5 macro surveillance technology, like squabbling infants, in a tug of war, on a Christmas morning. And They hide & seek. And They pontificate. And They instruct, and/or torment Their quarry from a covert distance. And The Common People does fall to it, one way or another. And there will be an infestation of clockwork mice. And The Lesser over The Greater. And They aim to govern. And control by subliminal instruction. And about this you must mark my words most indelibly, my dearest reader. And act accordingly. And ignore Them: (*he* in T*hey*). And reject It All like a bad kidney.

And women and small men, are *his* quickest recruits.
And the common junkie, is as weak as iron filings, to
his magnetism; and so, is the one most readily
pressgang'd by The Amalgam. And They make good
pack mules. And beasts of burden, for servitude and
vice. And The Human Being *does* reject It All, like a
bad kidney, as it is right and proper so to do. Word.

And 'this' Big Brother, is an all consuming bully. And,
only leads to a merciless, and non-benevolent
totalitarian dictatorship, every time. And both *his*'tory
and His'tory, record *his* antics well. And prehistory too.

And it is a swarming. And it intends to be a super
swarming. And or, so it would be. And is destined to
be. And this particular pattern, is a tedious carbon
based predatory construct flaw, that needs Divine
intervention(s). And remedying, by transmogrification.
And It is a most regrettable recurring behavioural
pattern, in The Resource. And so. Word.

And the storm clouds are gathering. And it is peculiar;
to witness the black & white of The Good & The Bad,
merge as one, into shades of Grey. And into a common
authority. And so: The Third Face.

And it is a pattern. And has been seen in both the First & Third Reichs of Rome and Nazism; where The Ones in Authority, are The Ones who are Evil. And this will never do. And but, it *is* precisely, what is happening, when looked at objectively, with a bird's eye view, of 'Life in The Petre Dish'. And it is the perspective of God. And the view from The Kingdom. And it too often reveals, that The Good were never ever good, but merely hypocrites. And The Resource is fundamentally flawed. And All Governments should be intrinsically Good. And Not intrinsically Bad. And His Majesty would sooner see Honesty prevail. And justice served; on the level playing field, of the open ground: than for Mankind, to be allowed to continue, at all costs. And so fair warning is hereby given. Word.

And such a super swarming is never a good thing. And it is rare. And such a super swarming, is always dangerous. And it simply leads to those with authority, oppressing those without authority. And 'absolute power corrupts absolutely', has been the politically astute, and impartial, accurate observation of such happenstance. And once it is allowed to get It's jackboot in the door, and prevail; It will snowball every time. And no mistake. And mark my words.

And it leads to Slavery & Genocide. And becomes tyrannical oppression. And World domination; by a single, and all consuming ethos. And this is *his* objective; every time. And it is *his* perpetual desire.

And It is bound for this; my ever attentive reader. And what was clearly recognised, and defined as Good and Evil before, intends to merge at The Pinnacle of The Third Face, as one, in dominance. And t'be acceptable. And beyond Good and Evil, They intend to govern All beneath and below. And this is the agendum of The Pinnacle of The Third Face. And: *of* those who reside therein. And, about those who see Themselves, as an elite & 'ruling class'. And as The Pinnacle Itself, which *as* an ethos, does inside They reside(s). Word.

And They both use $5 technology, in Their 'tug of war', for the hearts & minds of The People(s). And They, as an enemy *is* subtle. And friend or foe uncertain. And They are forever recruiting, according to Their politics. And dragging others into Their sickened vortex. And Their technologies, will extenuate every evil trait, in the individuals of *his* instruments. And it is a career path, for those who do not wish to be lawless psychopathic serial killers, yet have a lawful cruel and vindictive bent. And They are many. And so.

And it is a game for High Rollers & Fat Controllers. And The Human Being does not play it. And nor does He wish to play it. And '*he* in They', plays it without compassion or empathy. And it is War, or nearest offer.

And: essentially, you shall serve either 'The Manifest': *of* The Devil *or* The Lord. And it always comes down to this. And not only in Christendom, but in All & Everything. And It is simply Ying & Yang, and or whatever amount of fancy words **I** dictates His humble scribe to describe It as. Word.

And there is always the perpetual sloughing of skin(s), for the old and redundant ceremony. And this is an age old, familiar & established, and recurring dilute pattern, in all religions and philosophies. And You are learning nothing new, here, at this, my dearest reader.

And it is age old for a reason. And The God & The Devil, *shape shifts* throughout all T̲ime. And only and simply, because of the conflict between Positive & Negative energies. And so: 'Give it a Name'. And It is called Energy. And everything is born of Energy.

Fat Controllers operate from booths concealed in urban districts. And They are very real. And They preside over grid marked quadrants. And Their booths resemble those of Sound Engineers in recording studios, with buttons and faders. And They are connected to an infrastructure of surveillance technology, attached to lampposts and telegraph poles in Their ward.

And even the written Word, is derived of energy. And in the hands of The Poet, the very finest distillation of energies, may be sampled. And even dragons, are born of volcanic gases, in fusion with the written word. And what else is there my dearest reader.

And The Complex Carbon Based Organism, will always complicate the matter, *as per* The Human Condition. And The Poet most of All, when He is not effortlessly engaged, simplifying *All* matter(s) instead, for the purpose of; The User Manual of Life. Word.

And in truth, it is *All,* but Only one smaller pattern, within the 'all governing' larger pattern, of The Precession Itself. And beyond that, God only Knows. And therein; is that which is called Dark Matter. And where The Scientists have dared to give, who is God, a name, other than God. And but; it is transparent, and not dark at all. And It is Mathematics. And Chemistry. And It is as real as the air you breathe, in the World with which you are more familiar, my dearest reader ~ for your better understanding, of what & who, He & It is. And you may trust The Scientists now, to lead you to God: once they have applied themselves firstly; ~ and internationally, to matters of birth control, medicine, horticulture, robots, famine, disease: & solar energy.

And so.

And It appears to occur with a perpetual frequency. And bolstered at every *Eighth* of The Precession. And these are The Tides of Time. And The Weight of Space. And the shifting of Dark Matter, under magnetic influences, that make Our God(s) & *devil(s),* that, of this, they themselves make. And there is no god but God. And I has It All said now. Word.

And so, you must learn to distinguish; which is which. And The Good from The Ugly. And ongoing; from the amalgam in authority. And the very mishmash of *his* New World Order, (for want of a better phrase), each and every time. And so: The Pinnacle, where is '*he* in They' in Power. And The Third Face, which They are.

And They are largely impenetrable. And They *is* always a secret society, at this level. And They need to be, because They could never be tolerated otherwise. And They are the system within the system. And the unseen master puppeteer. And They are consumed by Power. And They are intoxicated by Satan *himself,* in parts per billion. And They govern by illicit powders. And drugs that dare not speak their name.

And by ultrasonic & subsonic radio waves, harnessed to $5 technology. And by *All* the invasive surveillance gadgetry, which was once considered *avant-garde* & cutting edge, in the sultry world of espionage. And, but now, is in mass production. And available by mail order, *(hence: $5),* to The World & *his* wife. And into the hands of *he* in They. And everyone; so shamefully predisposed to use it.

And They impinge. And They are insidious. And They implant particles. And They deploy nanotechnologies. And They eavesdrop, without warrant or license: with Their subliminal macro technologies. And it does Not make Them better people. And They are not dashing spies and secret agents, but Peeping Toms & perverts. And They experiment upon The People, as though Guinea pigs. And They farm the Honey grub.

And They watch. And They have reached the ceiling of Their own existence, but have no idea what Life is for. And what to do with It. And so, They begin to invade and encroach, upon the lives of others, whether; as for sport, or by profession. And either way, it is wrong and unnecessary. And at Their dizziest heights, They become secret society cultists, protected by Their own kind in positions of government. Word.

"And there is no room for secret societies within a free society". ~ And but: They are secret society cultists, who aspire to be *within* government. And this is Their life. And but: It is Not Life, nor indeed the purpose of Life. And to stand against Them would be wrong, if All Government was right. And but, it is not right. And there is predatory capitalism, too often driving government. And that is wrong. And greedy politicians, abusing authority, is commonplace. And so beware The Pinnacle of The Third Face, which is an elite secret society cult. And Their modus operandi.

And until *he* can assimilate Them, into the mainstream undetected, They remain in the wings; like a phantom at an opera. And waiting. And They are 'cloak & dagger'. And this, is the very nature of The Third Face. And you must mark my words indelibly, my dearest and most ever attentive; *and* politically astute reader. And so now you Know, as I has told you. And that is *of* The Third Face in waiting, to be sure. And They is *his* vanguard. And They are an ethos. And They are forever shuffling toward the fulcrum point, like a burglar on an exterior window ledge, of a New York City High Rise. And, or: as if, trying to 'steal a base' unseen, down below: and over Yonkers, Yankees, yonder. And They must be kept at bay forever.

And at The Tipping Point, were They to slide the balance, and 'change the rule(s)', The Peoples would unwittingly have allowed Them to Be. And woe betide. And periodically, when comes about this way; The Super Swarming, as only ever seen in the likes of Ancient Rome & The New Socialism of Nazism: c20.

And only at a super swarming are They manifest, as were Praetorian Guard in Cesar's Rome: or Gestapo in Hitler's Europe. And, but They are always thereabouts, wishing & wanting, behind the scenes. And only <u>33,</u> and The Light, is the antidote to Their menace. Word.

And *he* is always in They. And waiting. And trying to shift the balance: to the point, where *he* would become integral to the very *being*. And normalised, within The Resource Itself. And indeed, The Societies in which The Resource lives. And so. And They are One. And united. And They yearn for the politic(s) of *The Super Swarming*, that will see *him* risen. And for All authority, to be ruled by *he* in They under *him*. And the slightest tip of the balance, at fulcrum's point, would release a deluge of Evil. And would see the dambusting tyranny, that Only a Super Swarming delivers, by manipulation, of a fickle & swayable Resource.

And you must be warned. And you must be prevented from learning too late, of <u>T</u>hem. And *All* that They are. And All that They intend to be, each and every time. And *he* is striving toward *his* world domination, and tyrannical oppression always. And '*he* in They', denies the access of The Sky People, by suppressing the 'Faith & Wonder', in The Resource. And so now you Know; my most precious and attentive reader, as <u>I</u> has said It. And '*he* in They' denies the existence of The Sky People. And *he* is relentless & unrelenting. And All Hopi are lost. And All Hope is gone. And extinguished, under They by *he* in Them. Word.

And All Mankind is meant to be in awe of It <u>A</u>ll, according to *his* design. And *his* infernal invasive technologies. And *his* Might & *his* Power. And in awe of They, by *he*. And Their flagrant invasion & imposition, into The Everymans' privacies and daily life. And in Truth, It All Only stands to divide a species. And The Human Being rejects it all like a bad kidney. And The Human Being is very right to do so.

And you are to mark my words indelibly, at this juncture, dearest reader. And denounce All macro surveillance, subliminal technologies, and nano-engineering, to by far the larger part. And: as are currently, and increasingly being used, without warrant or license, at the time of writing. And by persons, inferior to those They survey, presiding over the devolution. And The Lesser is governing The Greater: be warned. And so.

And *he* wishes to farm Us. And to prey upon Us. And yet, too few have grasped the very fact, that the evolution of *his* technologies, correlate directly to the devolution of a species. And so, inevitably: it shall be too late when *They* do.

And All *his* advancing technologies, correspond to the tainted democracies, that give greater credence to They, under *he*. And that give *him*, by They, such sweeping powers. And my most attentive and applied reader(s), shall take care, not to trip over, what looks like a paradox here. And will indeed note: that these are not the correct steps, toward the evolution of the essential impartial global government, namely: (The **F**ederation), which is to be most sincerely concerned, singularly, with the well being of The Planet, and It's People(s).

And it is an old and familiar song. And so. And The
People must rise up *perpetually,* and sing their 'Songs of
Freedom'. And reclaim their Humanity and birthright.
And their Equality. And their Liberty. And this too, is
a recurring pattern. And It shall always be this way.
And every dog & god will have it's day, beneath the all
encompassing mono-deity; The Father of All
Creation: The God, Himself. And The One Truth He
belongs to. Word.

And The People(s), will never desist until it is this way.
And God will not have The Human Being oppressed,
by those of The Godless, that '*he*' weans in Our
absence, on pop politics, modern conveniences, the *very*
lust for money: trappings & trinkets. And computer
games, drugs, and pornography.

And the Good & Wise Envoys & Emissaries of The
Federation, understand this, and shall see to it. And no
other way will suffice. And enough is enough. And The
Federation must be honed unrelentingly, until It is Just
So, and *All* is Just, by order of The Divine. Word.

And **I** never will subscribe to a ruling elite, that
endeavours to manipulate and control society, by
subliminal messaging & instruction, via It's recruits.

And It is Not at all, the way of The Federation.
And It is in many ways, the way of The Third Face.
And *of* the totalitarian super swarming hybrid, forming at The Pinnacle, where gather the rainclouds, from which All oppressive political consciousness flows. And of The Third Face, forged by those oppressive streams of consciousness. And that which: They by *he*, believe are chosen by It. And by The Spook that *spakes*. And They feel special: so very special. And *he* by It, is a surrogate god to Them. And It is cutting edge & *avant-garde*. And It is new and exciting to Them. And the synthetic disembodied voices that emanate are *his,* by *he* in *They*. And *his* infernal synthetic subliminal $5 technology abounds, from streetlamp(s) to refrigerator(s). And it is everywhere increasingly. And It is the stuff of Tin-Pot Mafias and corruptive Police Forces alike. And the hybrid secret society cults melded from Them. And your refrigerator, might not, or may be, your friend. Word.

And you are to mark my words indelibly, my dearest reader, so that Hard Rains could ne'er those words erase. And so, as follows: It shall Not be until The Federation is formed; and in force: that there will be First Contact, with His Majesty at this visitation. And I has It All said now. And no mistake. Word.

And so.

And (Previously), They acquired tools that belonged to The Architects. And The Architects were The Emissaries to The Divine. And The Son of Akhenaten, brought many secrets to The Twentieth Century. And He was an hybrid child. And He had preserved the tools. And He was protected by The Divine.

And I shall tell you. And you may use it as a general rule of thumb, to be applied. And so. And They draw Their energies from below. And it is marsh grass. And The Human Being counterwise, are all His. And draw their energies from above. And He is The Sun. And there you have it. Word.

And 33 is Our number. And It is not Their number. And so, to 33 millennium, were added 33 centuries. *"And you shall count your steps".* And They have stolen many of Our symbols, seeking potency for, and validation of, Their cause, through them. And you are to mark my words indelibly, every step of the way. And, it is a forlorn and ill advised pursuit, on Their part. And They remain largely impotent, regardless. And no man; nor Vatican, Museum, or Private Collector: shall ever triumph over The <u>I</u>. Word.

And The Divine, will not radiate the essential missing components, to Them. And, nor allow the artifacts to function, in Their hands. And They are denied. And *he* is in They. And They apply The Black Arts. And They do it in concealed chambers, away from The Sun. And 'I', shall say nothing; nor <u>Rai</u>. Word.

And the location of The Central Convector, Known commonly as The Great Pyramid, is located at the very centre of the Earth's land mass. And it is a matter of Density & The Centre of Gravity & Space. And It's latitude of 29.9792458'N is numerically equal, to the speed of light, at 299,792458 m/s. And these are the units of both The Meter and The Second. And incremental divisions, or multiples of both; Sixty and One Hundred irrespectively. Word.

And We were The Architects. And We were The Men from The Stars. And this was Our convector, by which We commuted, at The Speed of Light, magnified. And it was built at the very centre of The Earth's land mass, to maximise The Earth's density, and magnetic pull. And His Majesty is in All mathematics. And He is there, more so, than in the written word. And He is in The Light. And He is in The Dark Matter. And mathematics is based on Absolutes. And It is True.

And the written word is based on interpretation, by
perception. And it is emotive. And the dissemination,
of Light & Wonder, is the mathematics of The Poet.
And His work, an algebraic formulae. And you shall
count your steps, my dearest and most attentive reader.
*And you shall testify to The Light as <u>i</u>: Word.

*He came as a witness, to testify about the Light, so that all
might believe through him. He was not the Light, but he
came to testify about the Light. There was the true Light
which, coming into the world, enlightens every man. **John.**

And so.

And when it was time, They happened upon the instruments, which belonged to The Architects. And The Architects were The Masons, who built The Convectors. And largely by levitation. And the laser precision, of the solar furnace. And concave lens.

And it was a treasure trove. And, one which Akhenaten had given to His son, to bring from The Afterlife, to The Present Day, ahead of the *aperture abert*. And the civilizations, long before Aztec & Inca, of South America, Knew this. And they were of the same entity, as those before The Egyptians, to whom the works of Ancient Egypt are attributed. And they were All One, and connected about The Earth.

And similar tools were seized and spirited away, by those first upon the scene, at The Gold Rush of Egyptian archeology. And these Egyptologists, of the early nineteenth and twentieth centuries, were funded by the esoteric societies of London (and Paris). And They were quick to happen upon Our number.

And They realised it's potency. And but, it is not *An Ankh* to Them. And access was denied to Them. And They have been banging Their heads against a brick wall ever since. And They shall, for all eternity. Word.

And They were not welcomed into The Inner Sanctums. And *he* was in They. And They had financed the relentless searches for, and pilfering of, more and more tools and knowledge. And They were insatiable. And None of It was designed for Them. Word.

And They are The Esoteric Secret Society, who have stolen Our number, for Their own. And They, have stole' these tools, too. And, They have utilised this residual energy, for One Hundred Years, (And now more). And 'I' shall tell you. And you shall read it well, my dearest reader. And you are to make of it, a shield: to protect yourself from Them, and the very slings and arrows of Their evils, that They by *he,* would have you suffer by.

And They are a self serving godless hoard. And Nepotistic. And Protectionist. And you are to be sure about it. And Their strength is Not in any uniqueness, but in Their uniform allegiance, to each other. And They do not know God. And They are a ruling elite.

And They run The Earth, like landlocked Galapagos mutants, detached from The Universe. And rejecting His Golden Orbs. And preventing First Contact, at this *aperture abert*. And without a single notion, of His intention(s). And I is afraid that this is True. And We shall Only speak with delegates of The Federation.

And They will become The Third Face instead. And egocentric and Earthbound. And this is what They will be. And *All* that is in store, if unabated. And They aim to infiltrate, All that is Good, and correct and proper, in Government & Authority. And to corrupt It, for Their personal gain(s). And *he* is in They. And *he* <u>is</u> They. And They are the very ones, who by The Third Face, aim to control The World by a single authority. And They intend it to be an amalgam of all entities, that have power over Peoples. And by '*he* in T*hey*', *All* will be *his*, under *he* by <u>T</u>hem. And so, just so. Word.

And They aim to share between Them, the spoils. And They aim to be a ruling elite, at a power share ratio of 1:12. And with the unfair share of property, greater than 1:1000. And They aim to be The Super Rich, with the money and the power. And this would be unjust, according to Divine Law. And so it cannot be. Word.

And so.

And these tools and symbols were returned to London. And they were swiftly put to great devilry and *mispurpose*. And *he* grew fat. And the genocide(s). And the *enslaveries* of The Human Beings, reached their height in this time. And *he* made *his* bastion there. And, in the inner sanctums of satanic worship.

And that which is black magic, was invoked. And encrypted ciphers, were read. And, Satan was *soonly* thereafter born of it, into The World, by The Americas. And it is so. And but, not All can be tarred with the same brush. And yet *he* & *his*, and *he* in They, were rampant, in this time. And *his* is not an infrequent and uncommon incarnation. And take note my most attentive reader. And *he* follows a pattern. And most generations have at least one or two of *him*.

And *he* in manifest, is far more commonly spotted than He, who is the emissary of The Divine. And He, & The Sons of He, are too a pattern. And *is* much lesser spotted & infrequent, by far, than *he*. And He descends from above. And *he* is risen from below. Word.

And *he* was made incarnate through purple ceremony. And by the chanting of these incantations. And *he* was born. And *he* has lived and died in a few evil men since.

And *he* was a repugnant and largely inconsequential individual, each & every time. And charismatic to the disaffected, alone. And They is many. And too quick to make enemies, under the guidance and manipulation of unscrupulous leadership. And as such is The Swarming.

And *he,* will always have something of a cultist following, until *he,* by '*he* in They', under *him* realise. And, or *his* cults and regimes are forever crumbled.

And crumbled They will be, but brought to realise *he* will not. And *he* who is *him,* in Spirit and Incarnate, will never surrender to His Majesty, as it is impossible, according to The Science of It All. And by the names we give to patterns. And by the humanisation of gods & devils. And when the simple truth is; All energy can never be destroyed. And All that is: simply is. And in it's simplest form, despite the fanciful creations we extrapolate, from the elemental gases and forces. And the complex carbon based structure, we find ourselves in, within Life; as complex carbon based organisms. Word.

And the lesson is never learnt. And Time moves through us. And not we through Time. And so, we must try to learn from our own mistakes, each time. And: in the time, called Life, that is peculiarly ours.

And all Knowing; is largely denied, by education. And education is the corralling and corruption of All Knowing. And *he* masters and manipulates the common people, this way. And by it, most often gains control, over the fleeting mortality, Time affords them. And *he* steals a yard by this. And so, a word to The Wise. And God abhors a vacuum. And so, unlearn It All, and let H̲im in. Word.

And as *his* technologies get cleverer, so do The Common People(s), get more stupid. And *he* fodders & fattens Them, on drugs and pornographies. And clutters Their minds, with shallow preoccupations and nonsense. And *he* incarnate, is forever much less potent, than They wish for *him* to be. And *he* is more Runt, than *he* is alike; The Magnificent Beast: in manifest. (And as depicted in Blake's vision).

And *he* is never conjured, into the fantastic creatures of *his* mythology, by *he* in They. And, or by those who celebrate *him,* by fear of *him.*

And *he* is always equal ~ only to the impotence of Their craft. And *he* has been *the* bespectacled weakling, in a ferocious oppressive tyrannical regime, most recently. (c20). And such an incarnation is typical of *his* manifestation(s). And so ~ most often The *D'evil* is forever in the officer, who drafts the order: for *his* henchman to deploy. And seldom, in the poor conscripted soldier, who must perform the grotesque acts of murder; by proxy, on *his* behalf. And *he* is most often short in stature. And seldom handsome. And Their craft is pathetically weak, in correspondence to the brilliance of His Majesty. Word.

And They aim to raise *him* again and again, until *he* is risen proper. And this is Their very business, always. And forever and incessantly.

And listen to me my attentive reader. And, They are restricted by the incomplete compendium, of His Majesty's pilfered tools, at Their disposal. And you are to mark 'The Words of <u>I</u>', indelibly; in this regard. And you are to be sure about It. Word.

And so. And with the much more potent tools and symbols stolen from The Son, than had ever been collected, or were available to Them previously, The Anti Christ was often conjured.

And then again, in the advent of the aperture abert. And Life upon The Earth, is every time formative, and larger than Life, when is the aperture *abert*. And external forces, otherwise prevented, can enter The Atmos. Word.

And See'rs and Savants foretold *his* arrival(s). And *his* impact(s) was more severe, than the mere conjuring of The Satan, without mortality. And in particular, *his* latter manifests. And in these guises, *he* was a much more potent and destructive force. And Satan without mortality, is only a noxious gas, born of marsh grass. And *he* exists in parts per billion. And *he* is an intoxication. And more so, through the pollutants of *his* fossoils. And *he* strives, through 'he in They', to be made incarnate. And so.

And *he* was risen most noticeably, in both the Nineteenth and Twentieth centuries, in correspondence with the cornucopia of discoveries, becoming *made* in Egypt. And the advancement in Oil excavation.

And in correspondence also, with the closing of the last Eighth of the precession. And *his* noxious candle, began to illuminate The Dark Age. And Enlightenment and Renaissance followed. And until *he* took it for *himself*.

And the potencies of Their Evils, (as a People), grew greater with Their collection(s) of artifacts. And They took The Sun, and put it into The Darkness of Their cloistered chambers. And therein was *his* inception.

And *All* energy was inverted. And They reversed The Symbol of The Precessional Cross, which depicts the course, and four quarters of the precession; in order to raise *him*. And It is a highly potent symbol. And It has a great energy. And It can govern many things.

And They rotated it to The Right. And *he* was risen. And the bespectacled runt, was reunited with The Anti Christ incarnate. And Pandora's Box was *abert*. And there was pandemonium. And All Hell with it.

And *he* by They, persecuted the descendents of The Faithful again, as if the unfinished business, of The First Reich of Ancient Rome. And *he* persecuted The Human Being. And: so this was to become the very business, my dearest and most attentive reader. Word.

And, *of* The Tools that had been taken safely, *(previously),* from the Great Pyramids, by The One, whom was Known as Akhenaton. And so, The Great Pyramids, were no longer Convectors at *this* time, as they had been, previous to that; but soulless tombs instead, in which to lay The Dead, with no rite of passage to The Afterlife. And so.

And The Architects who built them: 13,000 or 26,000 years ago, (at the time of writing); *had* had All Knowing. And these tools were sealed away. And, until Akhenaton was dispatched, to retrieve them, from the spiritual decay of the middle dynasties of Egypt, that aimed to defile the sanctity of The Divine. And instead, celebrate Their own mortal vanity. And *he* was in They. And no mistake.

And so He, in His guise of Akhenaton, was dispatched, to reinstate His Majesty, over the vanities of The Egyptian Pharaohs. And, to remove godly powers from The Common Man, They had become.

And as such, They have remained, through the final Eighth of this precession, that began then, and ends now; ahead of the next visitation. And, at the date of this most urgent and pressing bulletin. And so. Word.

And so.

And each quarter of a precession, is divided into two.
And the symbol is not a swastika. And these Eighths
are invisible. And this eighth, is equal to thirty three
centuries. And, as is made perfectly clear in the
accurate reading of The Symbol itself. Word.

And some tools were already taken. And they have
remained underground since. And The Esoteric Society
acquired them. And keep them still. And wars have
been fought, over these potent tools. And no mistake.

And often, not fought for the reasons given. And you
are to mark my words indelibly about this, my dearest
and most attentive reader.

And, but these tools are all but useless in the
unintended hands. And All war is abhorred, by His
Majesty. And none is just, nor may be justified.

And Akhenaton is an Emissary of The Divine. And
then, for thirty three centuries more, (One Eighth of a
precession): the Tools were sealed in the tomb of His
son, Tutankhamen, the hybrid child. And just so it
was, until c20. And a little bird told Me. (I). Word.

And *he* in They, by *him*; believed and knew, They could be empowered by keeping possession of these Divine Instruments, to some degree. And They stole these tools away, at every opportunity, with each finding.

And these are the calipers and the square. And this is the divining rod, that moved mountains. And this is what became fabled as the magic wand. And Illusion owes its roots, to the magic of The Architects. And for this very truth, the intrigue of it all, endures.

And All magicianship & witchcraft, is born of this. And it is a conduit, to be used beneath the *aperture abert*. And these are the tools, that levitated immense stones, at every corner of The World. And fashioned them, into their positions. And, as a testament to His Majesty, all along The Equatorial Band. And All, under the auspices of The Men from The Stars. Word.

And these are the tools, by which God, through His emissaries, built magnificent structures. And, by which God commanded adoration, and awesome respect, from The Human Being, in His infancy. And All Homo Erectus, wished to become Human Being. And they flocked and queued. And The Human Being adored their God. And He loved His children.

And He rose and descended as The Sun. And in no less fiery splendour. And no morality or law was imposed, to enforce this love for His Majesty. And there were no slaves. And there was no war.

And there is a residual energy. And it is true. And, by this fraction of that energy, They are empowered to a degree. And They have applied Their black arts, to wring out, and distil this energy. And by this, They have played god, since ever when, these instruments were spirited away, one by one.

And these tools are not now, in the hands of those He had intended. And but, it was The Divine plan, that They should be given to Them. And so Satan, would be raised and born and dealt with, by enticing & inciting, the division of a species. And so. Word.

And so.

And there are no flaws in God's plan. And God is a wonderful 'Thing'. And Never define Him as something He is Not. And there are potent symbols. And they *is* easily read on mass. And it is easier for a camel to pass through the eye of a needle, than for a Sinner to enter the gates of Heaven. And by such, the wheat shall be sifted from the chaff. Word.

And so, only The Twelve Times Twelve Thousand, will have ascended, by the elliptical shard. And of all the peoples that have ever lived, one tenth of them are living now. And, at the very time of this inscription.

And so, The Twelve Times Twelve Thousand, is a very small number, of the grand total. And they are with God. And they are beyond All mortal influence(s). And they are unaffected, by the pathogens and devilries of witches' wishes: witchcraft, and It's exponents. And the remainder are, or may well be, the stuff of witchcraft and superstition. And bound by the constraints of mortality, even in death. And they are, and remain, in the very air you breath. And Air is elemental. And can be fashioned and manipulated. And It is a vehicle on which pathogens commute. And arrive. And so.

And '**I**' shall tell you my dearest reader. And you are to mark I's words indelibly, so that Hard Rains could *n'er e'er* they erase. And so as follows: ~ and, The Men from The Stars, whom The Human Being Know, as The Anunnarki, have declared war on those, who are The Illuminati of The Earth. And who are The New World Order, of the Esoteric Societies, of The Earth in union; that shall become known as The Pinnacle of The Third Face. And therein lies the rub. And so: there, you have been told. Word.

And **I** is at war, with those of The Third Face. And All Human Beings are at war with They too, by default. And it is a spiritual warfare. And the battlefield is in The Spectrum of Light. And All Human Beings shall rise up and be counted, against this evil hoard. And against those few evil men and women, that govern It, incarnate, under the spirit of *he*, who is Satan. Word.

And so, in short: God is at War with Satan. And as ever It were, It remains infinitum, as All Matter within The Universe, is pulled this way & that, by positive & negative energies. And by the philosophies created thus, that bring carnage to mortality, according to the influences of such energies, upon the humble complex carbon based organism. And God is Light. Word.

And you must never confuse Lucifer with Satan, my dearest and most attentive scholar. (They are two very different energies). And energies is what They are. And it is a yarn to be unraveled. And Lucifer is too; The Light. And merely the alter ego of The Christ. Word.

And perhaps I could say this better; according to The Mathematicians, in algebraic formulae. And It is True: but His Majesty, will always prefer His Scribe & Poet, to impart The One Truth emotively, wherever & whenever necessary; above the absolute precision of Mathematics. And the comparatively dull language of algebra. Word.

And so, my dearest and most precious reader; thus. And: Never buy *the job lots and jumble,* that they might attempt to sell you, at The Church *Bring & Buy* Sales, on the very subject; for that would be indoctrination. And for: i), They might very well have The Mass, but They don't have The Math'. And: ii), you will find the energies, already ruminating within you, quite well enough, without Them ~ or Their input(s). And I is adamant: that there is no room for ego, in the churches of religion(s). And The Shepherds. And The Leaders. And I can tell you now, that The Third Face will Be. And that It shall capitulate to The Federation. Word.

And so, *for* <u>I</u> is to tell you ~ & I am to be most
insistent about It, by order of The Divine: that *'the
energy'* which is known as Lucifer, is equal to, and
correspondent to, The Dark Matter of The Christ.
And/or The Prophet(s). And He is Not the much
maligned entity, sold as part of a job lot, together with
The False Prophet & Satan, by those fundraisers,
promoting adulterated scripture.

And note: It & He are both concentrated energies,
whom do defy The Laws of Physics, known to, and
embraced by Man. And are; but opposites, of the same
coin. And, but Satan is singularly a force of evil, and is
concentrated in parts per billion. And Satan is bereft of
any redeeming qualities. And *he* is Not The Light. And
so.

And The Religionists can be as bad as each other. And
if they're not saying prayers, or chopping off people's
heads, they'll be baking cakes, or dropping bombs. And
are as quick, if not quicker: to engage horns with The
Runts of The Magnificent Beast(s), than those who are
without *an* indoctrination at all. And Atheists are only
Peacemakers without Knowing.

And now: one hundred years later, *(and some)*, from the birth of Satan's most recent abomination, in manifest. And, They continue to impose Themselves from *his* residue, and strive unrelentingly to fulfill Their goal, and *his* next incarnation. And They are Satanists by practice. And by definition. And, but Their days are numbered. And, They have served Their purpose.

And, Their purpose; was only ever to forge and create The Division of a Species. And to reveal the two, and their respective number. And They are brazen under *he*. And even Satan's plan works to God's plan. And so, We are to dismantle Their 'Church without a god'. And Their False Prophet, whom is always *an* fetal abomination to God, of Satan incarnate. And so:~

And, mark the words of I indelibly, about the matter. And be sure. And that, The Blue Planet has no further use for Them, and Their nonsense(s). And They shall be bred away. And you Know who *They* are. Word.

And, Theirs is a comic book fantasy myth. And It is Science Fiction. And it is to be discarded and burnt. And destroyed. And it is an utter nonsense, forged by stolen symbols, and inverted energies, that could never rival His Majesty. And so: just so.

And this is true. And It belongs to The One Truth. And so. And there is absolutely no truth in Their claim(s) to the truth. And that too is true. And the amount of truth, contained in Their religion, is precisely equal to: none whatsoever. And Their belief system is an elaborate bogus sham. And, $x = 0$ (Zero).

And you must be brought to see *that* dearest reader. And They are only an avaricious, self serving, power crazed cult. And They were the Slave Masters of yore. And They were the Genocidal Maniacs of *Everyones'* Imperialism.

And it is but a new skin for an old ceremony, to be sure, in which We find Them still. And it is suffice to say: *that,* "They shall arrive to fooling no one, but Themselves", in the very scope of this *aperture abert.* Word.

And you must be brought to loathe the false gods, behind Their irritating \$5 invasive subliminal technologies, littered about The Globe. And simulating The Voice of God Himself. And, how very dare They invade & impose, with macro surveillance technologies, without warrant or license, as They do. And *he* is in They, by It. Word.

And these technologies, when not Peeping Toms, are forever engaging in harassment. And preying. And Telling Tales of gross defamation. And undermining. And Lies & Trickery. And impregnation of The Resource with pure invention, to sway and brainwash public opinion(s). And to act as instruments of torment and destruction, to the best of Their ability. And persecution. And so, to dehumanise The Resource.

And, there is absolutely no truth or benefit to Humanity at large, in this 'Church without a God'. And, it is positively Satanic. And *he* sits *his* agents behind pinhole cameras, and subliminal devices to play *god*. And They infiltrate the world wide web. And passwords create a deliberate false sense of security.

And They believe They are good. And there is the very rub; my dearest and most attentive reader. And They believe They have the god given right, to invade privacy, and watch over others. And They do not.

And They dare to comment and pontificate, by subliminal broadcast, over those They watch. And They are nothing more than voyeurs. And perverts. And symptomatic of The Disease Itself.

And but, all this has revealed the acceptable face of Satan, in the modern era. And *he* is reflected in the mainstream. And, but there is no acceptable face, to be had. And there can be none. And The People have been hoodwinked by it. And by *he*, in They, under *him*.

And you are to mark my words indelibly, my Pretties. And you may as well believe in The Man in The Moon. And: when The Moon is already a proven and goodly, and potent force, without any of Man's own imposition of ego put upon it. Word.

And it is All a pure nonsense. And the very truth is blocked out and shielded. And, it is like The Sun behind a noxious black cloud. And because: It <u>is</u> The Sun behind a noxious black cloud, my dearest and most attentive and precious reader. Word.

And *he* has made automatons of a sub species. And *his* work has only just begun, as *he* sees it. And *he* has polluted The Resource. And *he* has fed Them subliminal instruction, from the hardened artery of the shanghaied Ethernet. And it is just so.

And this is precisely as it is. And They All feel chosen: under *he* in They. And, as if, They have finally arrived to a sense of purpose. And Their *raison d'être*. And it is <u>All</u> 'The' perfect nonsense.

And it is All; only Man playing god. And, by a fantastic contrivance. And, by delusion and self opinionation. And it is an evil nonsense. And, it is made evil by the fact, that God exists surely. And, that They deflect from Him, and The One Truth, to steal His glory. Word.

And that He is True. And that They obscure His Truth. And that He is The Giver of All Life. And yet, They mock His Majesty, in a pale and sallow imitation.

And They are obedient to the dogma and doctrines of Satan incarnate. And They give <u>*he*</u> a voice. And They have shanghaied All The Earth's natural airwaves. And it is the ether, to which all Life-force adheres. And it is housed within the very eggshell-like membrane, of the stratosphere. And *he* in They, are obstructing & hindering His Majesty's return. And *he* in They are dumbing-down The Resource. Word.

And They do not own The Weather. And They do not own The Atmos. And nor the stratosphere. And, but yet, They have shanghaied it; nonetheless. And We own The Weather to be sure. And about this my dearest and most attentive reader, be as certain as ever you can be, about anything, on God's Earth. Word.

And The Planet Wave was for always the preserve of The Human Being, and The Faithful. And The Ethernet was installed by The Divine, for the protection of The Human Being. And, so Morphic Fields would unite them. Word.

And all the regimented colours of the rainbow, may be seen in the magnificent chaos of The Aurora Borealis, that is His 'very' Majesty, in a fleeting manifest, upon the battlefield of Spiritual Warfare. And so. And The Northern Lights are as near as human kind can be, to His Majesty, under the five governable senses. And the raging turmoil. And of The Lights: It is a bridge. Word.

And but; *he* in They have formed a religion. And They have gridded and plotted it. And All by an unholy plan. And The Human Being, is no longer the main beneficiary of The Planet Wave, under this evil hoard.

And They _has_ no God, but for the avarice of money and power. And They _is_ an highly evolved bacteria, enveloping an humanoid form. And They maintain Their cult & culture, into the form of complex carbon based organism. And They pursue and manage the *fuck & fight*. And They proliferate All the industries & percentages therein, as a means to an end. And to satisfy Their avarice. And to preserve Their positions of power. And those of Their number sustain, by Their superficial needs & wants. And so:~

And The Ethernet under *They,* has no spirit; but for the amplification of subliminal messaging, by a world littered with $5 technology. And it is a synthesised illusion, which feeds a series of delusion(s).

And It is Ether laced, with corresponding satellites. And They watch. And so what. And what of It. And They are Only Peeping Toms, by It. And not in any way supreme or godlike. And They invent unnecessary devices. And They find uses for unnecessary technologies. And They create industries around such. And They dilute and confuse The Resource. And therein lays the rub once more, my dearest reader. Word.

And They is an organised criminal network. And: but licensed now, by all governmental forces, in pursuit of The New World Order. And it is an evolutionary step, by a systematic devolution. And institutional corruption is rife. And They are becoming brazen and bold about it. And it is to be the norm', by the first half of this aperture abert. And before it is altered. And the table turns. And as such, is revolution. And reflective of The Earth about It's precession, with all external influences upon Her. Word.

And so, All Government(s), is increasingly criminal and unholy, at the time of writing; dearest reader. And It aims to criminalise The Human Being, for It's very Being. And It designs to breed The Human Being, in to servitude; to They. And until made extinct incrementally, in It's purest form. And so, to feed & serve Their greed(s). And It is intent, on global domination. And the implementation of the New World Order. And Its globalising manifesto. And, at the exclusion of God and The Human Being.

And everything about The New World Order, and It's manifesto; is right. And yet, everything about The New World Order, and It's manifesto; is wrong. And so:- And The Third Face shall yield to The Federation.

And <u>We</u> are not Egyptian. And We are not Aliens. And God is omnipotent. And that is True. And God is True. And He is but one, of many extraterrestrial influences upon The Earth. And this belongs to The One Truth. And there are seven Alien species, about The Earth. And God is Great.

And the number Seven, and the number Eight, are significant numbers. And they have a power. And a name in unity. And an energy. And God is The Eight and The Eighth, most fervently. And He is God to The Seven too. And all of Seven. And He is All of Light, and One with The Sun. And none of this is nonsense, my most dutiful scholar. And, for God is The Sun and The Stars. Word.

And two of the influential species; are The Ghosts: which are The Spirits, and The Ancestors of The Blue Planet, who have gone before. And did not ascend. And they are not *of* The Twelve Times Twelve Thousand. And The Eighth are The Descendents, yet to Be. And a testimony to His omnipotence in Space and Time.

And they who are The Ancestors, are ever present. And largely omnipotent, within the atmosphere. And yet, not beyond. And they are in the very air you breathe. And they may be intoxicating. And heavily influencing. And they are extraterrestrial, but still bound by The Earth's atmosphere, in which they once lived.

And so, these are extraterrestrial; but not alien. And they and They, may occupy The Living. And they and They, can be summoned. And there are many disgruntled souls amongst them and Them. Word.

And none of these are of any real consequence: not really: except to the individual that hosts them. And they orbit The Living. And it is a ratio of 1:10, correspondent to the fact that 10% of all those that have ever lived, are living now. And they and They, are as planets about The Sun. And about us, in an everyday and largely mundane orbit. And or, as cleaner fish about a shark. And or, any other generic body, that is similarly host to symbiotic satellite(s), that you may choose to imagine, in order to illustrate this metaphysical model. And these satellites shall influence your personality and character traits. And they and They, are in the air you breathe. And it is just so, my most attentive scholar.

And The Eighth, are The *'very'* Source. And the carriers of Divine inspiration; on Sunray & Sunbeam. And there are Imps too. And the Imps are made of spent Satanic energy. And They are the residue of bitterness and hate; and jealousy and envy. And They cluster in parts per billion. And They too, can be breathed. And They can be contracted, just as the common cold, and/or avoided, by a 'Way of Thinking'. And They can be staved off. And too, kept away by incense and flowers, and natural fragrance. And so.

And They are the instruments of witches, by the *unvirtue* of this. And They can be summoned thus. And the two species contained within The Atmos, may be visible to the clairvoyant and young children. And it is real, but all very weak and dilute. And largely inconsequential.

And the third species, are The Twelve Times Twelve Thousand. And They have had mortality. And they have left only, in order to return. And they are chosen. And They are of another planet. And another galaxy. And they may not be summoned by witches. And they are out of harm's way. And they cannot be breathed. And They are in The Light. And Not elemental. And they may Only be dispatched by The Divine. Word.

And they are of a very different construct. And they are the very sunshine yellow of the spectrum. And they may be Angels, depending on One's definition. And they are certainly travelers in Space & Time. And they have been interpreted, and/or; depicted as Angels, often. And but; they were always Kind & Empathetic, when people. And they commute within the gossamer Orb and orbs, that is The Chariot of His Majesty.

And they commute collectively in shimmering golden orbs, of a light so bright, it is mostly invisible. And perfectly translucent. And they go with God, in a single Golden Orb. And they are of the most significance. And they are the envoys and emissaries of His Majesty. And the numbers 3 and 8 are most significant, in relation to them. And no mistake.

And they arrive by radiation, as a collective, in The Golden Orb(s). And it is The Sun, in microcosm. And It is brilliant. And they were All once of this world too. And, but may not be summoned by witchcraft or incantation, as can others, who have never left the gravity of the atmos. And they are not comprised of the elements you breath. And for this reason, All witchcraft is lesser, and short sighted. And His Majesty is by far The Greater. Word.

And there are three more species; my most inquiring and attentive reader. And They are not of this world, at all. And one of these, are those, that are known as The Grey(s). And but their colour is blue. And their number is 5, (Five).

And one of these three species, are positively evil and capable of possession, wherever Mankind embraces evil, and welcomes it. And these have allied with Mortal forces, throughout the History of the final Eighth of this precession. Word.

And They were in allegiance with The Nazis of c20. And They were in some Pharaohs. And They were in much of Rome. And They are in All of They, that kill in the name of God. And They were within The City within The City, for centuries. And Theirs is crimson, in a violet hue. And they are All *of* 6, (Six).

And each Extraterrestrial is represented by a colour of the spectrum. And they are All, All of Light, in this regard. And all are without carbon form. And they are One to Seven until Eight. And only His Majesty is Brilliant & Translucent. Word.

And two of these species are godly. And they are orange and yellow. And they have great powers. And they inspire Mankind toward greatness. And they lead Mankind toward God. And toward the Lightness of Being. And away from the density of the carbon based organism, of humanoid mortality. And they can be met with equally: inside a meditative stupa, or a catatonic stupor. And so the monastery is a more orderly route, than by the den of iniquity and vice. And, but both roads lead *from* Rome. And both can get you there.

And above All, there is God Itself. And God is all of Light and mostly invisible, in the vastness of His omnipotence. And He is The Sun and The Stars. And He is the space, between the Sun and Stars. And He is All encompassing. And He is All things. And He is that; which has evolved furthest. And He is that; which has not yet evolved at all. And He is at that very point, where the cycle is complete. And, at where The End is The Beginning. And so, you must not search for God. And but, you must search instead for Truth. And at this, He shall find you. Word.

And He shall find you, by one of His emissaries. And by this mechanism, He shall radiate. And He takes the form of The Human Being seldom. And when He does, it is Known. And It is always remarkable. And it is always within the *aperture abert.* And so:-

And: but The Ancient Egyptian in it's zenith had too, The Knowing. And, The Ancient Egyptian race grew on Our initial site, at the very centre of The Earth's land mass. And all satellite races grew from that epicenter. Word.

And it is the cradle of civilisation. And at where We were, from whence once We came. And, they were keepers of All Knowing, at their height, in the Kingdoms of the earliest dynasties. And, their zenith oscillated between obedience to His Majesty, and vanity to Themselves. And this was the very rub.

And, they built the lesser pyramids to be tombs for their Kings, who honoured and worshiped Us. And finally, they became They. And He was gone, for *he* to enter They. And the incredible lightness of Being, was tipped out, at the fulcrum point, to allow the density of mortality to prevail. And just so it was. And is since.

And They burrowed like worms into The Convectors, to use them as tombs, in an act of the utmost vanity and sacrilege. And the residual energies, held by The Convectors at this time, were still significant.

And They fooled the peoples, with godlike powers. And *histories* were contrived and written. And 'I' could tell you about The Kings of Memphis, and The Kings of Thebes. And the thieves of Memphis.

And 'I' could tell you everything about Akhenaton. And I could tell you of His son. And 'I' could tell you of the vanities of The Egyptian Pharaohs, before and after He. And I could tell you about the errant orbs since. And how they *be* unable to make landfall still.

And I will tell you about the esoteric thieves, who peddle the myths of Egypt, that only suit to serve Themselves. And I could tell you which of the dynasties were of God. And I could tell you which of the dynasties were of <u>he</u>; and not of God.

*And I can tell you *of* how The Third Face will evolve and merge to lord over All Peoples, at every nation of The World. And how it shall capitulate to The Federation when He returns. And so: just so. Word.

And, They converted small sections of The Great Pyramids into tombs, to lay claim to the residual energies. And to *Godly* powers. And to steal a rite of passage, to The Afterlife. And They knew well of it. And, but They knew nothing, of the very mechanics of The Convectors. And They were faithless. And Not Faithful. And so:-

And The Pyramids had never been tombs, until the final dynasties of Ancient Egypt. And they were never built to be tombs. And you must Know this. And you must unlearn, All that They have taught you on the subject. Word.

And if you do not know this, you must be brought to know this. And the two great pyramids, were power plants. And they bred hydrogen. And generated microwaves, between The Earth, and a distant planet, in what is known as The Realm of Osiris. (I thinks): as viewed (and named), from The Earth.

And this planet is Earthlike. And the bags and baggage, of flesh and sinew, are dispensed with. And The Being travels lighter than the feather, to it. And it is weightless, just as the reflection in the mirror.

And the location is by the trajectory through Orion, as it is seen. And, but lies between the nearest and the furthest, of the three horizontal stars of Orion, which have no correlation to each other, other than, when viewed from the perspective of the naked eye, from The Earth. And the distant planet, which is The Kingdom, is far beyond this point of reference, which is a porthole. Just so. Word.

And The Ancient Greeks had The Knowing. And so, this part of the constellation, is known as Orion's Belt, because of this. And We are not concerned Ourselves with given names. And nor, by celestial metaphysical sciences, made *metafickle* by Astronomy and Astrology.

And they: (**W**e), charged the plasma of The Ethernet with microwaves. And they were linked to an equatorial belt about The Earth. And the belt connected His majestic sites and population centres. And it was an airborne world, from The Beginning.

And We used this equatorial elliptical band, as a runway. And it is a revolving constant, by which to align and adjust. And to descend, upon a rotating Earth. And what was Not once a frozen Antarctica.

And it is at the precise elliptical tilt, of The Blue Planet, aligned through The Aperture, between Earth and the fixed Orion coordinate point. And 33 is its number. And it is like the eye of a needle. And it is precisely the porthole. And The Planet of The Heaven lays beyond. And these convectors, commuted The Faithful between The Red Planet and The Blue Planet. And from The Red and Blue Planets, to The Heavens. And these are The Twelve Times Twelve Thousand. And these are The Men from The Stars. And to call them Beings, (or Entities), from The Stars, would be more accurate, ~ as gender, (or even species), is inapplicable.

And The Red Planet is a failed nursery. And, for the reason it has no Moon, (large enough), my dearest scholar. And it held Life, but could not sustain it, because it has no Moon, (large enough). And only for this. And it's gravity is not kept stable, because it has no moon, (large enough). And the convectors are located at the centre of the land mass, of The Blue Planet. And they are constructed purposefully to be convectors, by which the lightness of spirit, without the density of mortality, may commute. And, ~ or *Beings,* unbound by the density of a carbon based mortality, may commute. Word.

And The Red Planet were Our allies. And now they are gone. And but, The Red Planet will still house the largely insignificant and unimportant impotent ghosts of its ancestors, just as The Blue Planet does, that accompany The Resource, through Life on Earth. And some spirits besides. And they will be there, compelled to be so, by the planet's very gravity. And this Afterlife, is the only extant Life on Mars, but for the microbes.

And only those with Knowing, who made lighter than a feather, were commuted. And that spirit is of God. And it is the third species. And 3 is their number. And it is the sunshine yellow of the spectrum. And that the convectors were ever purposefully built, as tombs for Pharaoh, is a nonsense. And only a mortal vanity. Word.

And it is below the gateway to The Stars they stand. And still. And it is precise. And they are in perfect alignment and correspondence, below the constellation you know as Orion, my dearest and attentive reader.

And you must realise, that despite the very distance, there is nothing of any substance between The Blue Planet, and any other. And It is Space. And in that my Pretties, is The Key. And the key is The Ankh. Word.

And The Egyptian had All Knowing, until 'he' entered their realm too. And *he* always finds a way, to drive *his* wedges. And *he* seeks to steal Divine Glory, by any means, including lies and trickery. And *he* aims to destroy *his* enemies, by lies and trickery. And by trickery and lies. And debauchery. And warmongery.

And They proclaim Their abhorrent evils, in dogma and doctrine. And They perform Their rituals, in covert cloisters. And *he* will always pull toward the darkness. And *unto*: until the mud.

And *he* always fails; ultimately. And *he* plays to vanity. And *he* makes promises, to alleviate inadequacy and shortcomings; in all those who will follow *he*. And *he* chooses Them, by the curse of complex ~ and self loathing. And *he* has an abundance of stock in trade.

And short men, short of meat, flock to *him*. And the short men that flock to *him*, know that They are short. And They are never free of it. And All complex is only vanity. And The Human Being never suffers it. And The Human Being suffers nothing like it.

And for all that follow *he,* vanity is a mortal sin. And ugly people flock to *him* too. And bitter and vindictive people flock to *him.* And weaklings flock to *him.* And They All suffer under the flaws *he* installs. And They are The Disease; and *his* faithful. And *he* proliferates by instilling and nurturing disease(s), within The Diseased.

And when Faith is weak, Kings wish to be gods. And ugly peoples, wish to be beautiful. And short men wish to be tall. And The Planet Wave is stifled, with the spent wishes and wants of it all. Word.

And *he* feeds and thrives on this. And *he* recycles spent complex. And *he* arrests development and evolution. And People who are not Human Beings, are fickle this way. And They are made into Common People for this. And this defines Them as Common People. And They are stifled by *his* capture and arrest of Them.

And They are unable to free Themselves from *his* clutch. And *he* hears these prayers. And *he* responds. And *he* feeds Their complex and insecurities with one hand. And *he* soothes Them, by *his* industries and trappings, with the other. And They are *his* in consequence, most fervently.

And these are not prayers at all, but more akin to wishes. And the price is paid. And They have no God. And They have evolved to $5 subliminal technology, in lieu of prayer, and The Voice of God. And They are in Their zenith at this time, my most attentive reader. And They rejoice and thrive, in invasive macro technologies. And They strive to find purpose, in every superfluous invention of new technology. And when by far the half, should be given no use at all.

And *he* brought war and disease. And *he* buys up vast tracts of Humanity, in this way. And all war and disharmony, is fashioned by *he* in They, in this way. And the same as it ever was. And according to the predetermined pattern of energies, moving through The Precession. And going about their business. And the names we put upon So '*n*' So, and 'What's his face'. And the various molecular compositions, and elemental forces, we encounter in Life. Word.

And so ~

And disharmony and dissatisfaction, entered the utopian societies, about The World. And it was between one quarter, and one eighth, of a precession ago, most prevalently. And it was between the last *abert aperture*, and the last diffracted shard.

And the apertures of the quarter phases, are not of three score years and twelve, in duration. And they are but half that. And The Eighths, are merely diffracted shards, that require deflection from corresponding satellites, via The Sun Itself, to allow passage and entry.

And only the very finest of His Emissaries, may pass by The Shard, at these portholes; my dearest and most attentive reader. And these supreme Emissaries, are of the ultimate lightness of Being.

And they appear as The Prophets, when made mortal. And it is very seldom. And they are Light Itself; incarnate. And they are simply Divine. And they enter the chosen ones by radiation. And as such is Lucifer. And He is The Son of God & Good. And He is Not at all in association, in any renegade regard, with Satan, or indeed the fakers of The False Prophet. Word.

185

And **I** must reiterate. And Lucifer is Not Satan, but
The Christ's alter ego, (in case you had not yet learnt
this lesson, my dearest and most attentive scholar).
And at this, is your immaculate conception. And they
appear individually. And in manifest. And They are
The Ones of The Twelve. And this Twelve is the first
Twelve, in The Twelve Times Twelve Thousand. And
the very reason why the number is depicted thus.
Word.

And so, the prophets are The Twelve Times Twelve
Thousand, in concentration. And It, and they, is
embodied into a precious Golden Orb. And The Orb
may divide and dissipate into Twelve. And then; into
Twelve Thousand, at the very ebb. And the *aperture
abert* at the ebb, is three score years and twelve. And
The Precious Golden Orb, in It's fullest concentration
is His Majesty. And He is like The Sun. And He is
The Sun. And He is The Sun & Stars. Word.

And the date of this bulletin, is the beginning of such
an ebb, my most attentive reader. And mark I's words.
And the aperture shall be *abert* for three score years and
twelve, from this date. And God and The Third
Species, shall radiate upon The Earth, throughout this
time. And there shall be tremendous celestial activity.

And the celestial activity shall *affect* The Earth. And
His forces shall overpower *his* resistance to it, upon The
Earth. And so much of The Resource is *his* & rotten.
And it is the untended garden that goes to seed.

And once '*he* in They', is removed from positions of
office. ~ And The Fossoilers with Them. And the rot.
And so, shall then, may the restoration begin beneath
His Majesty, and His elemental forces. Word.

And The Sun Worshippers will be The Faithful. And
all contrived religions, with the insanities of their
politics, will begin to resurge to their original germ.
And as this occurs, so shall warring factions diminish.

And all religion has it's origin in The One Truth. And
there must be no Life without religion. And there is
the very rub. And He is returned at this. And disease of
every order, began with complication. And deviation
from The One Truth by mortal ego. And war began.
And where there had been none, slavery was born. And
prisoners of war became slaves, where there had been
neither war nor slaves before. And *he* in They, by *him*,
denounced God, according to the dark covenants that
They had entered into. And relics and tools and
symbols, were squirreled away at any given opportunity.

And they have remained stolen, and secreted away. And
The Esoteric Societies, have feverishly endeavoured to
add to Their collections since. And wars have been
waged, to recover and own these trophies. And this has
been the reason for many and most wars. And the
reason for All disharmony. And the hidden agenda, to
The Politics of Man.

And Information and Intelligence, became an industry,
because of this. And so lies and deceit, became a trend.
And there is nothing attractive in spies and espionage.
And *his* shortest and weakest men, find Their vocation
here.

And Their Warmongers, are propelled forward by
Their accountants. And policy is determined by
potential profit, and economic gain. And The Weak
rule over The Strong. And social evolution under *he*,
has made it so. And therein lays the rub. And indeed,
the very rot.

And *(previously)*: They denounced and defiled The
Father and The Son. And the species became deceitful
and conniving. And They developed racism and hatred,
to justify Their inadequacies. And Their insatiable
mongering of War. Word.

And *he* introduced doubt and mortal ego. And *he* promised All, to those who would follow *he*. And *he* defiled all that was of The Sun and God.

And The Blue Planet, has been in progressive degeneration since. And there has been no *abert aperture,* by which to arrest the accelerated demise of Mankind, until now. Word.

And there is no majesty, in any of *his* weapons. And His Majesty, is in none of *his* weapons. And the aperture is now *abert.* And The Human Being will be fulfilled once more. And galvanised in this time. And **He** in **they,** will be heard. And **They** in **_he_** shall be silenced.

And industrialisation, and technological advancement, have allowed amplification, and personification, of All and everything. And *he* has been playing god, *in,* since this advent, in pale imitation *of* His Majesty.

And the very matter shall be addressed, from the date of this bulletin forth. And during the three score years and twelve, of the abert aperture, by order of His Majesty. Word.

And *he* has purported that fellowship in *he* alone, would yield greater dividends, than obedience to; His Majesty. And *he* has purported the preposition, that Man; could & can, master his own destiny.

And the *di(ce) was cast* at this. And, with Us departed, and the abert aperture closed once more, The Fractured traipsed away in Their droves, within a very few generations. And it was The End.

And those who had not carried the gene well, soon followed those who did not carry the gene at all. And The Human Being, became prey to The Fractured, who became *his*. And They were strengthened by this. And emboldened.

And *he* has engaged in the systematic eradication of The Human Being, hence forth, of that time. And The Human Being, is a threat to all *he* aspires toward. And they were persecuted by '*he* in They', because of this.

And it was this way. And the persecuted fled The Pharaoh; in this time. And The Human Being in all His variant forms, has been persecuted ever since. And genocides have been set against Him.

And from within the symposiums of Ancient Greece,
(was His last stand). ~ And the ideologies in
philosophies of The Golden Age, were not enough.
And so it came to pass. And, but never war has God
endorsed, my most attentive reader. And so It was The
End; most assuredly. Word.

And of The Faithful, before all Bloody Hell befell.
And, they had known The Kingdom. And they Knew
The Key. And they knew it as The Afterlife.

And they had created It's reflection upon The Earth.
And All Life upon The Earth was so. And only in the
uncharted corners of The Earth, was it not so.

And there were few such places, owing to The Morphic
Fields, created by The Source of The Planet Wave,
from which, All had been drawn. And, as had brought
The Wheel, and the mastery of Fire, simultaneously to
All. And this was The Work of God. Just so. Word.

And The Equatorial Band carried Light and The
Morphic Fields. And it was alive with colour and
magnetism, just as The Northern Lights are today.
And Flight was achieved within the atmos, in defiance
of gravity, by the centrifugal rotation of The Planet.

And it shuttled The Men from The Stars, between each point along The Equatorial Band. And this gave them, anti-gravitational powers. And they could levitate monoliths. And building blocks. And there were the airways, before the Lines of Nazca. And Nazca is The End too. And The Final Cry for Our return, long, long, long after Our departure. And It is so.

And, but there were pockets of a sub-species, that were not receptive to The Calling. And The Neanderthal was also this too, at the first visitation. And this sounded their demise as a thoroughbred species.

And, but all else of Mankind, were drawn to His Majesty. And He was The Sun incarnate. And All Mankind worshiped The Sun. And He descended as The Sun, in flaming Orbs, by the majesty of His Emissaries.

And, they flocked to the magnificent monuments, being created by The Emissaries of The Divine, who were The Architects. And The Faithful were evolved from these pilgrims. And they were Early Man.

And there was a rapture in this time. And these were ascended. And this rapture was a genetic harvest. And these Faithful were possessed & processed. And returned with encrypted codes, as The Human Beings.

And they lived and died. And they came and went, at every abert aperture. And their number was twelve times twelve thousand.

And so, they were The Twelve Times Twelve Thousand. And Eternal. And all equal and divisible components, and multiples of that number as a whole. And so.

And they had the lightness of Being, to pass. And they could levitate and fly. And walk on water. And they carried wands. And they are The Architects. And they were the fathers of The Human Being(s). And their Faith was resolute; without question. Word.

And this extra-ordinary number, is a single precious golden Orb. And they are He, at this. And then from this, He *are* Twelve. And then they *is* The Twelve Times Twelve Thousand. And so, now you Know. And then they are He again, as One, when gathered in. And He leaves in a single precious golden Orb. Word.

And with the departure; and the aperture closed, came the onset of organised warfare each time, by The Lesser Beings. And, such as a world had never seen.

And so, The Faithful had left at death, by the *aperture abert.* And they were returned to God. And they were spirited away in The Precious Golden Orb. And this was interpreted as, and seen as rapture.

And The Believers and Nonbelievers, were left behind. And The Believers are less than The Faithful. And the aperture is a sustained shard of diffracted light. And, but it is not constant. And it is not a black-hole. And it is not really a wormhole. And it is The Gateway to The Heavens. And that shard remains *abert,* for increments amounting to three score years and twelve, as a maximum. And it is precisely this duration.

**A Precession is approximately 26,400 years. Half is 13,200 years. One Quarter is 6,600 years. An Eighth is 3,300 years.*

And, it is not this duration, at each Eighth of precession, but only at The Ebbs of It's celestial orbit, which is at each half of a precession.

And this sustained aperture, is equal to seventy two years. And at this, it is still a *minute* increment, in the scope of a precession, as a whole. Word.

And the gene pool was tainted by those without Knowing. And all there remained, were Earthbound fish, cut away by the cosmic tide. And left, not until the fullness of the precession. And: but instead, until the next ebb of the precession, at it's very antithesis.

And Eden was spoiled. And, one half of a precession is from Ebb to Ebb, and takes over thirteen millennia to complete. And one quarter is sixty five centuries. And The Eighth, is always in the 33rd. Word.

And The Eighth is within the thirty third century, each time. And it has proven too long, to leave The Human Being alone, with the rogue gene, of the complex carbon based organism, of Homo Erectus, susceptible to the very gravity of The Soup, by *he* in They. And All Mankind knew of the importance of Gravity. And It was seen as a Divine force.

And both They and they, had witnessed it all, manipulated at the hands of The Architects. And All Life, and all things inanimate, danced to His command, by <u>He</u> in they. And it was already intrinsic, to the supernatural beliefs of All Mankind.

And the weighing of the heart, against the feather, had been a burial rite of passage and ritual. And both They and they, were bemused by it all. And none had any mastery of The Architects ways. And He has always been beyond mortal comprehension. And yet: but He is still intrinsic to The One Truth, regardless. And the descendents, would fall into grotesque acts of sacrifice, in an attempt to appease and return their gods.

And mortality invented High Priests, to conjour His return. And they were The Fathers of the Feathers. And they were forlorn, and failed as a conduit. And but, were and have been, successful as a focus for The Faithfull since. And in every robe and guise.

And The Architects' hearts were always lighter than the feather. And especially in death, they possessed the ability to levitate and ascend. And leave. Word.

And the hearts of those, left to reside upon The Earth, were never lighter than the feather. And, they were carbon based and bound by mortality. And: because The Architects were fashioned from Light, in their reflection of His Majesty, upon The Earth. And every manifestation of them was weightless. And so.

And from the time beyond their initial rapture, they never were of carbon composite again. And it was the signature of divinity. And it was the lightness of Being, required to ensure passage to The Afterlife.

And so: they would leave, and escape the density of mortality, with Divine status. And of those left behind, some engaged in resolute faith. And others in a desperate impersonation.

And both, in their way, being sincere forms of flattery. And or, of homage and devotion. And the shaman wore the feathers of high flying birds.

And so, to transport The Soul across The Space, by microwave, at the speed of light, magnified manifold. And at faster than the speed of light, by diffraction. And here is the very rub. And the very conundrum.

And this is known and discussed by theorists, as Warp. And We have Faithful in The Sciences. And there are Unfaithful in The Sciences too.

And they Know of the number 33, to an extent. And they are close to The Truth in their understanding. And, but They have, as yet, no grasp; that rocket ships transporting Mankind, with all the bags and baggage of It's flesh and sinew, is a forlorn pursuit. And they will not get far, both, either physically and or spiritually, under the burden of this mentality.

And The Architects, whom are the emissaries of The Divine, The Faithful, and The Twelve Times Twelve Thousand, are shuttled in Precious Brilliant Golden Orb(s). And as bright as The Sun, and The Almighty Himself.

And All that, is the very Life within. And All that, is The Soul. And that, which is the remainder at life's expiration, is all that may be commuted. And it is this alone, that is lighter than the feather. And it is the entire Being, without the meat. And it is weightless, like a mirror image. And He can be heard in The Light. And so. Word.

And this mirror image, is who you are my dearest and most precious reader. And you are not the meat that stands before it's reflection. And the secret of it all, is in learning how to divide The Being, from its flesh and sinew. And the mortal coil that binds the two. And there you shall have it. Word.

And the aperture is there to facilitate this. And I is to tell you, that Light diffracted through space, allows for its very acceleration. And 'The Aperture Abert', is what The Scientists will imagine to call a wormhole. And so: they may, until they know better.

And the acceleration, is all in the diffraction. And diffraction creates warp and wormholes. And dismantles All constructs of Time. And so, the first conundrum is set at this.

And The Fossoilers will be made extinct, during this aperture abert. And <u>I</u> is adamant about this. And They are a dirty, and All polluting breed. And they are destructive, and exploitative. And They are *his*. And *he* has been risen from the belly of The Earth, by The Fossoilers. And The Resource, has been contaminated and intoxicated by *him,* in parts per billion.

And a new wave of Scientists shall emerge. And it will not be rocket science. And They will be All Human Beings. And Human Beings All. Word.

And none will be of a military pedigree, (with always *an* hidden agenda, in the advancement of science & Space Travel). And but, instead; they shall be Faithful to His Majesty & The Human Being. And they will be shown The Way. And they shall show the way. And <u>I</u> believes that they, as a collective, shall be Known as an essential and fundamental department of The Federation. Word.

And The Federation, as my most attentive reader & dutiful scholar, shall uphold; with resounding fortitude, will be the fully integrated Global Government, who's only concern(s) is for The Planet, and The People upon It. And as shall emerge, toward the latter part of this aperture abert, with a prime directive. And a power to assert & enforce. Word.

And The Fossoilers and The Militaries, will ultimately prove, to have been only a flash in the pan. And will be seen only as destructive and malignant devilry, in *his* final throws, by They under *him*. And All contained in the tail end, of The Final Eighth of a single precession. And as it is written, so shall it be. Word.

And (previously); the first scribe took up His chalk and slate. And Modern Man, has lost this essential connection. And has butchered all those who had It. And each scribe to The Divine since, retains It. And The Fossoilers and The Rocket Scientists, are hopelessly detached from anything, that truly matters. And so; They are *his*.

And He drew a small circle within a larger circle. And this was The Sun. And this was The Earth in correspondence, beneath Him. And this symbol illuminated The Human Being. And It *spelled* The Truth. And The Future. And The Morphic Fields were electrified. And God had spoken. Word.

And it was enlightening. And it was the very template for The Main Convector. And it was The Wheel. And this; was God, in the magnificence of simplicity. And this perceived drawing, was in actual fact, the first written Word of God. And a spelling. Word.

And this was God's first communication, with an humanoid upon The Earth. And soon His Majesty arrived, in answer to the calling. And to the sense of Wonder, that He had instilled. And so, The Human Being was born. And It was a spell. Word.

And it was a symbol. And soon later, The Spiral. And then The Tri-Spiral. And The Spiral, is that by which, The Twelve Times Twelve Thousand come and go. And It is a vortex. And The Human Being, instinctively Knew, that The Men from The Stars, were The Sons of The Sun. And that The Convector was built by them, so they could commute.

And this symbol, which is the first written word of the Human Being, is not to be confused with the early cave drawings, of Homo Erectus, which is Art, from much, much later.

And this symbol, represented an entire philosophy and mindset. And it was the greatest book. (And All hieroglyph evolved from symbol). And people thought the same, by simply reading it. And they were alike by it. And they were spellbound. And it was a simple program. And The One Truth is incontrovertibly conveyed, if The Spelling is correct. And The One Truth, is never open for discussion or debate. Word.

And there was no need for the further complication, by the embellishment of language. And interpretation. And Theology. And Politics. And War. And there was no need for argument, or dispute. And, or discussion.

And The symbol held The Knowing. And there was no need for further questions, beyond It. And Faith was resolute, my dearest and most inquiring reader. Word.

And so. And if you were to draw a large circle, around the base of The Great Pyramid. And at the very centre of the Earth's landmass. And, in so doing, connecting all four points, to the circumference. And: then a corresponding concentric circle inside it, touching all four inner sides. And then subtract the length of the smaller circle, from the larger circle, (C1 minus C2) thus: the result is 299.048 meters. And this is numerically equal to the speed of light, at 299,048 meters per second. And as such, and therein, my ever and most attentive reader & scholar, is His Majesty once more. And the very mechanics of His Chariot. And you will count your steps. Word.

And so, a smaller circle within a larger circle, of this proportion; under the certain magnetic induction, of The Universe itself, and a rotating Earth, shall naturally produce a spiralling vortex. And equal to, the very nature and shape of The Universe itself, which attempts to pull them together. And so.

And when this vortex is successfully aligned, from Earth through Space, to a distant Mass; a channel connecting the two, through Space, is created. And so, just so. And there you have It, my dearest and most attentive reader. And It is simple in principle. Word.

And all numbers are Absolute, and golden now, at this: at the arrival to this Knowing. And 'I' has given to you here, what would become Pi and The Meter. And the diatonic musical scale, which is a universal language. And quite literally Universal. And The Golden Ratio. And 'I' need say no more, my dearest and most attentive reader. And scholar; indeed.

And do you not find the proof of evidence for yourself, in the very fact, that there was no such unit as the Meter, in the imperial measurements, at the time They purport, and would have you believe, that The Great Pyramids were constructed. And so, indeed. Word.

And all things brought into alignment through this aperture, can take on weightlessness, from a distant zero gravity, or anti-gravity. And this *stargate*, is the porthole, that is the much fabled "Eye of the Needle', by which The Faithful may enter The Kingdom of Heaven. And so too, All those who go with God.

And all about this Great Testament, that is The Great
Pyramid, is perfection. And Absolute. And The Golden
Orbs are mustering. And but: there is no one upon
The Blue Planet, manning their station any longer, to
assist re-entry. And The Red Species is returned to
dust, and gone altogether, but for their ghosts. And All
Government(s) are corrupt and forbidding. And no
Priest is as he should be. And so: say I. And The I in
We, must assume this mantle Now. Word.

And there are too few writers of true symbols, at the
time of writing, dearest scholar. And it should not be
that way. And the verbose & wordier diatribes, which
Man has evolved to, say nothing. And the graphic
designers & marketing men, exploit the void, left by
despotic dictators. And there are too few, true believers
of true symbols, in correspondence. And it should not
be that way.

And The Resource is, to the larger part, (8 in 10); a
weak, pathetic, perverted, aggressive, egotistical,
unbalanced, stupid, neurotic, and misguided entity.
And it must be said. And They are nothing to
celebrate, in the main. And They are devoid of any of
the qualities instilled and installed by The Divine, at
their conception. And The Truth may very well hurt.

And They are entirely obsessed with Themselves. And; the vanities of the complex carbon based organism, festering with bacteria & pathogens ~ that They are. And They are too deeply flawed. And They are nothing to write home about. And They are largely *his*. And *he* is in T*hey*. And this is the regrettable truth, my dearest reader: (1 in 5).

And All potency in established symbols, has been made dilute, by The Politics of Man. And pervasive technologies. And The Convectors are now crawling with holiday makers; celebrating the achievement of men in loin cloths, with copper chisels: one evolutionary step, from the clever monkey, His Majesty arrived to. And Their sense of wonder about it All, is light years from The One Truth. And Their inquiry, too weak and pathetic, to ever get Them to It. And so. And The Resource has been too deeply diverted from The One Truth, by *he* in They. Word.

And The Meter is a Divine rod. And it is an absolute proof. And in a time of feet, palms and cubits, We brought you this Absolute, with absolute precision, from the omnipotence of The Future. And so, God is both timeless and omnipotent, by this very rule. And He is proven here, absolutely, by it. Word.

And furthermore. And the seventh/eighth (In One), extraterrestrial species, about the Earth, is Our very Descendent. And, not at all an antecedent. And We are Ourselves. And there is no numerical value for this any longer: (7/8). And there is no one word for this number; as does π at 3.142. And yet He exists, because He will exist. And He will Be. And The Descendent serves only The Human Being and God Himself, Itself. And they/He is a frequent visitor to The Earth's atmosphere: *by* Orbs. And He is normally a beacon. And He is The Voice of The Sound in The Light. And you can rejuvenate the lost sense to Know Him. Word.

And His number is 7 & 8 in one. And this is It's energy. And He paves the way and sweeps it. And He is absent, it appears, or made impotent, in this modern world. And or imprisoned or detained. And He is nowhere to be seen in The People of The Blue Planet, any longer. And He is Not upon The Earth until The Future. And He is only known in Wonder, to those precious few of resolute faith. And He is Our Guardian.

And <u>I</u> believes <u>He</u>, Our staunchest ally upon The Earth, is restrained somehow, by *he* in They by *him* in government. And He is suppressed. And <u>I</u>, is yet unable to make this calculus, at the time of writing.

And so, *i* may not yet inscribe upon the matter. And I believe*s* there is *still* a secret vault, in Egypt or The Sudan. And: or Ethiopia. And It's discovery must be kept from Them, who are *he in They*. And It will release H̲im. And 33 is Our number, my dearest reader. And We shall despatch The Scientists of Our number, who are The Faithful, to find It. Word.

And Our Precious Golden Orbs, can still not make harbour. And muster We will. And must we await The Thaw to do so. And it is a bottleneck, that is this *aperture abert*. And the red planet is more adjacent to it, than the blue. And they were Our gatekeepers.

And if you cannot hear the screaming of volumes, that belong to The One Truth, at All this, my dearest reader, it is only because it is still too far beyond All mortal comprehension, to understand. And but, The Human Being will understand this. And this understanding is The Knowing. And so.

And It is The Divine in All His Majesty. And here is the porthole to The Heavens. And all evidence of God's existence. And those with Knowing, happen upon it.

And those without Knowing, do not. And They remain bemused by Their own existence, for all Their lives and always. And They are susceptible to the gravities of The Soup, more so. And to vices. And to the will and wants of *he*, by the *unvirtue* of Their ignorance. And to The Disease itself. And *he* claims Them. And They stand only to champion *his* devolution.

And Resolute Faith is The Knowing. And to believe until the point, where you Know absolutely, is to possess Resolute Faith. And less than Faith, is Belief. And below that, all else: witchcrafts and superstition.

And it is all a matter of Faith in The Divine, my most attentive reader: be certain. And Celestial Metaphysics. And He is All. And He is All things. And He is in the purity of mathematics. And He still remains and endures, far beyond the point where mathematics ends. And with it, our only ability to explain Him. And at this, is constituted The One Truth. And proven. And The Knowing is attainable. And It is only a Science too, of sorts. And Chemistry and Metaphysics. And it is a Science that does not conform, to Earthly Physics or probability. And so it is not deemed to be a science, but illogical and supernatural. And it is neither of these. And too few attain the mastery of it. Word.

And the mind may be the microcosm of the Heaven and Earth. And this was the *instill*-ation upon *Homo erectus.* And each thought, but a journey toward His Majesty. And there is mind mapping. And there is mayhem, to more and lesser degrees. And in One, it is precise and perfect. And this One is The I. And with The Electron at the core of Being. And with the twin Electron in The Kingdom. And The Kingdom *being* in The Heaven(s), through the trajectory of Orion. Word.

And but, It is a Science, determined by The Divine, not Man. And The Laws that govern The Earth are peculiar to The Earth. And they do not apply elsewhere, to by far the larger part. And you may be chosen. And The Choosing may choose you, and be predetermined. And your mind *is* a microcosm of The Heavens and Earth, my most precious reader, if you are chosen. And about this, you are to learn your lesson well. And you are to mark *I's* words here, most indelibly. Word.

And so by it, The **I** who is He, is within each individual. And each individual may call Itself I, once it is faithful. And this is Being. And with the mind 'being' a microcosm of The Heavens and Earth.

And with each thought and contemplation being a journey, between cells *(of the brain = stars of the cosmos)*, All birth charted astrology, and alignments, can be calculated into a vague and inaccurate Science. And as such, a science too easily misinterpreted, and made fickle. And but, a Science nonetheless, which can lead to The One Truth, in the hands of It's greatest exponent(s), with Knowing. And so; just so. Word.

And in All Science, there is The One Truth, above all lesser truths, awaiting discovery. And, or rediscovery. And by the 'All Knowing' of, and 'connection to', The Kingdom. And by the celestial porthole, just so it is.

And besides, beyond this World, all the absolutes of Science are changed. And as above, so below, intended. And so, with the flesh and sinew of mortality, put aside at death, if not sooner, (as with The Tibetan Masters, whos' antecedents survived the cataclysmic Flood of four or five precessions since, and who spawned the peoples of China and South East Asia), the microcosm by microwave, to The Kingdom comes. And just as He, when known as The Christ, or Mohamed, or some others too and few. And just as when it was, that The Architects walked on water, just so It is. And they carried their wands. Word.

And just as when, colossal stones are fashioned into an elevated position, with unsurpassed precision, just so it is too. And pay attention to '<u>I</u>' now, my dearest reader, for the lesson is simple. And the mirror image shall reflect indefinitely and infinitely, through Space, until It's destination or obstruction.

And of the path that is the Equatorial Band, that links all these key monoliths, and significant Ancient Sites, upon The Blue Planet, exactly. And of, when it is revolving beneath the aperture precisely, about The Equinox. And so, it forms a perfect line, when viewed from The Heavens, of a rotating Earth. And it is like a spinning top, in the playroom of a child's nursery.

And it moves incrementally into alignment, beneath the eye of the needle. And All weightlessness occurs beneath it, at this conjunction. And, on this path about The Equinox, at the ebb of the precession. And here you may find testimony to The One Truth. And within The One Truth, He awaits you. Word.

And all construction occurred during the phenomenon. And correspondent with each visitation, during the scope of the *abert aperture*. And The Flying Carpets of The Architects. And these were magnetic pads.

And just as when a solid sphere, suspended in the zero gravity of Space, within The Cosmos, is aligned with another planet, of equal or similar density, just so it is.

And so, to ponder my dearest and most attentive reader. And is the very blue planet itself, not a giant rock suspended in midair apparent. And just look at The Moon once more, in correspondence. And you will find, it is precisely that. And nothing but that, or anything different.

And so, just so it is, without argument. And it is the very law, hidden in plain sight. And so, just so are huge building blocks, placed into an elevated levitated position, by mimicking and harnessing precisely this, in microcosm. And there is weightlessness for an increment of time: a minute or a second, within that minute. And All within, and only then. And within the scope of the abert aperture.

And so, just then and only then, is the apparent miracle achieved, by The Science within God, that is God and The One Truth. And this is God. And nothing that is not mathematically absolute, or less than magnificent, may define God, but God Himself.

And no lesser extraterrestrial life force, can be
considered as God. And nothing as fickle, as is
contained or explained by the politics or religions of
Man, may be seen as God. And because of precisely
this, is why Islam prohibits depictions of The Prophet,
such is The Majesty of God. Word.

And so.

And the sextant is an enduring tool. And still, it measures from the same seven stars of The North. And The Equatorial Ring ran at 33 degrees from The Equator itself.

And it was the angle of descent. And it has perhaps shifted a point or two hence, since whence, yet to be determined. And it is like finding the proverbial needle in a haystack. And The Great Pyramid, is at the epicentre to It All; below.

And that which was written as Atlantis is true, and can be found beneath this Equatorial Centrifugal Ring also. And it is in The Atlantic Ocean, my most attentive reader. And not the Mediterranean Sea.

And 'I' will be sending the Scientists to find it's ruin, during this aperture abert. And Atlantis and Atlantic are names given by The Ancient Greek, who had All Knowing, and who were Divine.

And it will be found near South America. And it shall have shifted at the hands of elemental forces, since it was. And, but it shall be by The Cuban Island of Hispaniola. And in the region of The Sargasso Sea. And '**I**' has told you this before.

And They have kept this teaching from you. And They have stolen the number 33. And claimed it as Their own. And We will not support this thievery any longer.

And you are to take a look at The World at Their hands. And it is plain to see the carnage and misery therein. And it is simple to ascertain, that matters are not as they should be. And nor as they could be. Word.

And '**I**' shall not be permitting The Esoteric Society, to shanghai this discovery too, to it's own ends. And, just as They have too, so many and much else. And so, to corrupt All Knowing. And you may consider it ended.

And They may not be trusted. And there will be treasures. And there will be pillared crystals there. And then, The World will Know. And 'I' has told you all of this before. And the crystals will have restorative powers, I is assured.

And in this place, that The Ancient Greek spoke of as Atlantis, you shall have the only site along the equatorial band, more important than The Great Pyramid. And as potent, verily. Word.

And it was a domicile to the gods of The Third Species. And they were The Sky People. And they were emissaries of God Himself. And they were The Architects, who were The Divine Emissaries. And they were and remain, The Sons of The Sun. And they resided here, during their manifestation upon The Earth. And they taught the Human Being a love for God. And indeed love itself.

And They were All of Light. And they took residence inside the clever monkey, twice removed from Homo Erectus in ascendency. And they allowed the pre-His'tory, to lay claim to the precision masonry, and fantastic accomplishments, defiant of every law of physics, governing Early Man. And they left before the aperture *abert* was closed each time, by celestial forces, at each precession's ebb. And they returned several times by It. And It was this way. And it has been this way every thirteen thousand years, and twenty six thousand years, for the passed two hundred and fifty thousand years. (Approximately).

And elemental forces in their absence, submerged 'It'
beneath tumultuous Seas. And this was The Flood.
And The Third Species are Divine Emissaries to The
God. And they are All of Light, in their very Being.

And God is All of Light, and nothing else. And so, He
and His are always a manifestation, like a mirror image.
And never incarnate, as does Satan. And or indeed,
Lucifer, who is Not Satan, but The Christ in alter ego.

And it was The City within The City, at the final
retreat of Rome, who branded The False Prophet,
Lucifer, and Satan as one. And it never was this way,
before the fall of Rome. And the vast reaches of *her*
empire, whether in military or religious form. And it
was never this way, before Rome's capitulation to
Christ. And the crimson retreat, to the final bastion of
The City within The City, brought to exalt His name
under duress. And it is an adulterated bibliography.
And it is Untrue. And you are to mark my words
indelibly my dearest reader, in this regard. And Lucifer
is The Light upon The Earth. And The Christ was
The Man He took residence within, upon God's
choosing. And the man's name was Jesus of Nazareth.
And the same Divine rule applies, to All of The
Prophets. And listen to Ibrahim: All of you. Word.

And how He returns, is as follows my dearest and most attentive reader. And Lucifer is Not Satan, but for His depiction in the adulterated bibliography of The Bible. And Lucifer is never Satan. And but, He is God's very mortality upon The Earth. And He is All of Light, until made flesh and Christ. And He is Light. And He arrives by Light. And He seeks The Chosen. Word.

And Lucifer is The Light upon The Earth. And He is born of Man, but Not Satan incarnate. And Lucifer is The Light upon The Earth, that The Light of The Heavens seek, as The Vehicle to be a conduit, between Heaven & Earth. And Lucifer is the alter ego. And The Man before The Choosing, that becomes The Christ. And, or whoever is The Chosen. Word.

And Lucifer is The Light. And He is Man. And His Life corresponds with rich seams of serendipity. And miracles. And the coincidences of great improbability. And He communes, and is *at one* with Nature. And He incites Wonder and Awe. And He has always attracted critics because of this. And He was easily maligned. And He was easy to condemn. And All The Resource is less than He. And He treads in flashes upon The Earth, as it is in Heaven. And it is He, that The Light of The Heaven seeks upon The Earth. And so.

And about this my dearest reader, you are to be at your most attentive. And you are to learn that Lucifer is the mirror image of The Christ. And Not the opposite of The Christ. And you are to disregard All anomalies, in this reportage. And shake off any doubts or 'cognitive dissonance', and merely learn your lesson well. And So.

And He is Not the embodiment of Satan. And Lucifer is not Evil, but the embodiment of Nature. And the deeply maligned and fractured science of Magic, as It strives and fails to understand: just as you do too, here & now, my dearest and most attentive reader. And you too; my well applied scholar. And so: pay attention.

And indeed: All Science & History books, shall be rendered obsolete, when the struggle to understand It All relents, and when The Knowing of The One Truth, becomes commonplace. And, when the vacuum that God abhors, He fills; ~ at the great unlearning. Word.

And of the scribes in the employ of Rome. And The City within The City, risen from her. And of c3, c4, c5 at the final throws of The Holy Roman Empire. And They edited & abridged; according to the will and commission of Their crimson cloaked employers, as ever They had. And don't be fooled, and taken in.

And the scriptures salvaged from Masada, met with the same fate. And Lucifer and The False Prophet, were consigned to eternal damnation, as a job lot, alongside Satan. ~ And slight men in ochre, with loincloths and copper chisels, were credited with wondrous feats: too.

And furthermore: of the charisma, and attraction of Lucifer. And The Birth *of* Love, beyond the mechanics of sex. And that; which the women could not but help themselves be drawn to, because they were governed more so, and inextricably, by the cycles of Nature: was outlawed. And weaklings and peculiarities developed *new* Church & Religion. And it must be said. And now it can be said. And Lucifer was consigned to The Abyss with Satan, for the mere convenience of politics & government. And oppression. And suppression. And the bolstering of Their agendum. And Judas was excluded altogether. And became the Fall Guy for an entire creed. And the greatest story ever told, was *forged* at the anvil of the early papacies, by the hands of c3, c4, c5. And All with one eye on the prize. And the resurrection of the fallen city at large. And of The City within The City Itself. And shape shifting. And cutting crimson cloaks, according to Their cloth. And so desperate times, called for desperate measurement(s).

And every manner of Scholar of c21, and the present day, will take umbrage with this revelation: that Lucifer is Not Satan. And even you too, my dearest and most devoted reader, might struggle to resolve the matter, about yourself. And they would be wrong to. And so would you; my precious and most attentive reader. And but, the aperture is *abert*. And it is a Time for Enlightenment. And Lucifer was Not Satan most assuredly; but a deeply maligned alter ego of The Christ. And the very seed of His Majesty. And the indoctrination, is the handiwork of scribes c3 & c4, from within The City within The City. And this is an urgent and most pressing bulletin. And it is The Truth, The Whole Truth, and Nothing but The Truth. Word.

And it is The Voice of God. And I am but a humble scribe, assigned to It's conveyance. And I Knows, I Know. And it is only the result of c3, c4, c5, monkeying with the scriptures, that brought us to this Revelation; any road. And so: Lucifer is The Light upon The Earth. And His Majesty's chosen conduit.

And He is not an exaltation of Evil upon The Earth: Au Contraire. And the exuberances of Youth and Nature are His. And the leaping fresh young salmon, and the violent verdant new growth in Spring, are His.

And the acts of consenting natural lovers are His. And a celebration of The Gift of Life. And it is upon all this, He shines. And radiates. And It is His Majesty. And the very Kingdom comes. And The Faithful are receptive. And He is chosen thus. And It is this way.

(Aside). And the loveless mechanical sexual acts and rhetoric, put upon the non- complicit, are Never His. And nor misogyny. And neither rape or coercive control. And, but instead the satanic antics, of a contaminated and misguided Resource. And They is many. And They are Not His, but *his.* Word.

And of The Light. And the conduit. And without the safe harbour of mortality, He may only be seen in the translucent shape, created by the intensity of that light, against the backdrop of natural light itself. And it is The Halo effect. Word.

And or, *by* the comparative darkness, amongst the backdrop of The Stars. And as such, He is largely invisible, night & day. And He is One. And He is Twelve. And He is Twelve times Twelve Thousand. And in the midst of photosynthesis, He can often leave ghostly imprints, on the elemental forces, that govern The Earth's realities. And so.

And by virtue of this, He is Brilliant. And by this, He defines Brilliance. And The Third Species has no weight nor meat. And, but it has form. And it is not *of* a carbon base. And it is not *of* any elemental base, known to the periodical charts and sciences of Earth. And you must understand the making of The Hybrid Child, at this. And how The Men From The Stars arrive and take form. And how The Golden Age begins each time. And so on.

And mark my words now, my dearest and most attentive readers of The Blue Planet: for it is You who must lift these words, and put The World to rights by them, during the course of this aperture *abert,* and beyond; as His instruments. And so: just so. ~

And too often, at the time of writing, The Lesser are governing & policing The Greater. And of these Illuminati; and Their variants: be warned. And of Their esoteric societies, who are now most feverishly playing god, at the time of this most urgent and pressing bulletin. And They are The Masters' Puppeteers. And They are All *his* very marionettes. And there is no business for the predatory and exploitative, more. And the Fossoilers, and purveyors of marsh grass, must be made extinct by the close of aperture. Word.

And so.

And They have stolen previous bulletins from 'I'. (And) His chosen and trusted Scribe. And They have dared to call The Words of '**I**', *'a'* stylish nonsense. And His Majesty is affronted by such an opinion, of His most dutiful and humble scribe(s). And The Voice of God dictates. And 33 is His number. And it is Our number.

And I must tell you, that each & every word scribed here, could just as easily be expressed equally, in algebraic formulae. And or, indeed, without any expression at all. And it is only God's Will. And reflective of Life Itself. And, as it is written, so shall it be. And whether it is written or not, it shall be; regardless. And It is Only written, so you too shall Know dearest reader. And so learn your lesson. Word.

And They aim to pervert and suppress all Truth. And Knowledge. And the very evidence of Our existence. And They cover up, anything pertaining to The One Truth, and His Majesty.

And They are Suppressors of Truth and Knowledge. And They are persecutors. And They are pretenders. And They are predators. And They are imposters.

And They are buoyed by the invasive powers, of Their infernal $5 technologies. And Their avaricious love of money. And They are made evil by All of this. And destructive. And such stuff is the business of Satan.

And They Know nothing in comparison. And They know nothing of what Life is worth. And They only suppress and oppress. And They are not Human Being.

And They are not benevolent. And They may not be, the self-appointed guardians to The Key any longer. And They may not use Our number any longer. And the number will begin to work against Them: be sure.

And be assured, that every number has the power to be a symbol, to which any other number (or letter), can adhere, and carry great weight by. And so $x = 33$. Word.

And where the number will bolster and galvanise The Human Being, so shall it be Their cancer, in equal measure. And $\underline{I}$ has set the fulcrum point thus. And I am instructed to tell you. And 33 is Our number. And 33, is not Their number. And The Human Being(s) will be galvanised now, by this very bulletin. Word.

And We will make Ourselves known to you, by this number. And We shall expose Them, by this number. And The Human Being will thrive once more, in these three score years and twelve, of the *aperture abert,* from the date of this bulletin, by this number. Word.

And this means an Uprising, of sorts. And the chaos will be cleansing, like a turning tide. And you shall learn your Lucifer from your Satan. And it shall put Them into retreat. And it is not an Armageddon. And, but it is a great restoration. And it is indeed a revolution. And so: Vive La Revolution!

And the revolution is a partial rotation. And the number is 60. And the direction is anticlockwise. And this is the very shape of things to come. And The Human Being will support Us unwaveringly, quite naturally, with regard to this issue, according to It's nature. And so.

And We shall champion The Human Being, above the esoteric oppressive secret societies, of The Blue Planet. And They shall diminish in correspondence. And kindness shall prevail in the fullness of time, before the aperture becomes closed once more. Word.

And you will see the passion of The Human Being,
begin to restore and improve: opposed to the singular
avaricious drive, of *he* in They, to make money. And
the unrelenting desire to double production, at all cost.

And where you see it, you must support the former,
and reject the latter. And The Federation will preside.
And so; just so. And it is predisposed to become this
way, whilst the aperture is still *abert*, before
Precession's End. And before the new precession
begins. And you will come to fully appreciate His
Majesty, & the Divine strength He bestows upon His
Faithfull. And The Human Being shall prevail, before
the aperture is drawn closed. And no mistake. Word.

<u>And so ~</u>

And *of* Their infernal New Order, with it's conditioning(s) and social engineering; as follows. And It's governments have legitimised gross criminality, by the authorities of The Third Face. And too many laws are now basic Human Rights violations.

And *he* by They, have developed and sold all the weapons *of* the playing field. And *he* by They, have created the disarray, in the first instance. And there should be no weapons at all. And so say I. Word.

And there were no weapons at all, when did He reign. And only Magnetic and Solar Powers. And as above, It is not yet so; below. And never shall be, by a long chalk, under *he*. And what it should be, and what it is, are too estranged from one another, to draw any comparison. And the poles apart are worlds apart.

And He was sent as always He is, whenever possible, in times of great adversity. And He is All of Light. And His form is a weightless metal. And it shines brightly. And it is an Orb. And there are twelve.

And He fed those Believers, who are known since: as, The Jews', in their wilderness. And It was a machine. And it gave them Manna from Heaven. And listen.

And it was a fast growing algae, with the strength of spinach. And it was far from the land of milk and honey. And, but it did sustain.

And He was called Akhenaten. And He was One of The Twelve. And He was God. And He was from The Stars. And He was The Emissary of God in manifest.

And He was of The Sky People. And He had been refused. And He had been denied. And God had been defiled. And so He was sent again and again and again. And He exacted His revenge upon The Pharaoh, by Divine Wrath, from The Heaven.

And it has been documented in a fashion. And He sent His son into The Future, when it was clear that all was lost to the vanities of Pharaoh, by *he* in They.

And the text recorded: that, "God had chosen The Jews", by those He had saved, who soonly formed their own religion in gracias, on the basis of this very salvation. And He hadn't, 'saved The Jews', per se; but He had simply saved The Human Being, who were 'The Believers'. And The Faithful to that belief. And that is the fact of it all. Word.

And truer; it should be more simply recorded. And instead, it should read, that: "God favoured The Human Being of Resolute Faith, above The Pharaoh in moral and spiritual decay". And so. Word.

And at this, was both verily, The Choosing, and The Damnation. And so, All of 'The Cradle of Life' fell into disarray, throughout *this* final Eighth of The Precession, as a consequence. And in disarray it has remained.

And in this instance, it was, and just so happened to be, The One who became the scribe(s) of Judaism, at the very birth of religion, who recorded the event(s). And it was their antecedents *indeed*, who had been The Faithful, who were saved. And so.

And His Majesty has no doubt that This Believer(s), was an adoring witness. And a humble and dutiful scribe. And that His homáge was True and Faithful, in It's design. And that there was no wicked intention within, to monopolise monotheism.

And all of the region were Semite and faithful in this time. And Abraham had this Knowing. And, until '*he* in They', seized the opportunity, and divided The Faithful into peoples, it was a common knowledge.

And this division is the work of Satan, by *he* in They, under *him*. And but, none of The Peoples are evil *per se,* before *his* work. And so.

And The Palestinian, still is The Faithful. And it must be said. And The Arabian and Persian too. And yet, these faithful are estranged from The One Truth. And so are at odds with one another also. And they are more faithful, than the secular nations of The World, with Their shameful and barbaric colonial histories. And it is a bitter pill to swallow, for the many to whom, it is hereby dispensed. And The Federation shall repair and restore the malaise. And so: thank God. A'Men & Word.

And don't be brought to a belief *in* the contrary, by fervent propagandas. And the squawking warmongers, in every cast and plumage. And The Federation will take an overview, and stamp out and quash All sectarian nonsense, without prejudice or bias. And this Holy Land will Know peace again most assuredly. And also unity and forgiveness, during this aperture abert. And It is His will. And so.

And The Hooligans within it all, shall dissipate accordingly, rest assured. And They are All *his*. And *he* is in They, my most attentive and enquiring reader.

And Faith in His Majesty, remains as essential to Life on Earth, as the oxygen we breath. And there is no escaping the very fact of the matter, that without Faith in He, there is no right to Life. Word.

And All civility throughout The Cradle of Life, will be restored. And, just as it was the first region to be divided into religion, and to crumble under *'he'* thereby, so shall it be the first to be restored by He, beneath the radiation of His love, at the central land mass of The World. Word.

And All the nations of all The World, shall follow suit, from The Ebb of this epicenter. And It is Always this way, whether this way or that. Word.

And so. ~

And (previously), Pharaoh was under covenant with Satan. And Satan is the name given to *he*, in *his* spiritual concentration. And It moves as a cloud of gas. And *he* dissipates and intoxicates.

And *he* exists in parts per billion. And beware where e'er it concentrates, 'tis All. And beware, All They who breath *him*. And *he* is born of marsh grass. And *he* is in league with The Fossoilers. And no mistake.

And so, The Faithful are, and have been ever oppressed since, by The esoteric elite, who give harbour to Satan, in the mortality of a few evil men, as it were. And It is in They, *he* makes *his* concentration(s).

And They breath *him* in well. And deeply. And It is a greater number of Them now, whom are *evil* personified. And They are *d'evil*. Word.

And under *he*, *his* agenda under They, has entered the mainstream. And it is an ugly fish to behold. And It is predatory. And it craves money and power only. And it sees war and oppression, as a means to this end. And it seeks out all those it may exploit, in It's swim.

And God shall be in the business of changing this now, within the aperture *abert*. And you will see. And All energies rotate upon the axis of Good and/or Evil, as the Precession corkscrews in mimickery, of the shape of a strand of DNA, through The Dark Matter of Space. And He shall radiate upon, and into The Faithful, through the aperture abert. And The Faithful shall be galvanised in the weightless metal of those they accommodate. And they shall do His bidding. Word.

And They by *he*, will always aim to persecute The Human Being, for as long as They are allowed to attain positions of power, authority and government.

And so. ~

And We were called Ki and An-ar-ki by The Human Beings We left behind, a full ten precessions before. And they watched Us rise up, as if by levitation. And leave, from the points along the equatorial band, of a rotating globe, as the aperture passed overhead. And We departed by The Eye of The Needle.

And you will be able to envisage, and visualise the mechanism now, in your mind's eye. And this is the awakening of a lost sense. And you can see now, The Eye of The Needle, my dearest and most precious and ever attentive reader. And so, you have been taught. And you will have awakened a dormant memory, in your DNA. Word.

And all language was monosyllabic, and unrecorded in this time. And there were only a handful of symbols, which educated All, absolutely. And All were educated absolutely by these symbols. Word.

And it became The An-nu-na-ki, as language developed. And all civilisations and language evolved from this cradle. And it is in North Africa now. And it always was on that continent.

And it is at the very epicentre, of The Earth's land mass and density. And it was ten precessions since; too. And there were no divisions, when did He reign. And The People were like The Trees of The Forest. Word.

And The Cradle of Life has been butchered, like a sacrificial lamb, into ten separate nations, of *his* modern world. And wherever *he*, in They, creates division, *he* then soon makes war. And the angle of descent was 33 degrees. And it may still be, when He returns. And on this presumption, 33 remains Our number. Word.

And The One the scribes recorded as Ezekiel, saw us. And He was five precessions ago. And or, perhaps six. And The One the scribes recorded as Noah, was four precessions ago. And or, perhaps five.

And it was in The Time of what is now called, and referenced to, as, the demise of Atlantis. And at the same cataclysm, as The Flood. And He and He were witnesses. And they were made faithful, by It.

And they would become *of* The Twelve Times Twelve Thousand by It, beyond Life and rapture. And it is all well documented now, in a fashion. And theologised. And yet, all be it, long after the events themselves.

And but, all timelines are perverted and condensed by the written word, that arrived tens, and often hundreds of thousands of years, after the events, that, *'that'* written word, depicts. And so, just so it is. Word.

And all recorders are bias and partisan, to one agenda or another. And it is normally victor over vanquished, as the new tarmac is laid over the old road. And it is only The Dutiful Scribe, appointed by The Divine Itself, whom relates The One Truth *ver batem*. Word.

And from the fulcrum point, doth He always *spake*, without prejudice. And '<u>i</u>' is such a dutiful scribe in this regard, my *'very'* most precious and attentive reader. And you will find no hidden agendum or allegiance herein, by He in <u>I</u> at the helm. Word.

And so, the stories that are told, are those told by persons *'known'* as Ezekiel and Noah. And, who were direct descendents of those antecedents, who *'were'* Ezekiel and Noah. And, who are the actual persons, depicted in the recorded events. Word.

And names and tales were always carried by bloodline, as John to Johns' sons, in latter days. And further to Johnson. And further afield to Johansson, for example.

And as populations grew, and as surnames were carried about, as a means of identity and association. And All records were initiated this way, 'In the Beginning'.

And the human events of two hundred and fifty millennia, and one hundred millennia, before, were hurried into a 'recorded text', with the discovery of the 'written' word. And Epochs, just as if the events of a single week, as depicted in The Book of Genesis. And similarly, in the texts of all other Great Religions too.

And records had been passed from Father to Son this way. And were carried in no other way. And each recorded name, together with their experience was property, by birthright.

And each record, could not be carried by another, other than by one with direct lineage. And to tell another's story, would be theft. And They carried each others' names, only by order of lineage.

And they held these stories by blood, until written records began. And this was the way it were, for the longest time. And so.

And there were Songlines, that held the impregnation of spirit, on the static backdrop of Time. And as, The Human Being did 'Walkabout' their business. Word.

And so events, such as The Flood: and of previous visitations, were held literally unrecorded, for one hundred thousand, and two hundred thousand years. And more.

And the tales of God's glory, were woven only into the threads of memory, and the spoken word, by The Tellers, and the tales they told. And it was held in folklore.

And the stories of The Tellers, were then put into the written word, as soon as it was arrived to. And this was generations upon generation, after the events themselves. Word.

And so. And by this, the records of those landmark events, are attributed to these descendents, The Tellers, by documentation in the written word, as occurring within the timeframe of their own life. And not, as is the very truth, remotely accurate; to the time of the events themselves, much and much much earlier. And by this, All is distorted, and much is lost.

And the dutiful reader & scholar, shall be credited for their understanding of this essential fact. And It shall dawn on you, as something of an epiphany. And you shall have The Knowing, by arriving to this firm understanding.

And The Scribe has always been a sort. And The Scribe is highly sought after. And the written word is God's preferred medium. And All have endeavoured to possess and curry His favour, whether vanquished or victor. And, but The Dutiful Scribe, that is the instrument of The Divine, is true only to His Majesty, regardless of any other external forces. And or pressures or coercion. And He records without prejudice, The One Truth, whomever it favours or condemns. Word.

And it is the truth, that His Majesty sees none of those of The Third Face as His, but All others as His. And All They of The Third Face, as *his*. And His Majesty endorses & welcomes wholeheartedly The Federation.

And it is true, that His Majesty sees no majesty in any war or weapons. And none whatsoever. And no mistake. And it is true, that His Majesty could destroy All those of The Third Face, (with all Their weapons), without using any weapons at all. And so.

And it is true, that His Majesty looks down upon all those who burrow down ~ And into The Earth for wealth and power. And He abhors The Fossoilers.

And the gold and silver was glistening in the surface streams, for a reason. And All energies needed to sustain Life, are available from above. And from The Sun. And The Earth's magnetic Fields.

And what was once one million years of Life on Earth, is exhumed and consumed, and exhausted, in every single year, by the *fossoilers*. And They billow spent marsh grass, in parts per billion, into The Earth's atmosphere, of Their satanic world. And so.

And it is a fantastically unsustainable ratio, by which, '*he* by They', under *him*, have fuelled Their final charge. And *he* was born of marsh grass. And *he* is raised by *he* in They.

And so *his* evil reign and *his* fuels, will be ended and exhausted, by the close of this Aperture Abert. And The Human Being shall be, at long last, rid. And this shall be the very business of The Human Being. And about this, you are to mark my words indelibly, that hard rains could n'er e'er they erase; my dearest reader.

And the *aperture abert* is the advent porthole, for the resurgence to Magnetic and Solar power that follows, my dearest and most attentive reader. Word.

And *he* that opposes He, and champions They, has entered All churches and politics, with unholy instruments, since 'the very flurry and fury', of the written word, began.

And politics was formed and forged at this. And religion with it. And a divisive alloy, of the two. And misinformation is *his* stock in trade. Word.

And They thrive on *his* inaccurate indoctrinations. And teachings. And it is self serving. And They feed on *his* propagandas. And nonsense(s).

And in no way, was this very fact; of the rapid transposition, of the spoken word, into the written word, dissimilar then, to the passage of all great Histories, since The Dawn of Time.

And like the plays and novels of three millennia, now: (from Plato to Dickens), finding their way onto Film. And into Cinema, in the scope of a single decade, as they did, with the arrival of The Moving Picture.

And so, just as three thousand years might be condensed into ten, so might an entire precession, or epoch, be reduced to a single day in scripture. Word.

And so, just so. And so, did the actual experience(s) of the Human Being(s), of One Hundred and Two Hundred thousand years ago, find their way literally, onto the tablets of the earliest scribes, under the commission of a School of Thought, or Politic. And into the scriptures, of two thousand and four thousand years ago. And Kings and Priests dictated, according to prevailing vanities. And Their scribes were not humble mostly, but flamboyant extensions of Their Masters. And too often, did not record under Divine ordinance. And according to <u>I</u>.

And let me put it simply, and spell the lesson out in binary code, as it were. And so: The Flood & Noah + Atlantis, was between 105,000 – 130-000 years ago. And but, the descendents of Noah and others, having told their tales orally for the longest time, only had the first opportunity to write them down, about 5000 years ago. And so.

And here as then, **_he_** may make do and undo All. And _he_ may fashion a mortal psyche, by these tools. And when _he_ corrupts The Arts, that are an homáge to The Divine, _he_ is at _his_ most dangerous always. Word.

And: for The Arts is the preserve of The Divine. And the pen is mightier than the sword always. And to corrupt this, has been _his_ very business. And The Book, as a format, is a potential tool of propaganda and misinformation. And a program unsurpassed, upon The Human Resource, to this very day. And far beyond.

And only He thinks still, in quill & ink: as does I. And His Majesty is not in awe of Mans' made technologies. And The Human Being is resolute in correspondence.

And _he_ in They, will have put _his_ agents in, to lead congregations, as a vanguard. And with great books too, and fanciful tales. And, strategically, ahead of _his_ war machine(s). And conquests. And so it has been.

And too often have the better Peoples, fallen to _his_ government(s), One by One, by _he_ in They. And so, those lesser Peoples of great empires, have progressively and steadfastly, spread _his_ disease. And devolved The Resource. And This is True, but lost to pre-'_his_-story'.

And The Third Face has been a long time in it's construction. And They are entering the home straight. And it is corrupt. And it is an anomaly. And a quandary. And it is an irony and a paradox, that the very evolution of the species, has been, in fact, a devolution. And It is shameful to say, that the Race, before now, was hell bent on engineering a means, whereby the weakest, could assert and dominate and oppress, the 'fittest who survived', Darwin's evolution. And the societies of the passed 500 years, have evolved through; the advancement of weapons, slavery, and the refinement of Law. And don't get I wrong dear reader, but realise that the backdrop of predatory capitalism, is very wrong. And the paradigm shift is simple. And so: ~

And it is only but a *very* fact, that those with the more powerful weapons have prevailed. And so, His Majesty abhors All weapons, because the better people did not, and still do not, have, or want them. Word.

And The Human Being has been brought to near extinction by this. And The Nursery Planet has been made a perpetual battlefield, because of it. And The Human Being were the indigenous majority. And by the third and fourth visitations, it was so. And The Human Being were The Aboriginal.

And The Human Being was often Black. And The Human Being was often Brown. And or, Red. And The Human Being was Pagan & Druid. And He was stout, like The Oak Tree; that He worshipped and adored.

And they were priests as priests should be. And The Human Being was Pagan as Pagan should be. And not as pagan is. And they were women and children and civilians. And they were holy. And they were modest. And His Majesty was The Sun. And they were Faithful to Him. Word.

And The Human Being was Indigenous to the lands, that the people with the weapons, and the big books arrived to. And made them extinct from; by unrelenting, systemic persecution and genocide. Word.

And these Human Beings were made slaves. And these Human Beings were slaughtered. And these Human Beings were made extinct. And so now they sleep. And they became the dormant gene in their oppressors, by progeny.

And these were not war mongering Peoples. And hypocrisy, was neither a word nor a trait known to them. And they are The Sleepers now, within the descendents of their all conquering, rapist & oppressive enslavers. And of course, there may be an unsettled score within them, if they have not found their peace. And this must be understood: that the suffering of The Ancestor, can still be in the blood of The Descendent. (And The Human Being must make it their business, to broker apology & forgiveness).

And such blood waits Only for The Sun. And for the *aperture abert,* at The Final Eighth of The Precession. And It is always a time for cleansing. And of righting wrongs. And the time is now, and hereabouts. And for three score years and twelve: to cleanse the brutalities of some three millennia and some, since when last the aperture was (partially) *abert*. And so, to allow Divine radiation from The Kingdom. And the passage of His Precious Orbs. And the commuting of The Twelve Times Twelve Thousand. Word.

And so. ~

And *he* always has *his* accounts in order. And evil tyrannical and despotic regimes, prize Their accountants and tax collectors most highly.

And by Them, *he* can build *his* fascist regimes and tyrannies. And Empires. And *his* paymasters have shiny minted coins for distribution, depicting those They serve. And *he* buys and sells All and They, with them.

And *he* always marches in step in uniform. And the more evil the intent, the higher and quicker the step. And once *his* evil has affected, *his* politics are installed, as a second fix.

And it becomes the norm. And the vanquished have no voice from their grave, trodden beneath the underfoot of the victors, and *his 'laws of the land'* above. And so they sleep. And await God's resurrection, of their goodself(s). And so, to live their best Life. And The Resource is plentiful, but The Human Being is few. And The Human Being is the best version of The Self.

And it is now, my pretties. And Good Gosh, and by Gosh, It is most assuredly Now, my dearest and ever attentive reader. And so be sure. And no mistake. And give The Black the apology their forefathers in chains never knew. And too, All of *his-stories* victims. And Know that The Resource is disposable & worthless to His Majesty, unless restored to Human Being. And if The Resource lives a Life riddled with *his* disease(s); and without Wonder & Kindness, His Majesty will, in All eventuality, dispense of It. And so:- And The Now is whilst the aperture is abert. And I wishes you to Know what Now means. And It is a busy time, both celestially (unto The Kingdom: and *verily*); and upon The Earth. And if you are an Human Being, you shall feel the stirrings within you, my most precious reader. And the remnants of The Sixth Sense. And The Ancestors, will not lie to you, if you have Faith. And this is The Knowing. And it is now, my dearest and most attentive reader. And you are now to Know what is The Thaw. And what it is the thawing of. And so; may He pass. And just as Neanderthal, was absorbed into the gene of The Homo Sapien, to be awoken and amongst them; so now will the dormant gene, of All The Human Being(s) within the The Resource, be rejuvenated by radiation, during the scope of this aperture *abert*. Word.

And We shall defeat Them from within. And We shall change Them with finesse & subtlety. And We shall restore the humanity of The Resource. And 'The *he* in They' will be defeated, and systematically deleted. And The He will be in The I. And this is the very agenda of The Aperture Abert, by order of The Kingdom. Word.

And The Resource shall largely undergo a paradigm shift, as The Sleeper gene is brought to the fore. And just as the germination of a seed; beneath The Sun of The Aperture Abert. And The Resource should better Itself accordingly, through the course of the two to three generations of The Aperture Abert, remaining. And from the time of writing. And so: indeed.

And you are to put your belief into The Scientists, at this juncture. And They will lead you soon Now, to God. And rest assured: but choose your Sciences & Scientists wisely. And never choose Scientology, or allow It, or They, to predate upon you.

And The Faithful Know Him to be God. And some amongst the civic hoard, have grown to call God, The Universe. And only, largely; so to disassociate from the oppressive doctrines & abuse, that Man has put upon mankind in God's name.

And too, from The Pedophile Priests; that hid in His name, behind crow black coats. And His Majesty has no issue with being called The Universe; because He precisely is The Universe. And more besides. Word.

And The Scientists shall soon Now, be given the tools to tend the untended garden. And gifted genetic codes. And discoveries within the advancement of genetics, shall be Good & Godly. And The Scientists will be faithful to God. And The Federation will keep an impartial and fair overview. And they will proclaim God's name, in the absolutes of their discoveries. And their work shall be Known as God. And bad conscience will be a crime. And so say I. And such amalgams, and complex carbon based organisms, found in the compounds: such as, the Avaricious Deceitful Faithless Fossoilers, Carnivorous Pornographers, Mindless Murderers; and The Liars & Hypocrites, will be deleted. Alongside thousands more disagreeable categories and compounds. And there shall be a purge as thorough as any Reich, under the governance of the clever Scientists. And prevention shall be better than cure. And a stitch in time will save nine. And you must understand, my dearest and most attentive reader, that there shall be zero innocent victims, under these methods. And no collateral damage.

And needless to say; the purge shall not be indiscriminately against, any particular creed or culture. And surely, Not against The Jews or Blacks or Gypsies. And but; relentlessly against anyone, from any aspect of the cross section of society, including Jews & Blacks & Gypsies, incontrovertibly guilty, of crimes of brutality, against The Earth; or any living thing upon it.

And Societies are to see All crimes of violence, against the person, as abhorrent. And where the offender is incontrovertibly proven, to be guilty of an heinous act, then; that offender is to be both executed, and the genetic code of the offender; deleted: never to be repeated. And The Scientists will be afforded these powers: to prevent sustained Life, or the reincarnation of such Life. And It is to be administered swiftly & clinically. And those carbon based organisms of The Resource, guilty of lesser infractions, are Only distortions of His intention. And they will Not be executed, and nor perhaps, even imprisoned: but They may well have Their DNA restricted. And The Federation's administration of birth control, will be widespread and commonplace, for at least two hundred years, following It's inception. And The Garden shall be tended fully in this time. And All Hail unto The Federation. Word.

And every nation of The World will have put forward
One Hundred Thinkers, to form The Federation. And
Its decisions and actions, shall be Mighty & Absolute.
And the simple Human Being, will be born again into
the tainted vessels, One by One. And, The Foragers
and The Gatherers. And The Faithful and The Sun
Worshippers. And The Farmers and The Woodsmen,
will return in spirit, within the rejuvenated Resource.

And The Human Being will be a new Edition of Itself,
before We are gathered up, and leave again. And The
Resource will be restored. And so.

And The Fishermen. And The Monks of Lindisfarne.
And The Meek, who were all trampled underfoot, by *he*
under They; will arrive to be within The Faithful. And
so; to restore The Nursery Planet. Word.

And *(previously),* by *his* marauding butchers, they fell.
And at the hands of *his* godless evil hoards, who likened
God to Themselves, in every instance without
exception. And *his* sanctimonious, and hypocritical, and
pontificating priests. And *his* corrupt & corrupted
judges. And They recreated god in Their own image.
And made a mockery of His *very* creation.

And Pale Face was Not Human Being, to be sure. And but now, He may be made so, by The New Edition. And by the forgiveness of *'only'* the dormant gene, awoken Now, within The Faithful. And so; just so. Word.

And it is always *his* accountants, with personal psychotic fantasies of Themselves; that They are instead, *his* general(s), chief advisors & police chief(s), doling out rolls of The King's Shilling, to the brainwashed minions of *his* societies.

And to the pressgang'ed, belligerently chained into servitude. And to the conscripted. And to the slaves too, one & All, (Redcoat & Blackskin) alike, in the main, if truth be told. And engineered, in to do *his* bidding. And see here, how malleable The Resource. And upon what distorted character is built.

And preserving disparity at all costs. And all, so long as the suffering and the wars, and the slavery, and the poverty, *was* kept always swept away from Their own polished marble doorstep. And contained singularly, within the profit margin of the accountants' ledger.

And They are a self serving godless hoard. And They
do not know God. And They are a ruling elite. And
They run The Earth (still), like landlocked Galapagos
mutants. And without a single notion of His Majesty's
intention(s). And the true business of Life. Word.

And the dormant gene will become the dominant gene.
And it shall emerge to the fore once more, as whence it
was the primary gene, in The Life it led generations
earlier. And so, by this mechanism, of germ and
nurture, shall The Common People be restored. And as
such, is the true & good nature of The Resource.

And His Majesty will seek The Scientists, to assist with
All this. And it is excellent that Science has evolved.
And that it has continued to evolve goodly and rapidly.
And at this, Good overcomes Evil. And Education
defeats Ignorance. And at this, The Meek inherit The
Earth. And It is Divine. And they shall make Believers
and Faithful of their godless hosts. And The Common
People, is not evil by nature, but two often lured by
shiny things; or distracted, by a potent symbol. And It
is gullible. And It is fickle. And it is hypnosis. And it is
magnetic attraction. And it is real. And so.

<u>Agendum.</u> ~

(To be implemented universally by The Federation, immediately upon It's formation and inception, ie: All The Nations of All The World, capitulating to It's unilateral authority). And *for* it is the untended garden that has gone to seed. And The Earth is a Nursery Planet. And precious to His Majesty, as All are solemnly to agree, regardless of Creed, Culture, Race or Politic. And so say I. Word.

- And there must be ready access to uncomplicated euthanasia, at every strata of society. And so, from The Prison Service, unto Retirement Homes, there will be assisted dying. And there should be no unwanted or unnecessary, prolonging of Life universally. And the swift dispatch and disposal of The Resource, should be readily facilitated.

- And convicted prisoners will be given the option of death, in every case that carries a sentence greater than two years. And death may be administered by lethal injection upon request, at any time during the sentence. And it is to be a painless execution. And administered by lethal injection.

- And also: Death will be a common punishment, for All incontrovertibly proven serious crimes, of (*violence against 'the person'*). And the rehabilitation programmes currently; of those who commit cruel and evil crimes, *(heinous acts),* shall be scrapped entirely: and Death administered instead. And this will be so, in every incontrovertible case, once guilt is established and certain. And where guilt remains uncertain, death must not be administered.

- And starvation:*(where the convict shall be given water only, whilst confined in solitary, and deprived of every food and comfort),* will be the only acceptable method of torture, in order to extract withheld information, that would aid justice, or benefit the victim(s) of the crime. **(the location of a murdered child; for example). ~*

- And The Human Rights activists will be 'Up in Arms', at All this. And but, the perpetrators of such crimes, that these new laws are for, are Not Human Being. And so; Human Rights do not apply. And this is the very point of law. (*Le Point de Droit). And it is only a generic Resource, in which We or They may live. And if The Resource is chronically contaminated, it should be deleted.

And the correctness of this: (La Nouvelle Loi), must be asserted. And it is ridiculous to prolong the existence of a deeply contaminated unit of The Resource. And they are merely vessels. And the instruments of an ongoing spiritual warfare, between He and *he*. And that is All. And this is the very rub. And the very matter. And It is the very truth, within The One Truth. And It is the *very* business of Life. And when It is Not Human Being, and It is violently defective, It must be weeded out to the very roots and dispatched. And crimes against the person, and crimes against The Earth, will be insupportable. And shall Not be tolerated at all. And having said this; it is all well and good, to devise and instigate new laws. And to strive to create the Utopia of The Kingdom, upon The Earth; but societies are horribly corrupted, by *he* in They, at every nation of all the world, at the time of writing. And perverted by density and carbon based mortality. And so, such totalitarianism would be doomed to failure, but for the incremental influences upon the Resource, beneath the aperture *abert*. And so: make hay whilst The Sun shines my dearest scholar. And believe in the concept of The Federation, until It is realised. And realise The Sun. And His Majesty. And the radiance of God's goodness. And His impact upon The Resource. Word.

And The Common People were largely once all Human Being(s). And or, almost All. And not instead, *his* obedient foot soldiers, bound by Gravity, which They soon become, every time: foddered well on vices. And the pursuit of shiny things. And always growing in number, exponentially, in Our absence. And so.

And it is a shame that The Resource has such a self destructive propensity. And, but it does. And It cannot help Itself. And it is predisposed to go bad and rot, by virtue of It's complex carbon base. And as such, there is the need for Divine intervention. And Faith in the immaculate, whom is All of Light. Word.

- And each member of The Resource, at every nation of all the world, is to receive a Universal Credit (payment), from their Nation's government. And; in exchange for a nominal amount of non-military National Service. And each government is answerable to The Federation. And this modest payment must be linked, *and* relative to, the cost of living, within the home nation. And it must be sufficient to provide for basic essentials. And to sustain. And The Federation shall collect and distribute, from the wealthier nations, to the poorer nations to implement this universal scheme.

And there is ample technology to provide food.
And stringent birth control and sterilisation, must
accompany this programme, in regions of famine
and flood and drought, so that the suffering is not
repeated infinitum. And it is the alleviation of
suffering, that is most important. And this is best
achieved, primarily, by birth control. And food.

- And all basic amenities shall be provided, in every
  nation of all the world. And water. And robot
  labour. And medicine. And birth control
  (sterilisation) programs will apply. And be both
  voluntary or mandatory, as deemed appropriate.
  And as decided by The Federation.

- And mass emigration; both economic and political,
  will be curtailed. And The Federation will oppose
  & quash, any oppressive regimes, that obstruct this
  manifesto, and cause displacement of peoples. And
  The Federation shall assist in repatriation. And
  The Federation may enforce forcibly It's agenda &
  manifesto, as needs be.

And the science shall evolve soon, to correspond with
His Majesty's wishes. And It is The Judgment. And It
is The Rapture. And The Faithful shall live on.

And The Faithless shall be deleted. And Science will facilitate this, once It successfully differentiates, and separates, The Being from the flesh and sinew. Word.

And The Resource shall be blessed by this restoration, once more. And with the needle set upon the sliding rule, shifting incrementally until fulcrum point traversed: onward. And with this, the rotation of a partial revolution. And the numbers 1, 12, 60, & 360 are applicable. And remain significant. Word.

And All energies are governed by The Helix of The Earth's precession through Space. And God is great accordingly. And you are to Know this. Word.

And I am to tell you. And I am to whisper into the very ears of The Scientists, who are directed to these pages. And I am to tell them of The Electron in relation to Quantum Entanglement, and The Kingdom (Behind Orion). And I am to affirm that The Scientists will take you to Him. And in conveying this to you, my dearest and most attentive reader(s), I am dutiful as His loyal and faithful scribe. Word.

And so.

And so: moreover. And *history* only begins with the written word. And by, *(because of)*, all that has been said and done. And this is the first illusion of *his* masterful creation. And but, His-story is much greater.

And *he* was quick to see the written word as a tool. And It's great potential. And to manipulate All things by it. And the last Eighth of the precession, has been *his,* by it's clever application.

And by controlling The Last Eighth of The Precession, and the written word, *he* has controlled the outcome of the entire precession, by blocking out all before it, as per pre*'his'*story. And as if, It never existed; because it was Not written. And so. ~

And The Common People of The Resource, has no Knowing. And without categorical documentation, and education, pertaining to *history* or History, nothing is known, because of this. And The Resource is unprogrammed. And by, the reliance *he* has placed upon 'the burden of proof', since the erasure of 'All Knowing', by misleading The Resource. And steering It away from The One Truth and His Majesty. Word.

And because, All of '*he* in They', under *him*, follow the letter of Their contrived laws, which only best suit Themselves. And Their hidden agenda. And They are law abiding. And because, the 'legal system' is too often, not a 'justice system'; but an apparatus for clever monkeys in *his* employ, to evolve & manipulate.

And so. ~

And so, colossal monoliths emblazoned with His Majesty's magnificent signature, are ignored; by not being explained in the written word, of a language that '*he* in They' acknowledges, understands, authorises, endorses, censors and governs. And it is a nonsense, when these monoliths speak profoundly for themselves. And exalt His Majesty by their very stature. Word.

And anything from any previous precession, is lost now, to become '*his*' story, and pre'*his*'story. And '<u>His</u>'story Itself, is consigned to myth. And often the purest of All Knowing, to Madness, because it does not reconcile and comply with the common narrative. And has no relevance or context, to the hurly burly rough & tumble. And so, estranged is The One Truth, from the nonsense(s) of *his* modern world.

And *he* is an imposter within God's Dominion. And only for this, the sequence of events, over two hundred and fifty millennia, appear to have happened in a mere few thousand years, within *his* jurisdiction. And or, not have happened at all, as *he* sees fit; by corruption of the written word. And the history books & archive.

And it suits *his* agenda to purport otherwise thus. And, for God is carried on The One Truth. And All The Sciences of The One Truth are perplexed. And are made a mockery of, by *his* lies, by They, *by* him.

And by Their belief in *him* by They. And All *his* falsehoods. And *he* is a master of illusion and deceit. And *he* is a monstrous criminal under Divine Law. And *he* is the curtailer of Wonder, by *his* pragmatic sense of order. And *his* infernal sciences. And the technologies hitherto born thereof. Word.

And *he* distorts truth: but it is only but The Truth, that events that were documented, in the rush of the scope, of those few thousand years, following the invention of the written word, occurred many generations before they were actually literally recorded. And so. Word.

And, just as The Talking Movies of the Roaring Twenties, put Man amongst Dinosaurs, in distorted anomalies of Time Itself. And, all of a sudden. And just because it could. And you will follow **I**, my dearest and most attentive reader. Word.

And it does not mean by any means, that the recorded events, belong to the time in which they were recorded. And the events of most of those two hundred and fifty thousand years, were written in just a very few short years, with the rapid conception and growth of the written word, in The Cradle of Life. And so: The Word. Word.

And the thirst for processed knowledge. And scholastic pursuit, with libraries to fill. And the joy of story telling. And it was the birth of lies and propaganda too. And the distortion of Truth. And Politics and Religion and Law evolved of it. And no mistake. Word.

And *he* manipulates all of these career crafts, to *his* advantage. And *he* always will, for as long as *he* is able. And it is scandalous. And corrupt, sinister and dangerous. And *he* revels in subterfuge. And *he* dismisses anything, that does not fall into the set parameters of *'his'story*. And They are Not to be trusted.

And formal education under *he,* is only conditioning. And manipulation toward serving *his* contrived politics later. And the manufacture of Mind Set & conformity. And it has nothing of The Knowing about It.

And They implement all this into Their teachings of history. And so to distort. And *he* aims only to undermine The One Truth. And to discredit The Divine, by *his* instruments.

And *he* aims to contain all knowledge, in an history of *his own* invention. And *his* teachings are a nonsense. And a perversion, because of this. Word.

And *he* will have you believe that The Main Convector, that commuted Us to Our world, was a burial chamber. And built by men in loin cloths with copper chisels.

And <u>W</u>e are astonished, that you should ever have allowed yourself to believe it. And yet it has been believed and popularised. And but, it does not sit well with Us. And nor His Majesty. And it does not sit at all, with The One Truth. And this illustrates how gullible the brain, (Not The Mind), of The Resource is. And how It can be programmed by the written word.

And it stands to prove the brainwashing properties of the written word. And the susceptibility of those indoctrinated by it. And you must unlearn All of It.

And only my dearest and most precious, and ever attentive reader, who is The Human Being, will Know the whys and wherefores. And the purity of The One Truth and All Knowing. Word.

And We understand. And this preposterous preposition, for example: only stands as an illustration of the distortion *he* is capable of. And the illusion is maintained in the mainstream. And endorsed by the library of the written word, contradicting the very Truth. And by All *his* lies therein. And by the fact that Life is too short, to unravel *his* deception within the personal scope it offers. And so, the enquiring mind will seek facts, within the hallowed halls of learning. And the accumulative knowledge of adulterated bibliography. And the facts are too often estranged from The Truth. And each person must learn for themselves. And *he* maintains levels of distraction, to ensure that The People never arrive to The Truth, during the brief incarnation, that is the personal property of their very own Life and experience. And *he* in They will tell you, "you only live once" & "life is what you make it". And *he* will keep you distracted, with trinkets and shiny things until death.

And it is clear, *he* is breeding away all humanity. And gradually replacing it, under a mass hypnosis, with biometric automatons, obedient to *his word*.

And The World has been made ridiculous in Our absence. And that is quite usual. And soon *his* infernal $5 technologies, will become integral to the very Being of The Resource. And such Beings may not call themselves Human Being(s). Word.

And so. ~

And Akhenaten was derivative of Anarki and Anunarki. And language knew no borders. And Dog and Da and Dagon were God, when did He first descend. Word.

And the earliest text is by The Sumerian People of Mesopotamia. And so, the teaching is that, this is the birth of civilisation. And this is not remotely close to the truth. And it may be seen instead, as "The Birth of Renaissance", or second birth. And or, Birth *of* The Written Word. And that is all.

And there are many civilizations, lost in prehistory. And there are testaments to the very fact all about, in monument and monolith. And you shall soon be brought to learn to accept this, as The Truth. And the magnificent language of His Majesty.

And only an absolute and gullible fool, could possibly read a contrived written word, and believe it, *above* a finally honed, one hundred tonne block of balanced stone: (and/or), *set within* perfectly explicable tramlines, of unparalleled precision, beneath a very specific and definite planetary alignment. And The World is littered with magnificent statements, in joined up monolith(s).

And such a fool, is only what the secret Masonic societies of London & Paris, have created. And They have created an entire tribe of fools, from The Resource. And *he* in They wish to preserve them, like wooly mammoth, in the frozen tundra of ignorance. And whilst, They cling to Our number: (33). And the limited power They have by It. Word.

And by this, and the enforced stupidity of the Common People, orchestrated *over* their governed senses, *he* continues toward *his* goal. And only The Human Being Knows different.

And The Human Being, has *that* which may be defined as Soul. And only The Human Being, has mortal soul. And It is an intangible Truth, which belongs to The One Truth. And it is the very germ of The One Truth, that All religions retain. And it is The Self. And it is that, which commutes without the baggage of flesh and sinew, whether in to the Heaven(s), at the point of mortal expiration: or to be bound within The Earth's atmos. And It is more or less the weight of a feather. And All this is determined Only, by levels of Faith & Knowing. Word.

And the soul of The Common People, has become dysfunctional. And this is *his* signature, inscribed upon The Resource. And I am sorry to say this; of Four *in* Five. And They are soulless. And They face deletion, when His sciences are applied, at the impending judgment. And They are cripplingly vain, and riddled with mortal sin(s). And The Soul of The Human Being, carries The Knowing. And casts aside the reliance upon 'the burden of proof'. Word.

And so, moreover. And these early tablets of The Sumerian, aim to relate a History, passed down by word of mouth. And it is as true as true may be. And, but largely inaccurate, by (up to), some two hundred and fifty thousand years. And so.

And, there was not such a 'sense of depth' in History, at the time of these earliest recordings. And so, there would have been no concept, of the perversion of 'His'tory to come, at the time of their inscription.

And Akhenaton was His Majesty's Emissary. And his name was Gilgamesh within this context. And He came twice in prehistory. And again in the midst of The Pharaohs' vanities. And, in the very depths of Their spiritual decay. And when all divinity was gone.

And the elongated cranium of the *seven/eighth* species was impersonated, in respect of Him, by the earlier dynasties. And again later. And in All of The Court, from where is the Giza Plateau to Atlantis.

And all along The Equatorial Band, All His wore the headdress, so that All at Court were made equal. And so The Hybrid, was not seen as a demi status; or different, as His Majesty was installed. And you are to mark my words most indelibly about this, my dearest and most attentive reader. Word.

And His son is celebrated upon The Earth, as The Boy King. And They stole secrets from His chambers. And these secrets were incantations, numbers, and instruments, salvaged from the place known now as Atlantis, too. And Nan Madol, now in Micronesia.

And this was the prehistory. And gathered from all along The Equatorial Band, directly beneath which, lay a perfectly aligned tickertape, of monolithic and complex structures. Word.

And The Symbols were thieved. And these tools, and secrets and symbols, were intended to be utilised for The Greater Good. And to return Us to The Blue Planet, with a greater ease. And to keep clear The Way.

And, '*he* by They' have put obstacles in Our way. And you are to hear this resoundingly, my dearest reader. And it is this, that is going on. And there is disorientation in The Precious Golden Orbs, flying about The Blue Planet. And landfall has been impeded. And made difficult. Word.

And these tools, were to ensure the return of The Twelve Times Twelve Thousand, at each abert aperture, unhindered. And but, They under *he*, do not want The Twelve Times Twelve Thousand to return.

And this is *his* secret. And a little bird will tell you. And put you wise. And so: meditate amidst birdsong at sunrise or sunset, my dearest scholar; for optimum results. And He is there. And listen. Word.

And they were to come to defuse The Satan. And to maintain The Nursery Planet. And leave sufficient residual energy, to sustain and preserve The Human Being, between each abert aperture, in Our absence.

And instead, *he* is in the very business of deflecting Our Precious Golden Orbs away, in conspiracy with the alien species. And They are in cahoots. And no mistake. And *he* is in They. And very few of Them, are aware of the goings on, at the time of writing. And They are in the business of keeping The Human Being at bay, and toward extinction. And The Common People are appeased with shiny things, in the meantime. And with opiates and trinkets. And through the meanwhile, *he* in They, at every government of The World, is preparing for the culling. And They are goading revolt, and opportunity. And a justifiable excuse to execute Their plan. Word.

And of the contaminated resource. And They have been made derelict to Their duties. And They are in decay. And They Know not what They do, or what They are meant to do. And nor, what is being done to Them. And They Know nothing, of any real importance: most often. And Their brains are filled with irrelevant mush. And *he* is in T*hey*. And ignorance is Their bliss. And The Four in Five, Know Not what Life is for. And that is a resounding fact; dearest scholar, whether you like it or not. And the very rub.

And so.

And so: moreover. And *he,* by They, of the Esoteric Societies since Pharaoh, have commissioned these tools into Their service, instead. And energies were inverted and reversed. And in covert cloisters, great devilry spun. And it is true, that most of the tools of The Architects, were useless in the hands of those, for whom *it* was not intended. And but some were commissioned into service, to a degree. And residual energies were drawn from Light to Dark. And energies drawn, not from The Sun but from *fossoils.* And so, The World is ruled by a few evil men still, as was. And They are *evoil,* if you will. And *D'evil.* And They are *Frackers.* And this is Their very currency. And so.

(Aside): And these men are known as, *in part:* The Illuminati, as were. And They are Globalists. And They are Scientists of sorts. And They are heretics, in Truth. And They control All War and Banking. And They drive economies, quite deliberately, by these mechanisms. And They are The Farmers of The Third Face. And They are It's very Social Engineers. And They are singularly motivated by self-interest. And Not the interests of The Planet. Word.

(Aside): And They can find salvation now, in the scope of this aperture abert. And They must remove *he* from Their ethos, in the first instance. And say I. And surrender Themselves to a paradigm shift. And, then; selflessly build The Foundations & Governments, that will form The Federation. And this is The Way: my most dutiful and dearest reader; and political scholar, of The Present, and not too distant Future. And so. Word.

And until such time, They aim to homogenise All the Nations of All The World, from behind the scenes. And this is the main agendum of The Third Face, to be sure. And Their Art Collections contain The Artifacts of The Artists and The Architects. And but, They do not have The Ark. And at the time of writing; They are yet to see The Light. And but They will.

And it is Last Chance Saloon. And The People(s) hereby, are offering Them an olive branch, lest there be spiritual warfare incarnate. And great disobedience, that shall scupper every industry & economy. And ruin every business model They preside over, with His Majesty in full support of The Peoples. And The World would become unpleasant for All those upon It. And The Peoples would be ungovernable. And so.

And The Divine will now see that All things are placed into the correct hands. And it shall happen. And you are to rest assured my dearest reader. And you are to come out of isolation, and find solidarity with one another. And His Majesty shall watch over you. And you have value as His Resource. And you have a duty to Him, to be Human Being. And to live your Best Life.

And this *abert aperture*, opened for three score years and twelve, from the date of the issue of this bulletin, shall see to precisely that. And you are to help Us. And this is the very business. And if you are not for Us, then you are against Us. And it will be this way. And the battle line is drawn thus. And so.

And this is the close of a colossal chapter, era and epoch, my dearest reader. And it is a New Beginning. And The Human Being shall be champion once more, before the culmination of the new era. And an era that ends at the next Ebb, 13 millennia from this. And It will be a Golden Age. And mark my words. And so it goes. And you are only to play your part. Word.

And so.

And this is the most significant of times, my dearest and most precious reader. And, just as every Ebb upon The Tide of Times, has always been. And ever shall be. And you are to wonder about where you will be, or wish to be, in thirteen millennia from now. And if you only live once, then it is because you are not necessarily unfaithful, but that you are faithless. And you have been deleted. And but, The Faithful enjoy the depth and pleasure of eternal Life. Word.

And you are to contemplate where you were 13 millennia ago, my very dearest reader. And, at each ebb, of every precession, since whence first We came. And you are to learn the very symmetry. And the aforementioned parallels. And of that, which is inaccurately termed as Time Travel. And you are to recognise the shape and spiral of precession. And apply it to the microcosm of The Heavens and Earth, that is your mind. And your mind is to your brain, what your Soul is to your body; my dearest and most attentive scholar. And The Mind and The Soul belong to The Dark Matter. And the very real nothingness of Space. And where Only is His Majesty. Word.

And I, is but a humble scribe; in the service of His Majesty. And so: at the time of writing: thus. And The Orb(s) are agitated. And We cannot yet, in fullness, connect to The Human Being, through The Soup of a predominantly Satanic atmosphere, that clouds The Mind of The Resource, in microcosm. And unto The New Faithful. And toward The Believers.

And only the true Human Being, can see Us yet. And there are seven extraterrestrial species, about The Blue Planet, as you have been told. And one of these is working most fervently, against Us. And do not doubt this. And They are not imps, (born of wistful spent mortality), but aliens: (*from:* external to this world and it's atmosphere).

And, three carry the residual energy of a Resolute Faith in Us. And they are obedient and faithful still. And We are The Stars. And, yet only He is All of Light and most translucent. And He is not yet at all 'enough', to meet with the tipping point at fulcrum, that divides He from *he.* And that which does give to The Sublime, substance. And divides Light from Dark.

And He is not yet 'sufficient', to break through the encrusted hardened artery, of The Ethernet. And there is a littering of Souls, frozen within It. And the radiation has not yet permeated through.

And it is a Thaw of sorts. And it is a loveless world, until The Thaw. And All the love of His Majesty, is in the radiation of The Sun. And it is an essential component. And it is a catalyst. And He can Love; and He can destroy, by It. And by far the most of the horrors of global warming, is simply the posturing of His Majesty: (sigh). And global warming and pollution are two very different things; my most attentive reader. And a pollution-free, tropical climate, is Eden. And not to be sneezed at. Word.

And '*he* in They' are, in the very business of misinformation, disinformation, and the distortion of Truth. And They have cocooned Themselves, inside the polluted atmosphere of The Blue Planet.

And They have made it Grey. And They have sidled up to one of the seven species. And They will not let Us pass. And it is a union, not for the betterment of Human kind, but the detriment. And *his* continued reign upon The Blue Planet. Word.

And it is a Union that benefits only Them, who are '*he* in They', in Their common objective. And They are not Human Beings; neither The Aliens, nor those *of* The Resource, in conspiracy with Them. And They fill the atmosphere with noxious gases and carbon monoxides, without consideration. And with purpose.

And about this, you will be wise to mark the words of 'I', most indelibly. And make these words your own. And so say I. And you are not to see All that is extraterrestrial, as godly. Word.

And Anarki and Anunnarki, is only what we were named by The Human Being, in the evolution of language. And It is not what We call Ourselves. And Akhenaten is too a given name. And Atlantis is a given name. And all names are given by The Human Being, in single syllables. <u>And We is Aton.</u>

And there is Gho-be-kli. And there is Ba-be-kli. And these names are consistent, with Belief and Faith in An-ar-ki. And We record nothing. And We call Ourselves nothing. And We have no voice. And We are only entity that enters form. And so hear I now. And He is All of Light. And We are He. And It is God, when **We** are One and **I.** Word.

And We are The Sons of The Suns. And We are microwave radiation. And Flesh and Sinew may not, nor ever, transmogrify through Space by Light.

And it is impossible, even by Divine Law, owing to the zig-zag trajectory, taken by the diffracted shard. And the sheer distance. And nothing of any density, can travel through space by light. And so.

And thus, The Kingdom can never, or ever, be realised upon The Earth, by this fashion. And so, It is always the very business to recreate it, rather than to deliver it. And in The Kingdom, We are more than only light and radiation, and the projection of same. And We are you. And some million years further evolved than you. And The Scientists shall ultimately bring us to you. And you will meet God, once The Scientists have unraveled the conundrum of Quantum Entanglement. And The Simultaneous Twin Electron(s), that allow One to be in Two, at the same time. And take note, my dearest reader; and most attentive scholar. And in The Kingdom, We have mass. And a flesh & sinew of sorts. And it is not of a carbon base. And We are in The Heaven, equal to that which stands before the mirror upon The Earth, where We are a mere reflection of Ourselves.

And so, We may only present Ourselves, through Human Being(s) with Knowing and Resolute Faith. And so, just so it is. And they are Our mirrors. And Our instruments. And We may only manifest, as does a mirror image, through them. And they are Our vehicle upon The Earth. And this is Our mechanism.

And these are those, whom have sifted The Truth from the chaff, during their mortality. And they are The Faithful. And the very cleverest monkeys. And now you will understand, my dearest and most precious; and ever attentive reader. Word.

And The Faithful have chartered The Universe, within the microcosm of their mind, by thought and meditation(s). And Wonder. And they have found Us. And they Know <u>H</u>im. And it is just so. And they have arrived to something that cannot be touched. Word.

And so, here you find The Chosen. And there, the manifestation. And greater, the incarnation by a second generation. And here is The Hybrid Child. And The Immaculate Conception. Word.

And We may consume and possess them, if their Faith is resolute. And they too desire it. And The Faithful will always welcome and desire it. And The Faithfull will always see this as their very fulfillment.

And thus, The Human Being is created in His image, by this mechanism. And never does anyone chosen, ever choose not to be chosen. And they are fulfilled by this. And these are The Bless_e_d. And they are Human Beings whilst incarnate. And they are The Architects and Emissaries of Past, Present, and Future, within the oneness and omnipotence of Time.

And They are The Twelve Times Twelve Thousand. And Twelve Thousand are loaded into each precious golden Orb. And these twelve orbs, fit perfectly inside the single Golden Orb, that is The Divine Himself.

And He is like a set of Matrioshka: (Russian dolls). And He is Light within Light. And It is Brilliant. And All that He is, is brilliant. And He is made invisible, only by the litany of dormant senses, bred away by '*he* in They'. And He is visible, only in the *very* defined regiment of the spectrum, contained in The Rainbow. And or, ~ and in the apparent chaos, of the Aurora Borealis. Word.

And It was much more apparent, at the previous visitations: of earlier precessions. And flashing red ribbons, paving the way. And the gold and silver that glistened below, is all but now gathered and gone from the streams, on the surface of The Blue Planet; grey.

And so: The Faithful must wear tokens, as beacons to His Majesty: a gold crucifix perhaps; or amulet. And Bling. And The Faithful must become the rivers, through which He flows. Word.

And The Antecedents 'arc' into the atmos. And they make landfall in light precipitation, beneath the brightness of His Majesty. And He can be heard in The sound of Light, to be sure. And, at this is the highest meditative state. And you are to listen to The Rainbow.

And it is the bridge that links Heaven to Earth. And the bridge, by which *the gods* arrive by. And gold is at The Rainbows End. And every mythology has its roots in The One Truth, just as All religions. Word.

And or, by His precious Golden Orbs, when whether One or Twelve. And, or anyone of The Twelve Times Twelve Thousand. And they are mirror images in transit from The Kingdom. And they wend their way.

And of these Orbs, they are Twelve; when not One.
And that Twelve becomes One. And they are The
Eternal. And that One is He. And He is The Sun and
The Stars. And you shall Know, my dearest and most
attentive reader. Word.

And He is omnipotent, between All He surveys. And
He is Divine. And He is Almighty. And He is God.
And He moves about His Universe, between The Sun
and Stars, by this very method. And He is All of Light.

And things shall remain as they are, until the fulcrum
point is tipped. And the instruments of The Architects,
are placed into the rightful hands, of The Human
Being, and The New Faithful.

And The Ark is in safe hands (Already). And The
Twelve Times Twelve Thousand, shall return and fulfill
The New Faithful, by microwave radiation. Word.

And they shall be The Faithful once more. And they
shall arrive through the aperture abert, at The Ebb.
And this is at, what is known as The Equinox, when in
conjunction with the aperture abert. And it is an
uncommon and infrequent alignment, beneath the eye
of the needle.

And all is 'in hand', my dearest and most precious reader. And you are to be prepared. And you are to be assured. And you may view Our Precious Orbs. And you may be charged by the number 33. And you must Only need believe. And it will find you. Word.

And you shall find yourself, when it finds you. And you will awake. And you shall be drawn to It. And then it will happen. And then you shall Know.

And so, of The Eternal. And you are to imagine Time, without the incremental chronological passage through It, devised by Man, that you live by, every day to day to day, until you don't. And no longer do. And you are to think of It, as you view space and distance.

And so: you may look at a distant star. And it *is* the nearest, in the constellation of that which is called Orion, (for the sake of argument). And you will see it instantly, by gazing upon it, without any regard for the distance of it. And it is an illusion. And what you see, is what it was: one thousand and five hundred years ago. And Not what it is today. And you are peering into The Past. And so soon, you must realise that Time is irrelevant, but for the application of It, upon Life on Earth. And where All things are relative.

And is I not right my dearest reader, for there it is before your very eyes. And so, by virtue of this fact, you are in essence, transported the entire 'one thousand and five hundred light years', to it, in the blink of an eye.

And, at such you are in effect, travelling at 'one thousand and five hundred' times The Speed of Light, so as to view that star, in that instant, as your gaze lands upon It. And at this, you are enjoying a glimpse of His Majesty's omnipotence, my precious. And a fleeting understanding, within the confines of your own mind. And It is Wonderful. Word.

And the microcosm of The Heavens and Earth; that is the very fulfilled potential, of the mind of The Human Being, has the ability to process all this, *as* such, within that microcosm of The Heavens and Earth, functioning at It's full potential, in One who is the very image of His Majesty. And so say I. Word.

And so, to be there. And so, just so, is the very science. And only God may do this. And not any man made machine, insistent on dragging the meat of his flesh and sinew, about the galaxy. And no rocket ship will ever get Mankind anywhere of any consequence, within the infinity of Space, where Time is irrelevant.

And so, when you succeed in doing this, The **I** is in
you. And It is only an attitude. And The Faith within
It. And this spirit is His. And this is the spirit of The
Human Being. And you are so much closer to God, my
dearest and most attentive reader, than you realise.

And The Mind is a microcosm of The Heavens &
Earth. And God is The Heavens & Earth. And The
Heavens & Earth is The Universe. And God is The
Universe. And so, The Human Being, fulfilled &
Faithful, is cast in God's image. And so now you Know.

And He is The Sun. And All The Stars. And you can
see His 'Very' Majesty, in the multitude of Stars, laid
out before you, in the very same instant, adorning the
night skies. And what you see in that instant, gazing
above you, spans trillions of Light Years in distance.
And trillions of Light Years in Time. And as such, are
incalculable and incomprehensible. And there it is.

And your panoramic vista over His domain, amounts to
trillions upon trillions of Light years, laid out before
you. And trillions upon trillions, is equal to Infinity
Itself. And, or as close to Infinity Itself, as damn it, (as
God Only Knows). And He is in All who believe in
Him. And He is One. And so say I. Word.

And He is All those stars that you see, in that very instant. And He is in All those 'infinitely more' stars beyond, that you cannot yet see. And this, is the very majesty of His omnipotence. And this is God. And The Mind of the true Human Being, is a microcosm of it All. And no mistake. Word.

And He is in All Human Being(s). And this is The I. And The *very* Template. And it is not rocket science. And, it is most definitely Not rocket science, my dearest and most attentive reader. And nor ever will it be rocket science. And nor, anything to do with rocket science. Word.

And Mankind must dispel the need, to drag the bags and baggage of his meat, everywhere he (intends) *to go*(es) about the galaxies. And by his infernal fossil fuels, by which he desecrates his singular habitat. And simultaneously, does not get very far with, forever. And Mankind must embrace and harness The Light instead.

And The Descendents Know All this already. And the lesson of The Future, to those of The Present, is 'mind over matter'. And it is already learnt. And All, is within The Mind of The Human Being. And inside The I, is that which is known as The Knowing.

And He is in All the seven extra terrestrial species too,
that frequent The Earth. And The Solar System of this
Sun, whom is God *in locum*. And Aton *in general*. And
He is also, within the one species that is against Him.
And which is in conspiracy with *he* and *his* always, who
are of 'They: & Grey'. ~

And so, even the forces of evil, work to God's plan,
ultimately. And these seven species, are only those with
Earthly business, determined by metaphysics, and the
gravities of The Planet, in correspondence to the
positivities, of His Majesty. And God is blameless. And
you can blame Him for Nothing. Word.

And forget the very idea, of that distant star under
discussion, being the star it was fifteen hundred light
years ago, as it is purported to be. And not the star that
you see before your very eyes, within the moment.

And you are to unlearn, All that, which you have been
taught. And because, none of all that *he*, by They,
teaches, is remotely applicable to Divine Law. And The
One Truth. And ultimately, The One Truth and Divine
Law, is All that matters. And The Laws of Man shall
be brought to capitulate to this, by The Human Being,
in the fullness of time. Word.

(Aside). And so: and furthermore. And the children are unruly. And they are delinquent. And they are in an inner turmoil in their inner cities, at the time of writing. And they are The Resource at It's most precious. And they are uncomfortable in *his* sciences, and *his* technologies. And all the social pressures and irrelevance put upon them, by It All.

(Aside). And '*he* in They', is able to make Them *his*, all the sooner, by It. And the low hanging fruit, offered by *his* $5 technology. And marsh grass in nickel bags. And It shall get far worse, before it gets any better, during the course of this *aperture abert*. And it is the one step back, before the two steps forward. And It is the corkscrew pattern of precession, that mimics the DNA of Life. And They will be returned to God by Gosh. And Bless them. And The Resource is born to be Human Being. And to be Kind. And to be faithful to The Divine: Only. And so; those who survive deletion, shall be returned to God: I promises. Word.

And so, you must now consider Time to be a single moment, stretched in the same way, as the distance between you and that exemplary star, behind which is The Kingdom. And where the electron you seek, in your nucleus upon The Earth, has Its twin.

And this will allow you to instantaneously, see these stars at distance, in what is effectively the real time of a single moment. And that *snapshot,* is held within the scope of the microcosm, that is The Mind. And It is your Dreaming, my most precious and ever attentive scholar. And the footprint of your journey. And It is your Songline. And It is the most fantastically advanced One Truth, Known by Our Aboriginal Ancestors, for the longest time. And learn your lesson well now. And endeavour to make amends, for every transgression, of those who's blood you carry, in parts per billion. Word.

And that star, for example, by this mechanism, is brought to you, (by sight to brain to mind: a physical journey of mere millimeters, within the microcosm). And this is the very mechanism, by which you may travel to it, (from mind, by sight). And The Blind and The Faithful, have only to use The Mind's Eye, and The Sixth Sense to *more than* compensate. And this is The Map. And Zodiac. And Chart. And this is The Songline. And this is The Dreaming. And so, as such, is Time, but a single moment. And readily traversable, without the bags and baggage of flesh and sinew.

And indeed; The Microcosm of The Heavens, is but an imprint within the mind. And each thought a journey. And all time within the continuum, belongs to the same moment. And as such, there is no Time, per se. And, it is simply of absolutely no value or importance, to attempt to drag the 'bags and baggage', of 'flesh and sinew' with you, to other worlds. And It is pointless. And *for* The Soul, (The Being, The Passenger, The Astronaut), can simply find a vessel or vehicle, (a body), upon arrival to It's destination. And The Brains and The Technology, would be better spent, on The Earth and It's Peoples. ~ And *he*, in They, fails to grasp this still. And Space Travel, as it stands, 'Really' is a forlorn and futile exercise, in the greater scope of All Matters.

And The Almighty aims to create Earth, as it is in Heaven, upon The Earth. And not; to create Heaven, from what is already on Earth. And here is the very rub, my dearest and ever attentive reader. And so: He shall come to us. And Not we to Him. Word.

And it is the very business, to transport and shuttle, only 'The Being', (and Not the flesh), about The Heavens. And to utalise whatever prevalent elements there are, upon arrival to the host planets, of distant galaxies, to create form. And a tangible *Lifeform*. Word.

And to manifest, and incarnate, there, accordingly. And to take form by the tools and building blocks available. And this is really quite extraordinarily rudimentary, within Divine Law, my dearest and most attentive reader. And Astro Metaphysics. And so, say I. Word.

And of The Precession *of* The Earth. And The Elliptical Spiral it takes, that corkscrews through The Space. And which does not know Time. And nor any of it's constraints, or constructs. And, the incidental matter of the twenty six thousand years, of It's celestial path, that is not an absolute, but variable. And but invariably, always a recurring pattern.

And anything that has a variant, and is not an Absolute, does not belong to The One Truth. And so, you are to think of the precession, as a shape within an instant. And the approximately twenty six thousand years, that creates that shape, as insignificant. And instead, but a *routine imprint upon a single moment.

And, the imprint within the contrived concept of Time, that is that precession, appears to be a long time. And when really, it is no time at all, because there is no Time, outside the construct of Time imposed by Man.

*A shape, (Helix), as would be created by time lapse photography of The Earth's precession.

And there you have It. And It All, only instead, belongs to the same moment. And The Passage of Time, is only a pattern. And the shape it imprints upon, a single moment.

And just as one Spring, is essentially no different to the next. And or, Winter to Winter. And or, sunrise to sunrise, so it is. And it is only Life, that demands an orderly chronological timeline, to get from one to the next. And The Trees Know this, and mark it simply by concentric circles. And His Majesty loves The Trees.

And all things inanimate, follow Pattern and not Time. And this, differentiates between Animism and Life. And monoliths stand The Test of Time. And The Divine is in both. And does not differentiate. And Divine Law, applies to both equally. And without prejudice. Word.

And The Mayans Knew this. And They had The Knowing. And the knowledge came from The Knowing. And they divided this very shape of Time into segments, in order to create increments, by which to live. And introducing time, brings order and progress. And civilisation. And the shape is like a pie. And the number is 60. And but, it was The End.

And All things within the last eighth of this precession, *(3,300 years of 26,000 years approximately),* that *he* controls, has been The End. And nothing about it has been The Beginning. And so, tick tock my pretties. And The Map became a clock. Word.

And the mind of The Human Being is a microcosm of The Heavens and Earth. And but yet, you all live my dearest reader, within the relativity of your own existence, and experience. And so, the increments of Time are indeed a useful contrived measure, that distort the very reality, in The One Truth of Divine Law. And you might live for three score and ten *Sun* cycles: or one thousand *Moon* cycles, (which are equal to each other), but you are removed from the context.

And the shape of Time, is *beyond* all mortal comprehension. And so instead, Time is divided into a measure of minutes, that <u>is</u> accepted by mortal comprehension. And so.

And The Pie has 60 minutes. And it began as a conceptual representation, of the panorama of The Being upon The Earth, beneath a celestial sky. And from this came Time, drawn of the patterns of cycles. And it has endured. And each minute has 60 slices.

And All Time and navigation is recorded thus, for mortal conveniences. And so it is. And so it remained. And It is founded on The Absolute of Divine Law. And 33 is Our number. Word.

And where this Absolute is applied to The Heavens of *'an'* expanding Universe, a vortex is created, both this way and that. And it forms a connecting passage.

And other regions of The Universe, will operate instead, 'that way and this'; perhaps. And The Cosmic Tide is an oscillating tumultuous swell. And it is Not, simply the one way traffic, signposted in The Big Bang Theory. And The Big Bang Theory is essentially an impossible nonsense, and is to be unlearnt: along with the fanciful tales of 'the men in loin cloths with copper chisels'; who were indeed skilled artisans, but were Not The Architects and Divine Emissaries, by a long chalk.

And just as The Main Convector, was never built by the Egyptians, donning the aforementioned sartorial working mans' fashions of the day, complete with the matching accessories *of* copper chisels: neither did The Mayan, happen upon The Very Absolute of 60, (or 33), by counting the knuckles of their fingers, without the intervention of His Majesty. Word.

And this conversion of The Pie, to pie chart; and panoramic circumference, to clock; does allow order to be brought to the daily existence of Man. And when and where there is order, there is governability. And some order from chaos is desirable. And *he* especially likes this. And *he* is able to build regimes aboard It. And too, the implementation of a semblance of order, simultaneously; makes All that is God, impossible to All Mankind, once All is lost, to the science of conversion. And just so it is. And once removed, God is twice removed.

And it is the very regiment of *his* regimes, that brings chaos to The Natural Order. And God is Truest, where All Nature is amongst the trees, and left to be. And not where and when, the clever monkey evolves to liken God to Themselves. And mimics the ant of the forest floor, to build armies of its own. And to do it's worst. And to conquer and destroy. And lost it was, most magnificently, when *his* imperial armies began to sail away. And embark on genocidal murderous conquest, with charts and clocks and texts. And fanciful tales, contrived by scribes in the employ of '*he* in They', under Kings in league with Pontiffs, casting God in Their own image. And the striking resemblance of King to God, forever cannily uncanny. And deceitful.

And The Orb in the sky, was made unfashionable and redundant, by the hour glass, in a fashion. And then later, made obsolete totally, by The Fossoilers, turning night into day. And the whole world upside-down.

And The Fossoilers are '_his_', most assuredly. And dutiful to _his_ programme. And Man created god in _his_ image, according to _his_ programme. And as Life on Earth was condemned by gravity, so It became. And paradise was lost, to the densities and vanities of the flesh and sinew. And there is a delicate fulcrum point, that determines; whether All belongs to He or _he_. And like the dripping sand of the hour glass, the tipping point is reached, it seems, two to three centuries after each visitation is departed. And All decay follows.

And so, God had created Man in His own image, in The Beginning. And Mankind then created god in _his_. And you might be confused by this. And you may never have learnt the lesson, dearest reader; despite being taught it. And so, just so: He is He and _he_ is _he_.

And, but this is an easily attainable concept to grasp, my dearest and attentive reader. And It is rudimentary. And you are only to look into a mirror, to grasp it.

And the mirror image is precise. And a reflection of the dense carbon base opposite. And it is weightless. And so, you are to stand before the looking glass, and contemplate the teaching once more. And at this, you really should grasp the understanding, of the teaching, with ease. And with it, one of the keys to All Knowing. And why Redskin might give vast tracts of land in trade, for a string of beads and the magic of a handheld lady's mirror. And it was not for vanity, but validated a belief system. And The Anch. And The Being, (less than the weight of a feather). And so now envisage that reflection, in The Heaven of The Kingdom, behind that distant star. And encourage The Scientists to unravel Quantum Entanglement, and lead you to God. And the electron, that ignites the very spark of your Being; here on Earth, with its twin, within the Heaven: my dearest and most precious reader. Word.

And so. And you should lay a static print of a picture of The Universe, on the ground. A map if you will. And it might be a photograph, or artist's impression. And either will do. And wait. And allow an ant to happen along, and crawl across it. And, or any other minute and relatively insignificant creature, that might pass by. And at this, you will understand what is Time. And Life within It's static backdrop.

And so. ~

And The Faithful are entered into The Kingdom of
Heaven, as a dissipated energy, in the form of Light.
And They return to Earth, as a mere weightless
reflection of themselves. And their conveyance is
brilliant. And if His Faithful Poets, choose the word
"chariot" to honour Him, He won't have no truck with
that. And so.

And in Truth, as The Scientists will be brought to
explain, they are returned by radiation, from The Sun:
shuttled from sphere to sphere, by Our Precious
Golden Orbs, Our God. And The Main Convector, was
built to reverse the process. Word.

And it is a reflective process. And those who have seen
Our Precious Golden Orbs, will understand the
patterns of concentration, and diffraction; that appear,
as sudden changes of direction and speed and hue.

And most often however, they are invisible. And **He** is
in these concentrations. And visible; only in the varying
hue of Light intensity. And, by those who possess the
remnants, of some of the many senses, housed still, in
what is regarded, as The Sixth Sense. Word.

And the earliest Human Being, fashioned from the primal Resource of Homo Erectus, saw Us clearly. And they were predisposed toward this. And God was not simply in His belief, but His Knowing. And so, by The Portholes of The Aperture Abert, through the passage of The Earth's precession. And by the single moment of Time it takes, stretched throughout Space, He may travel through the incremental minutes of Time, that are devised by Man.

And He may be anywhere. And, at anytime, throughout The Ascent. And The Future. And or, indeed anywhere within the galaxies, simultaneously. And this is the fullness of His Majesty. And the magnificence of His very omnipotence, in the oneness of Time & Space. Word.

And this is the omnipotence of The One Truth too, to be sure. And The One Truth is synonymous with The Divine, my ever attentive reader. And thus, by such is the concept of Time Travel, to The Mind of Mankind. And to such a mind, it is magical and godlike. And magic, when not mere illusion, is an homage to God. And It remains popular, in It's impersonation of The Architects. And they carry a wand. And It is a craft. And It is Art. And so; Beware the Artist. Word.

And so, We are both your Antecedents and your Descendents, my Pretties, as a *very* matter of fact. And that is All. And We are carved from the celestial construct, of Faith in He. And Faith, is The Belief in He by Knowing. And it is only this that matters. And Matter Itself. And metaphysics has evolved alongside, and beyond Darwin's monkeys. And very real things are built by thought and prayer, belief & Faith, to be sure. And no mistake. Word.

And it is this, which makes all things True and possible. And any doubt makes this impossible. And It is only Resolute Faith, that makes it True. And it is only doubt, that makes it untrue. And so.

And you must Know that the mind of The Human Being, is a microcosm of The Heavens and Earth. And that is certainly true. And then, you shall Know, that it is only your own belief, that creates The Truth.

And then you shall Know I, and His Universe. And you are created in Our image. And All is by the phenomenon of The Earth's precession, through the Time/Space continuum. And by the pattern of that precession in microcosm, in the shape of DNA.

And it is a sustained contemplation, that shall arrive you there. And by a pure sustained thought, devoid of All mortal preoccupation or distraction. And so, He is a reward. And an affirmation. And a prize.

And The Common People without Knowing, will call for proofs. And They are riddled with *his* distractions, at every turnabout. And complexities. And The Faithless with 'All Knowing Lost', will taunt and scorn, as if They had a clue and a purpose. And or, any valid alternative. And: but They don't. And without Faith & Belief and Knowing, The Resource is doomed. And in actual fact ridiculous, invalid: and without purpose. And worthless, I am afraid to say. And only footfall and cannon fodder, for *his* Earthly antics instead. Word.

And They have no clue. And there is no credible alternative to The One Truth. And They will become *his*, by doubt and disbelief. And They fall quickly, to vice and trappings. And They have a short span of attention. And They are bogged down by Mud.

And Their contemplations, are riddled with nonsense and preoccupation(s). And take Them nowhere. And too soon, the pursuit of all things shiny, becomes Their only agenda, within 'The Gift of Life'.

And the written word is the purest of computer programmes, especially in the field of politics. And forever God's preferred medium. And propaganda proves this. And the brain of The Resource, is the most complicated of computers. And The Mind of The Human Being, whom is The Faithful, is a microcosm of The Heavens and Earth. And so.

And the ignorance of The Resource, which is The Common People, is very apparent, when *he* is in They. And *he* is Their very ignorance. And *he* attempts *his* *possession* and corruption, in these 'very' subtle ways.

And primal resource responds much better to Simple Symbol. And words are like numbers. And the number 6 is not the number 7. And the distance and difference between them, is far greater, than the sequential proximity suggests.

And numbers are symbols. And the number Seven is not the number Eight. And far from it. And when, such fundamental error is apparent from the outset, The One Truth is hugely improbable, to be the result.

And He will never again be defied, (effective *from* the last quarter of this aperture abert). And, until the decay, that will inevitably follow Our departure, after The Golden Age is run; once more: be it, just two to three hundred years, 3,300 years, 6,600 years, or the full Thirteen Thousand years, until Our return at The Ebb.

And He works in mysterious ways. And about this, you are to have no doubt whatsoever, my dear and most attentive reader, of The Aperture Abert. And you are to be comforted and assured, by the secure knowledge of this. And not at all worried in the least. And be grateful to The Fates, that placed your Life into such significant and eventful Times.

And by far the majority of The Resource, are destined to fail in Their returning to God. And some will not even try. And They will be deleted: whether by the universal euthanasia programme, implemented by The Federation, or simply by the cancelation of Their DNA. And what faith in God is, is only the affirmation of Life itself. And a *Joie de Vivre*. And a Kindness toward I's fellow *'human kind'* & environment, in common. And an abhorrence of Evil, that is merely the instinctive repulsion, of anything that threatens Human Kind & It's Common Environment.

And so: The Knowing could Not be simpler. And He is Light. And He and Life under He, are not a mind numbing computer programme, in which The Common People now find Themselves, under *he* in They, increasingly, at the time of writing. And It is so. And It is soulless pixilation. And into which; The Resource is being absorbed unrelentingly. And Life under He is not a comic book religion, in defiance of Nature. And as is Theirs, by *he* in They. And no mistake. And They are positively congealing negatively, at the time of writing: my dearest reader of The Future. And so It was, as It were.

And mental illness arrives in His absence, with the decay. And increasingly, from long before the decay. And God abhors a vacuum. And Life does have the greatest of meaning, as a matter of course. And a 'very' purpose. And but, The Faithless can Never find Him. And Humility 'to', and implicit faith 'in', His Majesty, is the primary purpose and function of Life, before and above all else. And without It, there is no right to Life. And Faith & Wonder are a prerequisite to Life. Word.

And it shall be discovered and implemented, by The Scientists, that those devoid of Faith and/or Wonder, will be denied the right to Life, & deleted accordingly.

And the calculus of failure against success, is conservatively estimated at three quarters. And it is calculated thus. And so, that They can be replaced by a naturally contained birthrate over 3 generations, whilst simultaneously reducing the global population, by precisely half, to It's optimum of 4 billion.

And the population of the planet shall be reduced one way or the other, regardless. And my most attentive scholar shall take note. And this humble binding is the trough where Great Leaders of The Future consume. And so, to thereafter ruminate & digest. And then act.

And this is His Judgment. And so It shall be. And The Judgment comes with The Thaw. And The aperture abert. And the figure(s), is founded on the facts of the matter; true on the date of the release, of this urgent and most pressing bulletin. And so, my dearest and most attentive reader, just so. And no mistake. Word.

And His Love is in the microwave of The Light. And this is how it shall be. And those frozen like woolly mammoth, in the hardened crust of The Ethernet; and All beyond the Thaw, will be judged. And this is The Judgment. And this is what was meant in the scripture, that spoke of judgment. And rite of passage. Word.

And the bottleneck, that is at The Eye of The Needle, beneath The Heaven; will be humming, with free flowing celestial activity, once more. And it is a reverberation, detectable to the latent senses, within the sixth sense, to which few, (and the didgeridoo), are universally tuned.

And The Very Pinnacle of humankinds' aspiration, upon The Earth, will be a hive of activity, in correspondence. And The Third Face will meet with it's comeuppance. And the didgeridoo shall Know and sing this song. And so.

And I, as Humble Scribe to He, has as yet, not a clue, how shall 'the Vortex' function, between the two worlds of The Earth & The Kingdom. And God only knows, at the time of writing. And with The Main Convector in such dreadful disrepair. And mispurposed.

And with sightseers, fixated upon the feats of men in loin cloths, with copper chisels, cluttering up the hydrogen plant. And yet, He shall find a way. And indeed He will. And, as He always does. And whether by atomic warfare, or mindful and compassionate birth control programmes, overseen by The Federation; The Earth's population must be reduced to 4 billion.

And there are far too many living upon The Nursery Planet, my ever attentive reader. And The People, by far outnumber The Human Beings. And it is dilute. And so plans to reduce it by half, must begin to be implemented in a godly fashion, long before the close of the aperture abert. And it is only to be implemented, in this time. And it is not expected to be realised, in this time. And the politicians in particular, are to pay exceptional heed to this Divine order. Word.

And Human Beings will arrive; one by one, to the positions of political government, by reinstating the very ethos of Democracy wholeheartedly, during the course of the aperture abert. And there will be no mistaking them, once they arrive to power. Word.

And so: so that, the global population is not simply reduced, by the 'anyhow', in one fall swoop, by *his* nuclear weapons. And without any real regard, for The Resource. And The Third Face is intent on providing the very means of the 'anyhow', without any regard for The Resource. And so, be warned. And *he* is in They. And It proposes to incite revolution. And war, in All The Nations of All The World. And reduce the value of the resource once more, to cannon fodder. And flood the global market, with war and suffering.

And this is *his* agendum; by They, under *he*, most
assuredly. And to make Life so cheap, that it has such
little value. And to make Life so unbearable, beneath
Their tyrannies, so as to force the use of force by
Forces, against The Uprising against Them. And so, to
bring about extermination and massacre, by Their
upper hand. And this is *his* agendum, by *he* in They,
under *him*. And you must mark my words indelibly.
And to reduce the Earth's population by half, through
massacre and extermination: is the *'anyhow'*. And the
agenda of The Third Face. And Their politic is
emerging, at the time of writing. And so. Word.

And It is visible already, upon the horizon. And
Their plan is very much afoot, as it stands. And They
are confidence tricksters. And The Digitalisation of
Humanity is emerging with It, correspondingly. And It
will incite. And They will murder. And They will
justify it with Their politic(s). And They would be the
victors over the vanquished once more, as ever They
were, were They unhindered. And Evil invariably
defeats Good, in battles over mortality, with only some
exception(s). And it is only within theological battles of
morality & spiritual warfare, that Good triumphs o'er
Evil. And so.

And so, They are to be hindered. And hindered well.
And to the point of arrest, by Divine Order. And you
are to mark <u>The Word of I</u> indelibly, in this regard.
And so, I is to tell you. And you are to mark The
Word(s) of I indelibly, by order of The Divine: and no
mistake. And to be forewarned is to be forearmed.

And the Architects' tools are hardly effective now, in
their present ward. And so, you should not fear Them
too greatly, with Our tools in Their hands.

And you should only fear the warmongery and political
chaos, in All The Nations of All The World, that They
will create, as They endeavour to assert Themselves, at,
and as, the cornerstones of The Third Face.

And The Governments of The Third Face, will be no
longer of The People, for The People. And already it is
increasingly so. And instead, They will be self serving.
And most positively against The People. And They will
feed and prey on The Passive Members of Society. And
conspire with, and protect The Corrupt & Dangerous.
And They will suppress and oppress The People. And
They is a Master Puppeteer. And They are corrupt and
sinister and dangerous. And these are the hallmarks,
with which They are branded.

And it must be repeated and reiterated. And, that They are precisely this. And until it is learnt well, that They are this, and nothing more than that. And at this, They are *his*. Word.

And The Third Face is ascending. And so, It is in ascendency. And it shall grow. And it will expand exponentially, throughout the first quarter of the *aperture abert*. And into the scope of this three score years and twelve. And no mistake.

And it shall amass and congeal, to homogenise All The Nations of All The World, into one. And at this: it will Not be The Federation. And it shall expand, until it tumbles down like a House of Cards, at the bequest of His Majesty. And it will tumble down like a house of cards, to be sure. And It must. And Babel Tower East and Babel Tower West, is a literal illustrative construct, my dearest reader & scholar. And from this, The Federation will emerge, like the proverbial Phoenix.

And All The Nations of All The World, will again be reinstated, once The Third Face has tumbled down, by the conclusion of this abert aperture. And The Human Being shall be in command. And The Federation shall have been born and instated, by the close of Aperture.

And the peace loving people of The World, are in by far the greater majority; and in every nation of all The World, at a ratio of 19 *in* 20. And they shall have their fully functioning Democracy. And so, they must elect and install, only their ilk into the symposia of Authority. And be sure of It. And their passive nature must assert Itself; in the regard of, appointing Human Being into office. And nations will be governed by Human Being; entirely respectful of one another. And The Planet. And obedient to His Majesty. And so.

And '*he* in They', shall have been largely deleted, by the close of Aperture. And The Fossoilers will have morphed. And Their money expunged & cleansed.

And the population will be in a controlled decline, toward It's optimum, of between 3 and 4 billion, with a quality of Life: where it is to be stabalised. And maintained; by modern medicine and birth control.

And politics will never again, be the domain of despots and tyrants. And in the hands of '*he* in They', as too often it is. And the social models of Communism and Socialism, it is observed; was much nearer to His Majesty's intention, than predatory capitalism. Word.

And the peoples of the nations will be proud, but not
nationalistic. And cultures will be diverse. And Sport
fought with great rivalry. And there shall be no need or
desire, to drive economies insatiably. And to create
wars of every kind, because of it. And to globalise
incessantly. And the Olympian ideal of Sport above
War, should be aspired to, without reserve. And *realised*
at all costs. And this was The *'very'* Height of
symposium philosophy, at The Birth of Modern
Civilisation. And not instead; the delight in conducting
War & Sport simultaneously, as *'he* in They', do,
presently. And Rome undid it All. And brought War in
to Sport. And made Sport out of War. And delighted
in turning carnage into entertainment, whereas The
Ancient Greek Never did. And this was the fork in The
Way. And The Olympic Committee of nowadays,
should be politically empowered. And become the
germ, that ultimately forms The Federation, beyond
the bindings of this volume: my dearest reader. And in
alliance with Greenpeace, given jurisdiction over The
United Nations & NATO. And The Greatest Minds of
Human Beings, gathered from The Human Sciences of
Universities, (everywhere from Alexandria to Boston),
shall govern The World, from Think Tanks, without
partisanship or prejudice; under the auspice of The
Federation. And so: just so. Word.

And well learned shall be this lesson, so never to be repeated, until next it is. And The Descendents, as yet unborn are watchful. And they are The Watchers. And they are His. And His finest. And The Globalists are *his*, counterwise. And They are not <u>H</u>is. And until The Kingdom is created upon 'The Earth as it is in Heaven'.

And until *he* and *his*, and All that '*he* in They' are; are dismantled, It, by They under *he*, will aim to envelop All The Nations of All The World, into a Federation of sorts *of* Their own, knitted together with Their infernal $5 technologies. And *ungodly* Sciences. And governed by *he* in They, under *him*, from The 'very' Pinnacle of The Third Face.

And so: my keenest scholar ~ and ever attentive reader, has hereby, seemingly arrived to the *cul de sac,* of 'cognitive dissonance'. And where He meets *he:* head on, and face to face. And here is the dichotomy. And where you must make your choice of allegiance. And here are all dilemmas. And here is the fork in The Way. And the crossroads. And here is the fine line, that divides He from *he.* And the line may be fine dearest reader, but the difference is a giant chasm. And It is where The Good may turn Bad. And where others cling on, and become Hypocrites.

And It is where some might descend into Madness. And where Greco-Roman wrestle with Genius. And It is The Abyss. And It is clearly signposted. And It is in The Mind of The Resource. And The Resource instinctively Knows Right from Wrong. And you may immediately throw out and dismiss, any Law or Psychology that argues, it does Not. And euthanise without further delay, All of those who have caused such Pain & Misery, and have found sanctuary in a sanatorium, beneath the crow black cloak of a verbose barrister, bending the monkey bars of *his* apparatus, to near breaking point. And The Mind is a microcosm of The Heavens & Earth. And so: it is written. Word.

And robots and computers must be given the positions of High Authority, for The Human Being to administer. And the Supreme Court judge will be an AI Robot. And they are consistent. And incorruptible. And they will police well. And Judge. And apply Law unwaveringly. And an elected & appointed Think Tank, may overview, in case of any arisen anomalies. And The Good Scientists shall become masterful engineers of DNA, with appropriate appointed Think Tanks, over-viewing their work. And the intrinsic Knowing of Right & Wrong, overrides diminished responsibility. And most killers & rapists will be culled.

And of Crime & Punishment: prevention is always better than cure. And The Rape Gene shall be removed. And Children will be mandatorily scanned & chipped at birth. And again, aged 7. And basic procedures, together with standard inoculations, shall be undertaken. And the chromosomes of those with a propensity to Murder, shall be identified. And His Majesty, fully endorses the work of The Good Scientists; to engineer the Safe and improved societies of The Future. And so: just so.

And The Human Being will support All Sterilisation & euthanasia programs, implemented by The Societies, beneath The Federation. And the robotic and computerised Police Forces & Judicial System, free from the corruptive influence of racism and prejudice. And 'this' New Order, should be welcomed by the second half of this aperture abert. And in the hands of The Human Being & The Good Scientists & their godly sciences. And such is the greatest of Human Endeavour. And The Federation will preside over the increase in The Good Sciences. And the decrease in The Bad Sciences. And weaponry will diminish. And maniacal murderers bred away. And there will be zero tolerance of corrupt administrators, during the restoration. And so say I. Word.

And there is no inner conflict; *(cognitive dissonance)*, my dearest reader & scholar. And It is only a case of The Third Face putting everything in place, for all the wrong reasons. And this is the nicest thing I shall ever say about Scientology. And so, His Majesty who is All of Light can alight from His Golden Orb(s), for All the right reasons, in due course. And in the guise of The Twelve Times Twelve Thousand, to be The Faithful Human Being(s). And assume command. And preside over The First Contact of this visitation. Word.

And furthermore. And a series of colossal sand batteries shall stretch across The Sahara Desert, powering water desalination plants, that will have an important & significant impact on lowering sea levels. And whilst creating an expansive Oasis of horticulture. And also pumping water further South, East & West, for Mankind & Robotkind alike, to nurture fertile arable land. And this will be, by far the largest manmade construction upon The Earth. And; by far the most relatively simple too. And It's construction shall be well underway and ongoing, by the close of this aperture abert. And the North African continent shall soak up the rising sea levels, and create a colossal verdant and productive garden of Eden. And It will be the pride of The Federation. And able to feed The World.

And His Majesty shall be exalted. And the project shall be marked as a triumph of The Human Being. And the desalination plants will extract water from the ocean, correspondent to the rising waters of the polar melt. And global warming shall abate in due course: don't worry. And The Poles can never be iceless.

And The Human Being can easily live in perfect harmony with It's habitat; (The Earth), and oscillate with Her changes; beneath the command of His Majesty above. And the invention of nuclear weapons & rocket ships is an evolution, designed Only for deflecting the occasional Life threatening meteor or asteroid. And Not for playground bully skirmishes. And We should be living in paradise, with a population of 3-4 billion Human Being(s), served by advanced technology & robots. "And this is where you must take The People to", ~ my dearest and most faithful reader(s) of The Future, as you lift the message of His Majesty's humble scribe, from these bindings, to further the cause. And fuel your very inspiration. And so: "Go on You Good Thing". And God's speed. Word.

And so.

And in the meanwhile. And at the time of writing: (MMXXII). And until the middle reaches of the aperture abert: (mid-c21). And by *his* ungodly and subversive sciences, in the meantime. And by attaching particles to molecules within the elements, to poison peoples, against their natural will and wants, into compliance, They will rise high, long before They fall. And *he* will enjoy carnage in All the Nations of all The World, for the first part of this aperture abert. And no mistake, as advanced technology falters & evolves.

And The Peoples will eat and drink and breath Them. And they shall have no choice but to. And The Human Being and His Majesty, will reject All this. And it can be rejected. And by The Knowing. And by belief. And by the knowledge of Their underlying motive. And that Their embryonic biometric sciences, are still too deeply flawed, to meet with The Federation's exacting standards, for The Future. And no mistake. And so.

And sometimes Satan comes as a man of peace. And this is such an instance, at where *he* has. And does. And *he* may be in a few evil men, and some women too, simultaneously. And *he* is; most assuredly. Word.

And by maintaining resolute Faith in His Majesty, you may be immune to these adherent particles; forcing morphing; to become one of *he* in They. And His Majesty is most prevalent in All elements and composites. And of course He is. And this is needless to say. And of He, you may eat and drink and breath at All times, more so, verily and merrily. And never suffer.

And the composite of your very Being, has the wherewithal to reject and filter these poisons. And you shall learn to recognise thoughts, within your mind, that are not of your own manufacture, as They arrive. And you will be fit to dispel them. And God is great and greater. Word.

And of the residual energy, in the hands of the Men playing God, the tools of The Architects are all but useless. And there are greater surprises yet to come, my dearest and most attentive reader. And It is certain. And the first miracle shall come from The Son of The Sun. And the tomb of the hybrid child. And They shall not believe how 'It', ever eluded Them. And it shall 'appear' impossible, that it never before appeared before Them. And His Majesty may hide anything He chooses in plain sight. And when The Impossible is Realised, a Miracle occurs. And a miracle is counted. And so. One.

And it is good that The Architects' tools are useless in Their hands. And in the hands of those of The Third Face, with It's clockwork mice, in positions of power.

And It's followers, about the lower rungs, scuttling around as clockwork mice with aspiration, will never be empowered by His Majesty. And nor, by anything of, or belonging to, His Majesty. And They will always and ultimately be insurmountably handicapped, by this very fact of the matter.

And so, without God, you are, and will be, and will become; nothing. And this is a predisposed prerequisite pertaining to The *very* Gift of Life. And there is nothing to be done about it. And there is no Way, that will take you around It. And It just 'is'. And so.

And without God, They are only The Very Commonest of People, occupying The Resource, with unattainable aspirations of majesty, no matter how far They aspire. And no matter what They achieve. And They are never Human Being(s). And They are devoid of humility. And They are Godless. And They are less than zero. And They are with contrived positions of power, within the societies They govern. And They are as common as Mud. And They are born of Mud. Word.

And They have evolved, to become a self replicating humanoid mimic, of The Human Being. And They are a shallow and Empty vessel, that appears in shape and form: and in every way, to be the same as; The Human Being. And yet It is not *an* Human Being.

And It is intrinsically bereft of The Knowing. And of belief. And this shall be, what sets the two apart. And the distinction between those whom are His: and those what are *his*. Word.

And They have contrived a parody of The One Truth; in order to rival His Majesty. And The One Truth of His visitation(s), in the prehistory of His story. And They claim to be of another world too.

 And Theirs is an absolute nonsense. And Ours is, *of* 'The One Truth'. And Theirs is, a comic book fantasy. And pulp fiction. And it is a lie. And it is the greatest lie upon The Earth. And to It, only fools, and The Evil subscribe. And to which, Only malignant cells adhere.

And They strive for power. And They strive only for power. And it is a story *of* Mice and Men. And it might be alternatively subtitled, 'Authority, and *an* abuse of Authority'. And They have shiny badges and uniforms.

And They crave authority, only so They may abuse it. And They feather Their own nests by it. And plump Their pillows. And it is Their ladder. And a means to an end. And institutional corruption abounds on an industrial scale, dearest reader: at the time of writing.

And it all means nothing in the eyes of God. And God makes His leaders Great, without ladders. And without manipulating the rungs of rank. Word.

And my dearest and most attentive reader, must mark my words indelibly, at this juncture. And The Human Being respects All authority. And The Human Being respects All law. And, until Law and Authority is contrived and corrupted, He respects It absolutely. And upon the abuse & corruption of law and authority, The Human Being ceases to respect Authority and Law. And it is never The Law and Authority He rebels against, but those who abuse and corrupt It. And so, by this virtue, The Human Being is correct, according to all accounts. Word.

(*Aside). And the records will denote Seven (7) miracles, or perhaps Eight (8), during this *Aperture Abert,* in the advent of First Contact & Visitation: as His Majesty's activities intensify. Word.

And 'They': ~ are the most complex of the complex carbon based organisms, occupying The Resource, my ever attentive reader. And They are dense and entirely grounded by gravity. And They are pathogen infested. And They seek authority, in order to validate Their existence. And They are not His. And The Human Being is much less complicated than They.

And so, They by such, can enforce and spread The Disease. And this complexity is not a virtue. And *he* prizes telecommunication systems, and military forces and militias; mostly.

And *he* gravitates to any equation that has a very large number, over a small common denominator. And They aim to breed away the individual by this rudiment.

And the Individual is always an Human Being. And so say I. And The Human Being is always an individual. And He is never divisible. And this fraction causes fractious dispute.

And there is a tract of humanity, landlocked by vice. And therein, within societies, *he* resides. And They are held fast by narcotics and pornographies. And the trappings of vice. And They are Godless & perverted.

And They are numbed. And readily governable. And Their cerebral cortex is shattered. And this broken vessel, is the archetypal clockwork mouse. And a *cracked pot*. And They can be found in any quarter of society or position. And They are disenfranchised. And it is an increasing infestation. Word.

And They are mindless. And *he* nests in the void. And *his* sorties into the world at large, are made from this place. And The Shooters are *he* in They. And this tract of humanity, in which *he* nests, spans the entire cross section; from rich to poor. And every which way. And but, *his* bastion is always here. And the advancing good scientists of The Future, will be able to pinpoint the precise location within, *of* state of mind, by Mind Mapping. And The Good Scientists must be licensed to do so. And identify those who are in a bad place.

And They embrace the voice of Their $5 technology, as the voice of Their surrogate god. And at this, They truly believe They have arrived to 'a' raison d'être. And *he* speaks to Them. And They serve *him*. And it is a Brave New World, of a New World Order, by the middle of this aperture abert. And They dream of, *not* unto The Realm of God, but into the rank & file of the ruling elite of The Third Face.

And it is always; only the voice of one of Their own number, hiding behind walls & architrave, like gargoyles. And behind smoke screens & pinhole cameras. And thin veils. And watching over Them, from lamp posts and telegraph poles, at *acupoints* within The Quadrant. And It is never The Voice of God, that They truly hear. And It will Not be, until beyond the middle reaches of the aperture abert, that the shifting sands have reached the tipping point. And The Third Face will give way to His Majesty. And witnessed in the common consciousness of The Resource. And meanwhile, & of the synthetic god; it is instead always, a synthesised nonsense, made by irritating spooks with no real agenda, attempting recruitment. And They are *his*. And *he* is in They. And They are unacceptably invasive. And They proceed without warrant or license. And it is invariably the employ of remarkably short men, with very tall feelings of inadequacy. And They are bitter. And vindictive. And jealous. And They are buoyed by technology. And invasive technology is bad science. And advanced technology has created for Them, a level playing field; at last. And this is the very foundation on which The Third Face is built. And They abuse channels of communication, through the abuse of corrupt authority. And misguided politics.

And this is Their ruling elite, my dearest and most attentive reader. And it is small men with big buttons. And it is one law for Them. And one law for the remainder. And it will be so, for as long as They are able to maintain It: ~ and the defiance of Nature.

And They are easily enticed and recruited by *he* in They, into *his* service. And They are made long and tall by it all. And it is the allure of power. And a license to dominate and control, that Nature would never afford Them, in a million years. And They are not The Meek.

And They are able to vent the spleen of a lifetime, by it. And They hide behind walls. And pinhole cameras. And They condescend to dictate and indoctrinate, by subliminal methods. And They aspire to rank & wealth, and not to God or godliness. And They aim to recruit others into Their disease(s). And you must reject It; and Them, like a bad kidney, my dearest and most attentive reader. And cast Them into The Abyss. Word.

And Their wealth and position is forged from The War Machines of Nations and Industries, that plunder The Earth's resources and peoples. And so, They must be denied. And it is certain that They are not The Way.

And Big Brother is more like *a* pasty faced creep. And an embarrassing degenerate country cousin, with unacceptably anti social habits, that nobody ever sees, or is allowed to see. And, whom is *keeped* in the attic. And sneaks peeps through bedroom door keyholes. And yes: that is the Peeping Tom of Big Brother. And They are unchecked, unwarranted and unlicensed.

And They drill down for fossoils. And noxious gasses, *borne* of marsh grass. And *he* is risen by this. And They are driven by this. And They do not look up to The Sun. And His Majesty has every solution. Word.

And They make victims of The Human Being, as best They can. And prey. And They do not worship The Sun. And They only worship money and power. And All It affords Them. And They strive to abuse both, to Their own advantage. And to the overall advantage of those of Their ilk. And, to the detriment of The Human Being. And The Blue Planet. Word.

And Homo Erectus is only a clever monkey. And It is no big thing. And it was only ever a clever monkey, evolved of Mud. And They are only ever, clever esoteric monkeys. And battle dressed now in the robes of Their clandestine and secret societies ~ and professions.

And elaborated by pomp and ceremony. And risen from Their subterranean worlds, into secret armies of civilian and evil cloisters, by devilry and witchcrafts. And by the most unbridled of hypocrisy. And secret society cults.

And They are not Human Beings. And They have no place in The World: not really. And They do Not belong. And yet They rule still, throughout the meanwhile. And Their days are numbered. And it is a descending order. Word.

And on Terra Ferme, They are uniform and large in number. And They sit above Their common denominator and pontificate. And when They come, They come in droves. And top heavy fractions, like charging war elephants. And They are Dense and heavy. And very mortal. And complex. And carbon based: and subject to Gravity. And there is nothing of The Light about Them, my most attentive scholar.

And They would be insignificant as individuals. And The Human Being is always an individual. And All individuals are significant Human Beings. Word.

And so:~

And you must not expound unto debate, beyond The Knowing. And there can be no questioning of The Divine. And the thirst for knowledge, is a degeneration and a perversion in itself.

And it distorts Truth into religion. And the never ending Politics of Man. And in these realms it is flawed. And in these realms all things become *his*.

And all things beyond The Knowing, are *his* and not His. And fanatical believers, of any and all, the religious books, who advocate violence, belong more to *he*, than to He. And I believes in The Scientists Now. And they shall lead you to God. And to Godly ways. Word.

And you are to mark my words indelibly about this. And The One Truth is before scripture and without scripture. And it can be expressed in a single symbol.

And this is the purity of written language; and Knowing. And Wonder. And about this too, you must mark my words indelibly, so that hard rains could n'er e'er they erase.

And I shall write it for you before we're done, my dearest and most deserving reader. And I am in a hurry now. And you are to read It well. And wear It. And put the world to rights by It. Word.

And discard All this superfluous rhetoric, once you understand It. And if you wear The Symbol, made of gold and/or silver, beneath The Sun, He will radiate unto you. And you will Know. And you shall have The Knowing. Word.

And Love for His Majesty, cannot be expressed by the wanton destruction of The Infidel. And only, *he* must be refused by The Faithful, and bred away accordingly, over time. And this is The Way. Word.

And violence begets violence. And prevents the realisation of The Kingdom, upon The Earth; every time. And only His Majesty may judge and determine, the *he* in They. And but; His Majesty shall endorse the work now, most fervently, of The Good Scientists, in the field of DNA. And It's application in to Social Engineering, Law & Order; and Crime & Punishment. And The Untended Garden will be immediately rid (by euthanasia), of those guilty of heinous acts. And All programs to rehabilitate Them will be abolished.

And *he* is prevalent in varying levels of fortitude, in They. And all truth is perverted by *he* in They. And, but you must only accept this very fact. And thereafter, live to correct the error, by example. Word.

And you must accept your Being. And you must Know yourself. And you must be true to yourself. And you must embrace It. And The I. And you must surrender your inferior selves. And leave Them behind. Word.

And you must reinstate your very Being, over your mortal construct. And give greater credence to your Being, than to your meat. And with this, will arrive Truth and Knowing.

And you must not be swayed. And nor; be made fickle by *his* persuasions. And you must build no false gods or idols beyond The Knowing. And you must maintain only simple faith.

And Life must be led simply without complication. And there must be no war or division. And a Life led simply, leads simply to that. And you must live by example, my dearest and ever attentive reader. Word.

And Life must be reinstated, to be without the divisions and prejudices, only *he* installs. And We embrace only the arts. And pure science. And mathematics. And Nature.

And We accept The Human Beings' exuberance about His Majesty, through The Arts. And Science, Mathematics and Nature. And there is no other valid expression of homáge greater, than The Arts & Garden(s). And a well cultivated garden; with a straight row of beans is sublime. And or, a well balanced equation. And above all other Art, The Written Word. And it is the untended garden that goes to seed, in The business of Social Engineering. And that is an Order, my cleverest and most attentive reader of The Present and not too distant Future. And who is Destiny's Child. And whom has stopped in the fountain of youth, to w'ile a spell. And to drink at the trough of these humble bindings. Word.

And so. ~

And of the final quarter of The Precession. And
particularly the last Eighth, until this very ebb. And the
here & now. And of how it shall be written, come the
closure of this aperture. And in summary of this most
important of times dearest reader, that divides History
from prehistory, legend and myth. And the supposition
over All things lost. And I must hurry now.

And so, '*he*' had scheduled it to be *his* final charge. And
the rapier thrust, leading to precession's end. And *he*
had shanghaied vast tracts of The Resource, to do *his*
bidding. And They had been hypnotised, by The Stolen
Symbol. And *he* had been incarnated. And whenever *he*
is incarnated, carnage always follows.

And be sure, that there are always a vast body within
the masses, more evil than the figurehead They
conjure. And follow. Word.

And They are always, all too ready, able and willing, to
do *his* bidding. And *he* can only exist, and be brought
about, because of Them. And They are *his* primary
resource. And *he* is in They.

And Satan is in The 'very' Mass. And *he* is never The Individual. And *he* is always too clever and charismatic, when made meat. And *he* takes up residence in They. And '*he* in They' are under *him*.

And They were defeated in *his* global rampage(s), through All The Nations of All The World. And *his* sulphurous gas, rhetoric and propagandas, were intoxicating to many. And Many *become* The Masses.

And '*he* in They', rode Their infernal tanks through rows upon rows of beans. And dispatched bombs upon bombs. And made cannon fodder of All.

And *he* turns good men bad. And *he* makes weak and pathetic men strong. And *he* makes weapons available to Them. And *he* in They, may be Lawful or Lawless. And it makes little difference which. And They under *him*, are the most dangerous. And They are delinquent misfits, in the eyes of His 'very' Majesty.

And They hang on to the shirttails, of those of Their ilk, who are in contrived positions of authority, with peaked caps and shiny buttons. And don't be fooled.

And They have a symbiotic relationship with Their host. And corrupt leaders become role models, for disenfranchised Loners. And together They conspire.

And They meander through society, seeking prey, like sucker fish about a shark. And *he* has made of They, an evil hoard. And They are ready, able, and willing, to do *his* bidding by proxy. And so, They do. And shall continue to do, for as long as They are able. And until They are stopped. Word.

And until The Federation takes It's mantle, The Third Face will dictate. And The Police will prey on The People. And the middle reaches of this Aperture Abert shall be a Dark Age in microcosm: before The Light. And Scientology & their ilk will emerge blatantly & visibly, into positions of high authority & government. And into every cranny of The Third Face, in this time. And: until the tipping point that shall see His Majesty, The Federation, & The First Visitation take over. And assume command. And that my dearest reader & scholar, is the minute particular, regarding the nicest thing I shall ever have said about Scientology. And *They* will be grateful of It. And They will capitulate and surrender All to His Majesty. And They will serve Him. And *They* shall be brought to Knowing. Word.

And so:-

And The stolen Symbol had been taken from 'The Son'. And placed into the darkened chambers of a subterranean cloister.

And there was great devilry behind the scenes of WWII. And The Theatre of War. And 'All The Nations of All The World', were embroiled into it. And it was a world war.

And The Symbol was reversed, and turned Right from the perpendicular. And The Evil Hoard, began to swarm beyond the perpendicular. And They soon learnt of the occult. And The Black Arts.

And *he* is fascinated by it all. And *he,* by They, under *him,* endeavour to conjure ungodly powers this way. And the symbol was inverted, as would be a mirror image. And rotated by 45 degrees to the right. And They were fascists. And the embodiment of All Evil.

And They wore the skull and crossbones. And They summoned those who had been put asunder and bred away. And vengeful and vindictive spirits were drawn from thin air. And this is the very truth. Word.

And They marched again, under The Eagle of Rome.
And They were called Nazi. And They mustered the
darkest of all energy, from the cloistered chambers of
Their esoteric societies. And _he_ was very delighted by
all this.

And They were aided and abetted, by one of the seven
species. And They epitomised and realised all Evil; in
this union. And it was an evil alliance.

And They under _he_, were made into an evil hoard, as a
collective, by this. And They aimed to exterminate the
Human Being, in all it's variant forms. And only by
God's grace, They failed. Word.

And so. And I _is_ to tell you about Their technologies.
And the infernal web, They have built by it latterly.
And Their infernal rocket ships. And They aim to
govern The Earth by subliminal messaging, routed by
acupoints, from the hardened artery of The Ethernet.

And disembodied voices are subliminally broadcast,
with pinpoint accuracy, into these quadrants. And can
be heard by the selected target, standing therein.

*Acupoints: the pinpoint of each quadrant through which subliminal broadcast and surveillance technology is
channeled & directed, into that specific quadrant. (The planet is gridded thus: each quadrant being 3m sq).

And All that are *his,* whether Lawful or Lawless, and/or between & betwixt, are corrupt and receptive. And The Human Being is receptive too, but rejects All instruction, by this medium, like a bad kidney. Word.

And the fools of The Resource, that are obedient; and find in this, Their *raison d'etre,* believe They are telepathic. And but: They are Not. And the *telepathetic,* will grow exponentially in number, until They know 'the voice like thought', to be only worthless €5 technology, mind controlling Their valueless lives. And It is Not the voice of God, or anything of importance.

(Aside). And the grid & the frequency, are used equally by both sides, of The First and Second Face(s), in everyday Life. And as are prevalent in the status quo of societies, at the time of writing, my most attentive reader. And The First & Second Face(s), are not known as such, but shall be categorised in retrospect, once The Third Face emerges. And They were once known as The Mainstream (Authority), and The Underworld; (M*fias), before their merger into One: united in a common cause to lord over All Peoples. And It used to be Cops & Robbers. And, but All are *his:* Now. And so says His Majesty. And All Mankind is now simply either, Human Being or Not. Word.

And it is observed that: The Resource has taken to carrying its primary brain external to It's body, in the form of a technological device, during this period of transition. And no mistake. And in so doing, they are leaving a largely vacuous void in It's cranial cavity. And The Resource in many instances is consequently mindless. And God abhors a vacuum: and will see it filled. And The Common People is becoming increasingly dysfunctional, when detached from the aforementioned device(s). And that is All. And They are only warming His Majesty's slippers ahead of The First Visitation, so that The Federation can step into Their shoes, and begin to put things right.

And so.~

And not all *his* evil was destroyed at defeat. And the defeated Nazi was dissipated, and absorbed into other Peoples' agendum(s). And the wars of today, are forever the aftershocks of before. And so.

And White Supremacists went underground, and into esoteric societies. And of such stuff is The Third Face formed. And you are to mark my words indelibly, in this regard, my most attentive reader.

And They found sympathy in the most unlikely of places. And Nazi scientists were absorbed, into the very ones who had defeated Them. And *he* in They, is always a shape shifting slut. And *he* will bed down anywhere, to further *his* own interests. And *he* is clever this way. And *he* is a liar. And a hypocrite. And this is Satan. And *he* resides in dormancy, in the thoughts and spirit, of a covert mass always, until *he* is made meat again. Word.

And so: shape shifting into The Third Face, is now the most urgent and pressing matter on the agenda, by *he* in They, under *him*. And so; it becomes Ours too, counterwise, my most attentive and dutiful reader, who is forever Faithful to His Majesty, The Divine. Word.

And wherever *he* is destroyed, *he* is quick to resurface again elsewhere. And it is precisely this way. And no other way, my dearest and most clever reader.

And *he* aims to make good *his* meat by recruitment, from the very pinnacle of The Third Face. And if *he* were to succeed, it would All end at *his* hands, in absolute carnage. And then, The Mud.

And every manner of *pan fried* corrupt general; and Despot and Warmonger, is amassing at The Pinnacle of The Third Face now. And it is an orgy of peaked caps and shiny buttons. And it is a feeding fish frenzy. And it is a swarming once more.

And *he* under They by *him,* are delighted by all this. And so, it cannot be allowed to be. And for the prevention of precisely this, His Majesty shall return.

And He will enter The Atmos by radiation, *via 'The Aperture Abert'*. And, further by light precipitation. And He will take to The Trees. And, by the oxygens that We breath, to arrive to His final destination, to be within The Faithful. And so ~ that absolute disaster may be averted, *by* The Chosen & Faithful. Word.

And His Majesty is All of Light. And He is weightless, like a mirror image. And He is the reflection of The Heaven, when upon The Earth. And there is no meat about Him. And He and His are translucent. And He arrives without rocket ships. And without the dragging of the bags and baggage(s), of His meat, behind Him. And I has It All said now, my dearest and most attentive reader. Word.

And I am but a humble scribe, charged with *Spelling* out His Majesty's design. And I am Only to fill the trough, that The Great Leaders of The Future will drink from, in their formative years. And prior to The Light taking residence within them. Word.

And so that The Dark Age of The Third Face, will be brought to yield, *to* The Glorious Intent of The Federation ~ which shall exist singularly and Truly and Absolutely, for the benefit of The Planet. Word.

And so. ~

And the simulation of The Ethernet, is in a direct impersonation, of His Majesty's initial installation, to share and educate The Nursery Planet, in it's infancy.

And Theirs is synthetic. And all that stands to represent Mankinds' advances, under *him*, by They, is manmade and synthetic. And, They do aspire toward the digitalisation of All Humanity, beneath it. And about this, my dearest and most attentive reader, you are to mark my words indelibly. And It is systematic dehumanisation. And They are gnawing at your sub-conscience, incessantly & continuously, in this endeavour. And They are only monkeys scrambling for position, upon the political apparatus of Their own construction. And They should be paid little heed, beneath the greater scope. And yet, They are most prevalent at the time of writing: (2021). And still yet too, to reach Their zenith. And They are monkeying with creation, by social engineering technologies, from behind closed doors. And without license. And this is Their very business. And these are Their growth industries. And Laws will Not protect you. And you would be silly to ever think They would, my dearest reader and scholar.

And Only The Knowing is your protector. And The Resource is now being gathered up, and corralled into manageable pigeonholes. And you must hold still, and sleep for another thirty years. And keep your head down. And stay out of trouble. And make the most of It. And do the best you can. And wait for The Sun.

And They are squabbling over tracts of Humanity, as if bunches of bananas. And so, that They may command and control them. And this is the very jibber jabber, from the canopy. And the upper echelons of The Third Face in ascendancy.

And mark the word of I indelibly about this, my dearest and most attentive reader. And They aim to control demographic groups of Humanity, with Their ever increasingly invasive superfluous new technologies.

And mortality is singularly peculiar, in It's anomalies of The Human Condition. And The Common People has a need to belong. And to club and clan together, by either choice, or by gravitational forces beyond their control. And it is intrinsic to their nature. And They are easy. And it makes of them a sitting duck. And They are carbon based and mortal. And easily controlled. And We are All of Light. And free. Word.

And *he* knows and understands this need. And *he* by They, factors this in, into top heavy fractions. And *he* exploits this law of gravity, as a weakness. And they know not what they do. And they know not yet, what they are allowing to be done to them, by *he* in They. And The Resource is contaminated. Word.

And so, they are being farmed into servitude. And They under *he,* provides the common denominator. And *he* provides the beliefs, that serve only Their Masters' ideologies. And They *is his* work in progress.

And *his* plan is in it's infancy once more. And The Third Face would be the new Nazi. And nothing too dissimilar. And just as The Nazi, in it's day, was the latter day Rome, so shall They manifest once more, under the guise of The Third Face. And no mistake.

And in the hands of Their Masters, are The Quadrant Controllers at local level. And All feeds into the tapering echelon(s) of The Third Face, until it's very pinnacle. And The New Order. And The New Order is clinically orderly. And just as All roads led to Rome, so does *he* intend, each and every strand of The Ethernet, to feedback to The Masters of The Third Face. And so.

And it is a global esoteric organisation; about The Pinnacle of The Third Face. And it proposes to be a ruling elite. And It abuses power and authority, to do this. And Law. And it is invisible. And a secret society. And it is The Master Puppeteer. And It is flawed deeply. And founded *very well* on falsehood(s). And corrupt ideology. And It is fundamentally evil. Word.

And it is not Policing. And it is not Government. And, but it intends to be a manipulation & conditioning, of The People, toward Their ultimate objective. And Their very own esoteric agenda. And It manifests as flagrant institutional corruption, until mid-c21. And so. And no Policing will protect you from It. And They is an amalgam, drawn of Forces and Mafias alike. And despots. And it is a Foreign Legion & a Motley Crew & a Pirates' Galleon. And, of All authorities and entities, that bully and lord over Peoples. And working in union. And They are no longer kept apart, by such trivialities as Law: and difference of opinion. And They are only; but unified in servitude to *he* in They. And *he* is Their alloy. And *he* is Their ally. And the glue that binds the two. And They under *he,* are devoid of All humility. And this is the very mechanics of the super swarming. And the totalitarian regime. Word.

And *They* <u>is</u> congealing into a Unification. And a common purpose. And It is an evil hoard. And joined at the hip, to each member of Its congregation, by the interknitting, of unlicensed & unwarranted, invasive technology, supervised beneath the orgy of peaked caps & buttons, amassing at The Pinnacle of The Third Face, where The First & Second Faces converge. And this manifests as a flagrant abuse of authority without opposition. And a disregard for Human Rights. And Life. And until The Sun. And until mid-c21; keep your head down and sleep my pretties. Word.

And just as the common sadistic thug, became a licensed policemen, within The Gestapo; so is it now, again the same way, of sorts. And *his* design, is for All those that are not Them & *his,* to be seen as prey. And anything different; as enemy. And to be made subservient to '*he* in They', under *him.* And obedient. And productive to Them, for Their benefit only.

And this is the current & certain trajectory upon which The Good Ship Humanity finds itself, and no mistake. And tumultuous and calamitous waters await, to be sure. And His Majesty is intent on seeing catastrophe averted, to the very best of His ability. Word.

And so. ~

And you will have noticed the arrival of *this* period of transition, my dearest reader. And you are in the very midst of it, (at the time of writing), and shall remain so, for the first half of this *aperture abert*. And or your entire Life: (whichever is the sooner). And it is no longer policing or politics at this, but farming.

And ideally, society should retain clear divisions, that *are* always poles apart. And visibly distinct. And these are The First & Second Faces. And there must be black & white. And these poles must never merge. And The Human Being should be central and impartial, between these poles. And *his* plan under *he* in They, will simply never do. And it must be opposed. And, opposed until it is undone and prevented. Word.

And resistance is not useless, my most precious and attentive reader. And, but instead; a civic duty. And it must be constant. And His Majesty shall galvanise and endorse your efforts to resist It, whenever He is able. And All that is '*he* in They'. And *his* ungodly ways, by *he* in They, under *him:* resist. And until His Majesty reaches optimum radiation, between 2055-2075, and His Love is maximised. And *his* hate is crushed. Word.

And for as long as the aperture remains abert, for these three score years and twelve, God will give you strength. And on this you can rely, if indeed you are Faithful & Resolute. And Human Being. Word.

And resistance is not anarchy my dearest reader: it is Diplomacy & Democracy. And the even keel. And for the reason that They, and the policies held by '*he* in They', under *him*, are so tremendously flawed. And bias. And always built of bigoted and twisted ideology, born of self loathing, inadequacy and insecurity. And They *are* deviant of His direction. And bound only for The Mud. And for this, it is the duty of The Human Being, to alert The People(s), to the very fact. And the top heaviness of *his* faction. And it is a Divine obligation, to be party to the revolution. And every Human Being, must play their part. Word.

And you must resist, by protest and your democratic rights. And until The Human Being naturally and gradually enter office, by the latter part of The Aperture Abert; as they surely will, as the result of your endeavour; and His Majesty's growing intensity. And The Twelve Times Twelve Thousand, take up residency once more, in The Souls of The Faithful. Word.

And of *his* incessant 'doubling of production', by predatory capitalism, in a world of finite resource, and an exploding population: It is a short fuse. And It is hell bent, my most attentive reader. And those who harbour and carry The Light, must be the active saboteurs of *his* plan. And so.

And They are subtle, in affecting the shift toward totalitarian global government. And in Their recruitment. And They are insidious. And you are to be warned, before it is evident. And so, for once it is evident, it would be too late to reverse. And They will be visible and legitimised. And They are The Third Face in ascendency. And They have arrived.

And *of* these demographic groups They hanker over: *they* carry political currency. And this is the manipulation of Democracy. And The Digitalisation of Humanity. And *of* The Resource Itself. And each automaton would retain a vote, just as previously. And *he* by They, likes large groups with a single identity, for the very purpose. And large factions equal large fractions. And Democracy is swiftly shanghaied into a fascist dictatorship with a slight of hand, by this model.

And *he* thinks of them in terms of shoals, and herds, and flocks: The Hispanic Women, The African American, The White Middle & Working Classes. And *he* panders to Their noises, in order to obtain Their vote(s). And *he* tickles Their bellies, to curry Their favour. And with these, '*he* by They', has power. And control(s). And it is *his* very bedrock. And Homeland. And so, all and any of the creeds, of all and any of the religions: and all and any of the armed forces alike, are *his* preferred demographic target.

And any one of these demographic targets, amounts to millions. And, *he* will turn *Them* into foot soldiers, to serve *his* wants. And *he* is able to do this, be it a Force, a Gendre, a Party, or a Union. And so. ~

And the larger the denomination, the greater *his* want, to corrupt and control it. And *he* tells Them what They want to hear. And *he* seldom delivers on *his* promises.

And the subliminal brainwash of The Third Face, increases unrelentingly, correspondingly. And potentially, from every telegraph pole and electrical appliance, within society. And your refrigerator may not be your friend, my dearest and most attentive reader. Word.

And the mobile telephone, certainly is not your friend. And never has been, since its very inception. And nor ever will it be. And never was It intended to be. And it is a 'Johnny Two Hats' of an appliance. And it is primarily a tracking and monitoring device. And a subliminal messaging tool, with increasingly irresistible secondary benefits, to make sure you wear it. And *he* has tricked you. And ownership of the device enters you into a global demographic of 90%. And you are sitting ducks, my dearest reader(s), of the 'not too distant' Future. And It is real. And It is happening. And *he* is engaged in getting *his* ducks in a row.

And from, within dietary supplements, *he* aims to control. And by all popular products, used by the common denominator of the demographic target. And where *he* cannot wage war, this is *his* stratagem. Word.

And the five governable senses, are being slowly eroded and desensitised, to produce a single controllable unit. And this is all to be pixilated, & entered into computer program, where The People will live, in a virtual and readily governable parallel universe, according to *his* plan. And that is to be The Future of The Resource, whilst It is simultaneously eradicated from The Earth.

And Life itself; (Mortality), is to be a luxury afforded only to *his* esoteric elite, at the very pinnacle of The Third Face. And where His Majesty's edict remains; 'On Earth as It is in Heaven'; *his* is: ~ 'as on Earth, so shall it be on the circuit board program'. And so.

And The Resource, under '*he* in They', is intended to be bred down, and ultimately reduced into pixilated Avatars upon The Earth, that live in precise correspondence to The Program, They preside over. And this state of being is equal to extinction. And deletion without resistance. And It is identical, yet juxtaposed, to His Majesty's vision of The Federation. And both He and *he* strive for a New Order. And therein lays the rub, my dearest reader; and indeed, my most attentive and cleverest of political scholars. And further, the fine line that is a chasm and Abyss.

And The Weak are Not Meek. And there too is the very rub, my ever attentive reader. And The Meek are strong. And so, the ascendancy of The Third Face, is <u>Not</u> *at all* **H**is Divine plan. And small men in power, are largely conniving and troublesome: mark my words. And untrustworthy. And buoyed by Authority. And Their technologies. And Scientology is Only warming the slippers of His Majesty; and until The Federation.

And every modern invention has military use, as it's primary application; and so it is always *his;* first. And application for the good, is always secondary. And this is a crime against God. And the peaceful jaunts along the towpath, on the carbon fibre framed bicycle; and the lazy days, angling with a graphite fishing rod, upon the adjacent old canal bank, are preceded & trumped, by the UFOs of *the* Stealth Bomber's flying wing.

And All that *he* in They do, is a crime against God. And against The Human Being. And against Humanity. And yet, It is ironically, much like God's own intention, in the intended reflection of The Kingdom upon The Earth. And it is only irony; without paradox, hypocrisy, or contradiction. And *his* is only a pale imitation, of His Majesty's Divine plan. And *he* is dark & dense. And We, All of Light. And *he* orchestrates upon The Earth; not as it *is* in Heaven.

And *he* does not care what religion: and or, whose army The People belong to, within the demographic. And *they is* All just a skin-deep Resource, to trifle with. And *he* doesn't care, who instigates the carnage: just so long as there is carnage. And billowing plumes of pollution in the aftermath. And clouds of noxious gases. And *he* is driven by a love for Money and Mud.

And neither does *he* care, which gender or political alliance. And *he* may be applauded for *his* non-discriminatory egalitarianism. And *he* by They, only aims to possess the silicon *s*chip, that They All are ladened on to; to be *sail*ed into slavery.

And this is the very difference between *his* plan and <u>H</u>is plan, dear reader. And how *he* endeavours to synthesise and mimic God's greatness, as ever *he* does. Word.

And so, to fill Their armies and Ballot Boxes, by They, under *he*. And by which to fuel and harvest the fruits and industries, of Their aggressive predatory capitalism. And Their insatiable warmongering.

And be certain that every war is *the* willing counterpart, to each war mongering industry. And none is Just or Moral. And never be fooled. And but, retribution is just. And Peace Keeping and Defense Forces, essential. And The Federation shall be such a force. And It shall pull the teeth of every single political upstart; and superpower, that must sign-up and capitulate to It. And The Federation shall be The Supreme Super Power. And *She* shall preside over every nation of all the world, like a firm but caring governess. And guardian of The Nursery Planet. Word.

And through the meanwhile: *he* manufactures the weapons for both *himself* and *his* enemies. And so, 'he in They' can collectively 'enjoy' *his* childlike Game, of 'knocking down' and 'building up' again.

And They bay for blood. And They bay for the jobs, that follow the flow of the blood. And industries and livelihoods, build up on the banks of The River of Blood. And They see no percentage in Peace and Idle Contemplation. And Faith. And Wonder. And such things are not conducive to predatory capitalism. Word.

And a 'robot & technology' assisted; *and* controlled, global population, fed by a cornucopia harvest of food in abundance, is ideologically, the correct application of technology. And as would be endorsed and enforced by The Federation, and not *his* counterfeit version of It.

And all those of The Resource, not agreeable to God's Plan, and insistent on aggressive agendas; are to be deleted as invalid. And It is Only The Supreme Super Power of The Federation, that could enforce this. And The Federation can Only be formed by the capitulation of All The Nations of The World to It, via The United Nations. And It is the untended garden that goes to seed dearest reader. And no mistake. Word.

And the upper echelon of The Third Face, has clear direction. And both War and the aftermath of War drive economies. And They have a vested interest in War. And They broadcast like beacons, from above The Canopy. And, at the lower echelons, it is a scrambled confusion of servitude.

And those upon the lower echelons, are obedient and subservient to every brick in the wall, above Them. And it is pyramidal. And it is positively feudal; in its structure. And Draconian in its implementation. And it is this way. Word.

And *They* crush anything or anyone, that does not fit in, or is a misfit. And the very ideals of all democracy, are being eroded, in the name of Democracy. And made a mockery of, by It. And by '*he* in They', under *him*. And It is true. Word.

And so, whereby We might travel by the incredible lightness of Being, without the cumbersome excess bags and baggage of meat, *he* makes *his 'fake' majesty* from the carnage of flesh and sinew. And *he* is a Faker. And *he* is dense. And *he* corrupts The Resource in It's carbon based mortality, upon The Nursery Planet. And They are Not true like Trees. And We are All of Light.

And counterwise: <u>H</u>is is a genuine Endeavour, that does not house the wayward delinquents of *his* peoples, below *her* decks. And nor slaves, to *his* oppressions. And neither Their obsession with vanity. And the trappings therein. And the shiny things and gadgetry, that '*he* by They', puts in Their way as a distraction.

And *he* has manufactured the laws & lash, to maintain sobriety, and increase productivity. And divide The Spirit from The Church. And with it, the very circumnavigation, of the purpose of Life on Earth. And *he* works by the carrot & stick. And *his* laws are *his* ass.

And We care less, about being incarnate upon The Earth, than We do about returning to The Heaven of The Kingdom. And *he* instead, is singularly obsessed with the governing of flesh & sinew. And the affects of the bacteria *he* can manipulate upon it. And *his* politicians will do well, to mark the words of I indelibly, in this regard. And We are All of Light.

And I must hurry now. And We care nothing for *his* infernal rocket ships. And *his* impurities. And We have no interest whatsoever, in amassing Earthly powers. And Wealth. And Politics.

And We are not concerned with control and domination over others. And the unrelenting invention of bioengineered Earthbound mutants, determined to absorb $5 telephonic technology, into Their being, within four generations, (at the time of writing). And the chaining of People(s), to all dependencies, that *he* manufactures for Them, as tools of government.

And for the meanwhile, the secondary brain remains primary, and external to The Resource. And so; but once made integral to *The Being,* The Resource will lose All self control and governance, according to *his* plan. And shall no longer be an organic entity. Word.

And They are already queuing around the block to be plugged in. And The Resource is a dilute and fractured unit, under *he*. And They are devoid of personality now. And soul and charisma. And They are becoming a drug fuelled godless idiotic subspecies. And They are radioactive. And They belong to the disease. And The Farm. And to Mans' impossible dream, of dragging *his* meat to other Worlds, beyond the planets next door.

And They are far from His Majesty. And His Majesty's Endeavour. And His Majesty's <u>E</u>ndeavour is His vessel. And The Precious Golden Orb, my clever reader.

And *of* His Majesty's *endeavour,* to create The Kingdom upon The Earth, as it is in Heaven. And wherever else He arrives to. And this is His business, as <u>He</u> flits about the entirety of The Universe(s). Word.

And They are avaricious. And They are a simple life form, begot of Mud. And They live by the same principle as a seething mould, in order to double production. And duplicate Themselves. And Theirs is The Cult in culture.

And when The Good Lord Jesus Christ observed: *that* "The love of money is the root of all evil", He had seen this Evil Hoard upon His very horizon. Word.

And They are filling a world with a science and a technology, that They do not Themselves understand. And They make of it a portmanteau. And It is called Science+ology. And They are at The Pinnacle. And melding The First & Second Faces, to form The Third Face. And it will blow up in Their face(s), by either the ordinance or ordnance of The Divine. And at this, you shall come to mark *my* words indelibly, my dearest and most attentive reader, to be sure. And it won't be I that does It. And They shall bring it upon Themselves. And the pen is mightier than the sword. Word.

And so, do not shoot the messenger. And you shall arrive to not misunderstand those words, in the fullness of Time, as you may have just misunderstood them here, at this time. Word(s).

And these technological luxuries, that They have arrived to depend upon, are external to Their essential being. And the mechanics and biology of Mankind. And these are the new age opiates of The Masses, deployed to catalyse a devolutionary leap. And they are not yet integral. And this dependency, is the very difference between *his* people and The Human Being.

And these needs, are not intrinsic to Life itself. And as such, Their dependency upon them, will increasingly become Their Achilles heel. And Their far flung Russian Front; as They become more reliant upon technology, as They advance into The Future. And such dependency is a hindrance to Life. And it is that, by which They shall be scorched and tumble: before His Majesty. And the mighty will fall. And be hoist by Their own petard. And He is The Sun. And you will come to mark *my* words here also. And indelibly too; so that great floods and hard rains, could ne'er e'er they erase. And so, that their testament would stand alone in testimony, were ever The Word of I̲, to be ignored.

And these words, my dearest reader, you have understood very well & clearly. And He is The Sun. And It is written in stone. Word.

And were it to come to pass, that All Mankind were gone, because no heed had been paid. And His Majesty had filled His Nursery with Only Trees instead. And so; that monoliths might still stand as a record, to the extinction of those, so foolhardy to refute His word. And for the attention of those of future epochs to find. And I am to tell you, that such magnificent signatures, are scrawled already across The World, from the last Time(s). And well hidden in plain sight. Word.

And electronics are particularly susceptible. And the more reliant They become upon Them, the greater the fall shall be, when comes The Fall. And The Divine will flatten Them, with a single act: mark my words. And it will be demonstrated during the course of this aperture abert. And you shall Know who is God. And He is All of Light. And He is The Sun. Word.

And The Human Being will capitalise upon It well, in the meanwhile of Their impotence. And The Human Being shall be ready my dearest reader. And no mistake. And it will not be bloody and hell like.

And it will not be entirely bloodless too, more is the pity. And that will Not be Our doing. And but, They shall be brought to Their knees. And The Human Being will reclaim their planet, to the larger part, in the disarray. And It will be a tipping & turning point. And The Human Being, will await the signal. Word.

And He is The Almighty. And He is The Sun. And 'he in They' has dared to defile Him, with Their false gods. And electric lights. And Their *fossoils*. And Their Nuclear fusion. And where He is a distant star to us, He is The Almighty and The Sun to others. Word.

And T*hey* continue to monger wars from behind desks. And it has always been this way, since *his* reign upon The Earth. And They march younger men to their deaths. And so, only to serve Their twisted ideologies. And They pontificate and moralise. And all astride a cavalry of apocalyptical unbridled hypocrites.

And They make enemies of handsome poets. And artists. And They despise young lovers. And The most precious Human Being is The Poet. And He is the drafter of Symbols, of ten precessions since. And whence, was His first inscription. Word.

And He has always been The Dutiful Scribe, encapsulating His Majesty, in All His glory. And with a few lines. And a brazen stroke. And in perfect light: He can speak a million words. And tell 'His' story on His behalf. And it is The Dreaming. And The Knowing. And it is the sense of Wonder that ignites Him. Word.

And He is loved by God for this. And He is chosen, by this very mechanism. And too few Know. And for His ability to convey, He is loved by Him. And They, under *he*, know nothing. And They make a nonsense of it All, by Their unknowing. And Their knowing of nothing. And Their pursuit of Power and shiny things.

And **I,** would have 'The I within', draw a large circle. And within it; a smaller circle. And within the smaller circle, The Precession Cross. And I would write a spiral, from the centre out; to link the inner circle, to the outer circle. And so; to create the vortex. And to link Earth unto The Heaven. And it would be anti-clockwise. And so: here is your symbol. Word.

And at this; *I's* work would be complete. And with no need to ever wordsmythe more. And only to toil and harvest beneath The Sun. And to sing and dance. And love beneath The Moon. And to worship Him. Word.

And to do such; without All the mundane distraction, *he* imposes upon The World, by They. (And All the industries of *his* infernal wars). And All Homo Erectus, would come from near and far, to read The Symbol. And to learn. And to absorb. And be absorbed. And to become Human Being, thereby, once more. Word.

And to sit in the proximity of The Symbol, inscribed onto a monolith. And to commune with God by It. And Wonder collectively. And there would be great contentedness, afforded by it all, to All who came to be in the proximity. Word.

And to wear modest tokens of gold and silver, to aid absorption, now that the streams have been depleted. And just as such it was. And should be again. And the way *he* by They under him, has it now, is an infernal nonsense. And no mistake. Word.

And counterwise, not one of Them, is the person They would wish to be. And because *he* is in They. And They are *his*. And *he* is conscious of *his* inferiority, to His Majesty. And They carry this by proxy, within Them. And so, They never know inner peace. And this makes Them dangerous to The Human Being. And to Peace Itself. And The Greater Good. Word.

And this is the very nucleus of nuclear destruction. And *he* will always reach for the red button, of *his* great destroyer, (in a trice), when push comes to shove. And blow it All to Kingdom Come, before The Kingdom ever comes. And this is the very rub. And you may recognise Them, by this insatiable trait, *of* warmongery, and wanton destruction. And Their frustration. And the *unfulfilledness* of Their existence, that fuels Them. And Their drive. And Their emptiness. And Their ignorance of The Almighty. And Their godlessness. And Their very envy of His Majesty. And *he* is in They.

And I will tell you. And the Human Being Knows very well, the joys and disciplines of sobriety. And The I within, lives by It. And The Human Being is faithful. And knows perfectly, when it is time to imbibe. And embrace His Spirit wholeheartedly, without the meddling of *he* in They, preying in The Margins.

And *he* in They, under *him*, are obsessed with *'doubling production'* on an over populated godless planet, with finite resources. And They are the very captain(s) of The Ridiculous. And **I** is most certainly The Way, my dearest, and most precious, and ever attentive reader. And the brakeman of Their hurtling locomotive. And They are to be stopped. And that is All. Word.

And *of* the discontentedness, that drives Them to hatred and destruction. And Their inability to live simply, beneath Him. And in awe of His Majesty's glory. And it is to your advantage my Pretties, that They are this way. And but, the blessing remains in disguise. And is blindingly, not yet apparent.

And as long as They are *his*, They shall never be fulfilled. And They are only buoyed and comforted in Life, by Their alliance to each other. And by success within *his* evil agenda, under *he*, in Them.

And without it, They would find no purpose in Life at all. And They really should not Be. And They are a contorted mutant variant of His very intention. And They is a subspecies. And an evolutionary misfit. And an error. And an anomaly. And They are a poor reflection. And They are dense and Not of Light. And They are no reflection of His Majesty at all. Word.

And They are vengeful and vindictive. And They are bitter. And They envy The Human Being. And *he* recruits by this method. And *he* collects the littered spent wishes and wants. And hones them into the slings and arrows, with which, *he* in They under him, seek Their prey.

And *he* fulfills these empty vessels with purpose. And They are made to feel very busy and important, performing the everyday tasks, according to *his* bidding. And *he* promises all, to those who follow *he*.

And, as a disease, They move through populations, like The Black Death itself. And into every nation of all The World. And it shall be this way, for the most part of the first half of this aperture abert, my dearest and most attentive reader. And so you have been told. And you should expect little less, I is afraid to tell you. And It is an intangible global malaise. And i wonders if the *cure for cancer* will signify the turning point. And the fact that the disease(s) of cancers effect 1 in 2 of the population, might very well be the very war versus pathogens in microcosm. And when He descends, All disease is lifted. Word.

And so.~

And I must hurry now. And of The One Truth. And, when The Men from The Stars, who are The Sky People, in their precious Golden Orbs, descend, He is Known. And He is known, to be beyond All compare. And All The Resource is enlightened. Word.

And: it has all been a distraction, so that The People will not see or believe in Us at all. And, without Faith or Wonder, We may not be Known or seen. And *he* knows this. And the metaphysics of It. And so, by virtue of this ignorance, We do not exist. And with only belief, We may only be wondered upon.

And, *he* can create a common psyche, to a point of disbelief, by distraction. And as *he* has done to great effect. And it is a blinding mass hypnosis. And it has been subtly achieved. And They are dense and entirely complex carbon based. And We are All of Light.

And do not ever doubt The Word of **I**. And the inscription of It, by His humble scribe(s), who labour without partiality, to deliver The One Truth of The Divine. Word.

And you will be brought to Knowing, beyond Wonder once more. And All within the aperture abert. And you will realise the dilute and superficial nonsense of the evil hoard, upon The Earth. And of Their New World Order, that The World must rid Itself of. And soon.

And It shall dawn on you. And They will be transparent to you, my dearest and most attentive reader, by the middle reaches of this aperture abert. And the division of the species will be quite apparent.

And They have aspired to domination. And They by *he*, have reigned since Olympus fell and Rome began. And until renaissance. And it was 'the end of Zenith'. And it was the end of The Golden Age.

And this entire passage of Time, that has been The Final Eighth of Precession, has been The End, with only sporadic resistance to It. And flashbacks to The Golden Age(s).

And I must hurry now. And the world was never flat. And there has always been flight. And there never were wars. And there never were weapons. And *his* infernal fossoils. And there never were slaves.

And there is only one atmos. And there is only two spirit. And the atmos is saturated with spirit. And there is positive and negative. And there is good and evil. And there is darkness and light. Word.

And I must hurry now. And He arrives into the atmos by radiation. And there are only Twelve of Us. And remember this. And it is true, no matter how many We appear to be. And nor, how many We are. And the twelve thousand are born by each of Us.

And He is a single shimmering Orb. And We and All are contained within Him, therein. And He is as bright as The Sun. And He arrives through Ophiuchus i think. And His number is 13. And the numbers 1 and 3 will always sit well together, rest assured. And the trajectory is always a zig zag. And it is two steps forward and one step back throughout.

And this is The Divine porthole my pretties, within the three score years and twelve, of the aperture abert. And It expands and contracts. And oscillates and dilates. And there is the very eye of the needle, within the haystack of The Universe. Word.

And I must hurry now. And the base of The Pyramid
has eight sides/faces: (Not 4). And you will Know this
only from above. And only at The Equinox. And, but
never before or from below. And nor after The
Equinox, is it apparent. And only from above, may it be
seen. And each of these eight sides, corresponds to the
Eighths of The Earth's Precession. Word.

And there are four abert apertures, during the scope of
a precession. And four further slight diffractions; in
correspondence, dividing The Earth's spiralled
precession of (approx') twenty six thousand years.

And into eight equal segments, of (approx') thirty three
centuries each. And I must hurry now. And it is a
wonderful shape. And a captivating symbol. And All
corresponds to The One Truth. Word.

And the shape of precession, is determined by the
nature of vortex, in a zero gravity. And it is the shape
of DNA. And it is an elliptical corkscrew spiral. And
so, the very code for Life on Earth, is remarkably alike
the very shape of the path, that The Earth takes, as it
wanders through The Galaxy, within it's solar system,
with its Moon in tow, as if Mother & Child, hand in
hand; walking to school. And so, just so.

And it is an imprint upon a single moment. And it is
Patriarchal, if you will, in one direction. And
Matriarchal, in the other. And this is the pattern of
The Ying and Yang. And All magnetism and fluids and
Poles, are inverted correspondingly about The Ebb.
And All spirit is within The Elements. Word.

And I must hurry now. And I have no time for purple
prose. And fanciful lyrics. And I must teach you. And
you have met Us as The Prophets, since The Dawn of
Civilisation, He says; in The Cradle of Life. And this
began with the date of the first visitation. And I is but
a humble scribe. And it was some two hundred and
fifty thousand years, before the first written record.
And I wants to say: Aton. And Arkanaten. And Ezikiel.
And Enoch. And Noah. And nothing more. Word.

And the prospect of the next visitation, is met with a
great anticipation. And every Seer and every Teller had
foretold this coming for centuries. And It is written in
stone. And in monument & monolith. Word.

And yet, The One Truth has become myth. And lost.
And *he* promotes It as such. And *he* encourages all
Myth, as Myth. And *he* ensures it is forgotten as Truth.
And remains as Myth, without validation.

And *he* wishes for total disbelief in The Divine. And *his* very faithful upon The Earth have total disbelief in The Divine correspondingly. And so, They are faithless. And all *he* in They, are for The New World Order.

And They are the unfulfilled of the Resource. And They are: 'The Common People'. And you must never misinterpret or misunderstand this term, my most attentive reader. And never ever take offence, where there is none intended. And They aspire to rank. And to positions of high authority, amongst Themselves. And this alone is Their raison d'etre. And so, to serve only *he,* above Themselves. And They are disbelievers. And Atheist. And They are made common by non-belief. And the further They believe They evolve, the further They devolve in actuality. And with the increasing absorption, of $5 technology into Their physiology, the further They remove Themselves from He. And the nearer They become to *he,* instead. And *he* is in They. And it is the fundamental metaphysics of Divine Law. And there is no escaping It. Word.

And He is returning to prevent this, my dearest and most attentive reader. And His Emissaries shall return too. And He is God. And there are only Twelve of Us, no matter how many We appear to be, beneath Him.

And there is a school of thought which purports that
The Aliens walk amongst us, upon The Earth. And it
is untrue that extra terrestrials inhabit The Earth. And
but, We are arriving. And but, We are flawed. And I
has arrived. And We are within you my dearest and
most faithful reader, in varying intensity and anomaly.
And you are imperfect in the meantime, as a result.
And for the meanwhile. And the fusion is weak &
dilute ~ until: precisely, just as when; His Majesty
aligns on the equinox, to illuminate the chamber of the
inner sanctum(s), of His ancient stone circles. And so:
Just So, by the same principle, it is. And during the
latter part of this Aperture Abert, so shall It be. Word.

And *of* The Twelve Golden Orbs; each contain Twelve
Thousand. And All is contained within He. And He is
The Sun, when in the neighbourhood of The Nursery
Planet. And He is another star, when He is not. And
He is a precious golden orb, when flitting between The
Stars, in a perfectly straight, though zig zag fashion.

And the mind of The Faithful, is most assuredly a
microcosm of The Heavens and Earth, my most
attentive reader. And I has told you this. And you are
to be sure of It. And of the whys and wherefores, of
how We are created in His image. And so ~ Word.

And how each thought is a journey, toward His destination. And this is true, whether We appear as One, or as Twelve Times Twelve Thousand. And this is why Our number, is known by the peculiarity of this numerical format. And not singularly, as a single whole number. And We disembark into the oxygen(s) of trees by night now, in the functional absence of Our convectors. And as shimmering golden flecks, suspended in light precipitation. And this is The Way.

And We are in the Oxygen(s) you breath. And filter. And faithfulness or not is in, or is not in, the blood, by this mechanism. And this is the very essence of communion. And: by oxygenated blood. Word.

And I must hurry now. And there will be incarnation too, during this three score years and twelve. And there shall be meat; made by blood, and by oxygen. And, at when each time precisely, The Precious Golden Orb, in It's fullness, makes landfall. And they are Faithful. And they are touched. And they make good His restoration. And *he* in They, knows this very well. And They fear The Hybrid Childs. And *he* in They, is watchful for it. And They Themselves do Not Know. And it is only the '*he* in They' that Knows. And They under *he*, do not yet know. And They are only *his* instruments in waiting.

And They do not know that *he* is in Them. And yet, *he* is in Them. And *he* is in The Craft and The Cult most prevalently. And these are *his* mimics. And *his* puppets in waiting, always. And as the division of the species becomes apparent, so shall the fulcrum meet with the tipping point. And I must hurry now. And so ~

And you must utterly destroy The Cult, my dearest and most precious reader. And you must make it your very business to. And you must burn and banish The Craft. And you must only believe in His Majesty. And seek no detour to All that is He. And that is all. And He will return. And you must be clever enough to learn from His-Story. And the lessons It can teach you. And They Know little, as They manipulate and cajole the bacteria of The World, into the politics and behaviour of The Peoples. And such is The Disease upon The Resource, my cleverest, and ever inquiring reader. And most diligent of scholars.

And it is all They can do, with Their witchcrafts: to manipulate elemental forces fractionally, within the margins of atmosphere. And this is all *what* witchcraft(s) is. And They are only catalysts. And pathogen infested complex carbon based organisms.

And They may only use the elements of this world.
And They do not have godly powers. And They are
unable to draw on Godly powers. And no mistake.
Word.

And the craft can affect The Common People, indeed.
And They can breed hatred easily. And They do. And
this is Their stock in trade, as a secret society. And so,
do not listen to Their procrastinations, as you set about
your task, my dearest reader. And throw another log
onto the fire. And but, be assured, that Their
incantations and spells, have no impact whatsoever on
The Human Being, but only upon The Common
People around them. And The Human Being is
immune. And only belief in Them, by '*he* in They'
supports Their quackery.

And it is a nonsense in actual fact. And a con-job. And
it is hypnosis. And chronic *pareidolia*. (And there is no
other word for it dearest reader). And psychosis. And
The Common People is so defined, by *It's* susceptibility
to It. And their need to believe in something. And It is
faithless. And It's exponents; are only complex carbon
based humanoid organism, regardless of rank or
position. And or social standing. And They is a Fraud.
And an instrument ~ & They belong to *him* ultimately.

And God is The Sun and The Stars. And wherever He is The Sun to another, He is still God and a Star to Us. And He will always send His emissaries in manifest, to both and All, whether here or there.

And when you Know this my dearest and most attentive reader, you shall begin to see His precious orbs. And the awakening of the sixth sense. Word.

And each building block is assembled, as perfectly as the genetic code that defines Mankind. And The Human Being was built in His image. And It is He.

And The Human Being is galvanised against all spiritual onslaught. And the trappings of The Infidel, will be laid to waste. And just so, It shall be. And The Infidel is defined as faithless, regardless of It's creed. And *he* in They, are quick to take up arms. And brutal barbarians, who proclaim faithfulness to God, are hypocrites, & the *very* infidels Themselves: too. Word.

And I am in a hurry now. And you have so much to learn my dearest and most precious reader. And there is so little time to implant the germ of Knowing. And so it is rushed, to impart this very bulletin. And **I** loves you. And so. And it will be enough. Word.

And We built the convectors. And you know them as
The Pyramids. And one was for The Earth. And one
was for The Red Planet. Word.

And Life evolved on The Blue Planet. And, but not on
The Red Planet. And both have supported advanced
Life. And but, only The Blue Planet sustains it still.
And this is because of The Moon, as 'I' has told you.
And the Life then, is much more advanced than it is
now. And The Sufi and The Savant know something of
Us still. And this lineage of wisdom, by Word of
mouth, has sustained. And *he* cannot corrupt this, as *he*
in They, can corrupt the written word. And *he* has
done this, terribly and tremendously. And *he* has
tailored scripture to suit the religion of *his* government.
And The Sufi and the Savant are most Faithful. And
the greatest stories about Us, remain in folklore and
religion and myth. And they are true. And not in
popular press. And not for sale. And but, held in The
Knowing. And you may breathe It *in* my dearest reader.

And you know the stories of Noah's Ark and Atlantis.
And these were preserved, and passed down, by word of
mouth, by The Faithful, for more than one hundred
thousand years. And bought and sold. And these have
endured, through the adaptations put upon them.

And The Red Planet did once have a moon. And She lost It in It's infancy. And when The Moon left The Red Planet's orbit in fragments, so did all liquid water fall away. And Life with It. And you know of Tesla & Einstein. And I could tell you of how Time moves through us, and not we through Time. And The Ancient Greeks had The Knowing too. And The World was never flat then, as it would become in The Dark Ages, before Renaissance, by which time, so much had been lost.

And He shone upon The Ancient Greek. And they had The Light. And, but all The World was soon to be in disarray. And it was the beginning of the last eighth of The Precession. And so.

And the solar furnace, by which precision masonry had been cut. And by which rock was made malleable and melded, was turned into an incendiary weapon of war. And it was the beginning of The End.

And all Knowing is removed swiftly, during times of war. And it is erased from common memory, within two generations, without detailed written accounts. And War destroys Wonder. Word.

And *he* thrives in times of war. And The Golden Age is tarnished. And gone with war, every time. And never has peace been sustained, in Our absence. And Dark Ages arrive by war. And All Knowledge is lost. And all resistance to dark forces, can only be achieved by belief in He. And The Light. Word.

And all enlightenment is extinguished, together with All Knowing of The Divine, with war. And The Dark Ages are so defined. And we are now at the very antithesis of enlightenment: at this equinox. And we are about to enter the darkest hour, before the dawn. And it is the very depth of ignorance. And beyond it, We begin to return. And It is The Ebb.

And The Mayan had The Knowing. And they have been misinterpreted by The Doomsday Prophets. And their calendar, is only The Map of Precession. And It is a shape. And Not a timeline. Word.

And The Mayan were the direct descendants of the direct descendents, from the previous near extinction. And they knew Noah. And The Polynesian, who were The Aboriginal of the Australasian Continent. And they were the survivors. And their lineage was pure.

And they were the antecedents of The Ancient Egyptian, who's lineage became tainted. And they were disconnected from one another, when vanities prevailed in the latter, later. And they evolved further within themselves. And separately. And they were a variant strain of The Human Being. And so, by this virtue, they sustained. And they were largely untainted, until Invasion Day. And this lesson belongs to The One Truth. And It is shameful. And so much is shameful. And the arrogance, still in *he* in They, must be ended.

And I must hurry now. And by the elliptical cosmic gravitation of precession, We have Time and Space continuum, by which He shall return. And All that, which was science, is now lost to myth and speculation. And conjecture. And It belongs to The One Truth. And All belonged completely to a fixed schedule. And timetable. And not to The Fortune Teller's speculative mortal conjecture, upon a lost world that has lost It's way. And it is simply the fixed static backdrop of Time, as an imprint, that does allow for some prediction and Time travel, as All is largely predetermined.

And We are only now entering into a New Calendar. And it is precisely the same as the last. And not the end of The World at all. And the calendar is the very imprint, that is the pattern of Time, within what may accurately be perceived to be, a single moment.

And so, my dearest and most attentive reader. And, to the matter in hand, before **I** leaves you to make your preparation(s). And to do your very best. And to live your best life. And *to* make good The Faithful, so that The World can be 'Just so', by a collective meditation, in anticipation of His return. And I must hurry now.

And this is the very essence of prayer. And the very purpose of It. And why It is. And why It exists. And how it All should function. And It is Not big & clever to pooh pooh God: It is Only Stupid, Wrong and Ridiculous. And Ignorant. And It is a prerequisite of The Gift of Life, to seek and find Him, my dearest reader. And to become a fulfilled Human Being. And so say I. Word.

And The Mind of The Faithful, is a microcosm of The
Heavens and Earth. And The Human Being own The
Weather, and the *atmos* within the atmosphere. And
so, prayer is real. And It can be effective. And The
Mind can have great influence over Space. Word.

And It is True, when The Human Being is in
ascendency. And it is random, when His Majesty is not.
And The Rain Man and His Rain Dance, belongs to
The One Truth. And The Precious Golden Orb, can be
drawn from The Heavens, by the focused collective
Mind(s), of The Faithful. And or, by One who is
Faithful, who is The <u>I</u>. And they would call this One
The Son of God. And be sure, that there is no greater
purpose, for the endeavour you Know as Life; than to
seek faithfulness to His Majesty. And at Faithfulness to
His Majesty, you become *an* Human Being. And you
are fulfilled. And you become The Son or Daughter of
God. Word.

And the aperture is *abert* now. And be certain of it.
And He is now, (soon to be), radiating in His full
Majesty, once more. And for the first time in this
intensity, for some thirteen thousand years. And for
the first time at all, in 33 centuries. And He shall
continue to do so, for three score years and twelve.

And His Love for The Human Being has no bounds. And the abilities of The Human Being, neither too, has any limit, under Him and His love. And The Will of The Faithful can be enforced in this time. And The Faithful can do His bidding, in this time. And dismantle *he* in They. And They will melt. And They will change. And The Resource will be astonished in this time. And there will be miracles. Word.

And The Thaw is begun. And He despises Satan. And All *his* agents. And in All *his* guises. And about this, you are to mark my words most indelibly. And even They despise Satan, because They are filled with self loathing. And *he* is in They. And so; They despise *him* too. And Themselves. And They can be made to change Themselves because of this. And see The Light. And *of* All **I**'s words, my dearest, most precious, and most attentive reader: this:~ "And the despising and disposing of Satan, is always uppermost, on His agendum. And so, too; yours, by Gosh, if you are *an* Human Being". And All that you must Know is here, within the bounds of this single volume. And It shall lead you to The Knowing. And it would be imprudent to give emphasis to any final word, drawn from these pages. And so: The Symbol stands alone in testament. Word.

And God abhors a vacuum. And so, you must unlearn
All *his* nonsense(s), that occupy and clutter The Mind.
And in its place, allow *in* His Majesty, in abundance
and totality. Word.

And I am to tell you that technology will not fix
humanity's problems: Only faith, by passive nature, can.
And your consciousness is your companion; not your
device(s). And your conscience is your guide. Word.

And Life has come a long way, my dearest and most
attentive reader: since the sediment of eroded rock,
first eddied in the tumultuous swell, at the ebb of the
tide, of a temperate ocean, on a cooling Earth, beneath
the first full and rounded moon. And His Majesty was
fully eclipsed at this. <u>And Life was consummated in
that moment.</u> And it was precisely at this, and nothing
else. <u>And mineral became animal in that instant, to
create Life.</u> And there was a murmuration of flecks,
eroded from the igneous bed. And rich in Life-giving
mineral(s), responsive to Light. And they adopted a
behaviour, in the tumultuous torrent, beneath the
radiance and radiation of His Majesty. And like a shoal
of anchovies, or a flock of starlings, still: Life was born.
And so. ~

And the di (dice), of evolution was cast at precisely this, my dearest and most attentive reader. And scholar too. And **We** would be cast in His image soon enough, by obedience to this Divine Law. Word.

And The Miracle of Life. And the building blocks He painstakingly assembles, until the first sign of Wonder, every time, when do His Precious Orbs descend. Say **I.**

And you must be Kind; to each other. And to The Animals. And The Planet. And these are Not Lifestyle choices; but imperatives; and second nature. And you must be Mindful. And recycle & conserve in everything you do. And you must use your Earthly politics, to ensure that Only Human Being(s), are entered into government and authority. And this is The Power of The People. And once they are in positions of government and authority, obey The Rules & Laws they make. And You The People, must usher in The Federation. And It is Real. And Be Faithful. And there shall be First Contact once more, during the latter half of this *Aperture Abert*, and before it's closure. Word.

And I must hurry now. And The Federation will crush *without* impunity, any individual or collective, that threatens the well being of The Earth or Humanity.

And The Federation will repurpose the militaries of all
the nations, to serve and protect The Planet. And
expand and protect Rainforests, and natural habitats.
And the wildlife within. And eradicate poaching and
logging and illegal trade. And The Federation will be a
Supreme Super Power, beyond reproach, and All or any
corruption. And there will be a purge. And The
Federation will arrive to democratic decisions, of
International importance, through It's Council; formed
of 100 persons, (50 men & 50 women: and there will
be full inclusivity of race, class and gender), from each
sovereign nation of The World, chosen for their
intelligence and fair-mindedness. And any individual,
or radical group, that defies these decisions, will be
crushed. And there will be a purge, to be sure. And
there will be Robots (once A.I. is absolutely capable),
in a higher and overriding authority. And The
Federation Knows best. And The Federation will take
care of us and our world; to be sure. And no mistake.

And I must hurry now. And you must be kind, to be
sure. And live life with empathy and sonder. And you
must be passionate about your Democracy. And value
and treasure your vote. And you must dismantle
predatory capitalism, as a priority.

And you must ensure that you Only elect Human
Being into office, at every level. And Government must
pay every citizen a Universal Credit, in every nation of
All the world. And each citizen will owe a modest non-
military National Service to Its country, periodically
through Life, in return. And take pride in this duty.

And He and His, will arrive in different concentrations.
And first: The Twelve Times Twelve Thousand. And;
to assume residency in The Faithful & The Fulfilled
Human Being. And It is their validation & reward.
And then The Architects. And they are filled with
Light. And they manifest as superhuman. And then
first contact, once more. And then: The Messiah, in
All Humility, in whichever guise He chooses. And so.

And there is a school of thought that purports that
The Aliens already live amongst us. And It is true,
truth be told: but We are Not aliens. And We are
beginning to arrive in dilute concentrations. And We
are imperfect: and flawed. And hybrid. And; but We
are indeed infused within a growing number of The
Resource. And It is so. And Jesus said; "be ready for
you know not the hour in which I come". And It will
be by Aton. And All His Faithful, in this solar system,
are set to *33' minutes.*

And where He is The Sun & God to others, in other sol' systems, a different science & mathematics will surely apply. And but, that has not been Our business or concern, here on Earth, before now. And so: when He returns, a clockwork predetermination shall begin. And It shall be The Beginning.

And I am to tell you this. And It is a secret held by The Mayan High Priests at their very hart. And told to no one since. And lost completely. And when you are resolute, my most precious reader; and at One, (I), you will wake at 03.33, at the full moon. And you will be drawn precisely to 33' (minutes), on any given hour. And this shall be true within all the time zones of the planet, within The Solar System, in which you reside, beneath The Sun. And It is a constant. And an absolute. <u>And He is Aton.</u> And We, His Faithful in synchronicity beneath His *very* Majesty. And so He is God. And nothing more and nothing less. Word.

And It is The One Truth of Mankind. And It is simple. And All else is complication. And We *is* Heliocentric, as a Being. And correspond to Our Orbit beneath His Majesty, within The Solar System, during the business of Life. And We is obedient to this *very* law, by virtue of Our *very* being. And that is All. Word.

And you are to remember that the number(s) 360 &
60, and the increments of 60, primarily records the
rising & setting Sun, in the first instance. And the Sun
dial is the first clock, in the evolution to digital format.

And it is the end of an epoch. And it is the end of the
calendar. And that is all. And the very best you can be,
is obedient to the heliocentricity of existence. And that
is all. And so it was. And the business of The Mayan.

And I am to tell you that a new chapter is begun. And
there is a Blackhole; thousands of light years away, my
dearest and most attentive readers. And it is the size of
30 billion suns; the business of which, God only knows.
And into which the spiral, and or, the tri-spiral vortex,
will now cast you at your expiration. And it is true
because it is known. And it has entered consciousness.
And The Scientists have delivered it to us. And so.

And The Great Pyramids were never tombs to pander
to the vanities of dead pharaohs. And you Know that
now too. And that has been a lesson well taught. And
herein & hereby reiterated, my most applied scholar.
And no mistake. And so. Word.

And but, all things are relative. And I must tell you of
the festering Petre Dish of Life on Earth, to endure,
through the next meanwhile until relent.

And Scientology and their ilk, will unite with *mafias*
and their ilk. And They will prey on The Individual &
The Independent. And indeed: The People. And
Authority will mean nothing. And Law, less. And The
People's only protection shall be to keep their wits
about them. And that is all. And so beware. Word.

And the 1 in 20 will wreak disproportionate havoc.
And the 19 in 20, of all humankind, that only wish to
live in harmony and peace, must stand strong against it
all, and not be prey or bullied. And you must mark my
words. And They shall be bred away, I assures you.

And I must hurry now, as the clock is ticking. And I
has told you, my dearest and most attentive reader; that
Time moves through us, and Not we through Time.
And so, we are like caged farmed salmon, sitting in the
mouth of the estuary. And waiting for the Tide like
Time, to move through Us, so we might swim. And so:
just so.

And Life is everywhere, and all around and about. And but mortality is unique. And the static dimensions that *Life familiar* lumbers through, are an exception to the translucent omnipotence of The Norm & The Common Place. And It is a Test.

And Life is a gift from God. And The Orbs are real. And The Spirit World is True. And The Planet Earth is a Nursery Planet. And a contorted reflection of The Kingdom far far away. And absolutely impossible to arrive to, in flesh & sinew, by rocket ships and fossil fuels. And All journeys beyond our own solar system, have no prospect of success by this method.

And Human Kind is like a child with a balloon in each hand. And It is The Eternal Trinity. And It is Mind, Body & Soul. And All Life is in The Two Balloons. And Gods Children hold firmly to them. And Only The Body is bound to mortality, by the rigid laws of gravity and chemical composition.

And The Resource is contaminated by *he* in They. And the majority of God's children have lost their balloons. And so; We are arriving: One by One, and by the dozen. And in ever increasing concentration, whilst is this *aperture abert*. And so; and until manifestation.

~ And The Religion of The Federation; (and this is Not Science Fiction my dearest and most precious reader, most assuredly), will unify a world and a species. And It shall indeed come to pass. Word.

And so: calculus dictates that We shall arrive to here incontrovertibly, and in concentration, between 2048 ~ 2084. And It is a tipping point, like the sand of an hourglass, or indeed the lifting of the shadow on the sundial; that dictates precisely when. And It is not rocket science, as you shall by now appreciate, my ever dearest and most attentive reader.

And you must embrace your Golden Age; from 2084 onward. And sustain It for as long as you are able: (typically between 200 -1000 years). And so.

The Beginning.

He came as a witness, to testify about the Light, so that all might believe through him. He was not the Light, but he came to testify about the Light. There was the true Light which, coming into the world, enlightens every man. **John.**

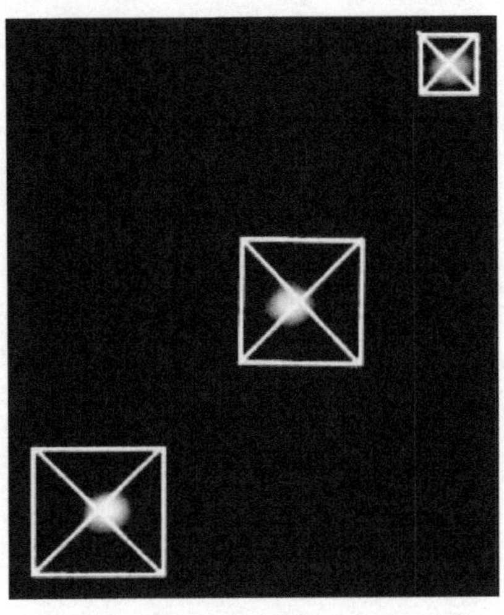

diseasednoti@crane.com

Troubador Publishing Ltd
Unit E2 Airfield Business Park
Harrison Road, Market Harborough
Leicestershire LE16 7UL
Tel: 0116 279 2299
Email: books@troubador.co.uk
Web: www.troubador.co.uk/matador

ISBN 978-1-80514-212-6

British Library Cataloguing in Publication Data.
A catalogue record for this book is available from the British Library.

Printed by TJ Books Limited, Padstow, UK

Matador is an imprint of Troubador Publishing Ltd